The Custody Wars

Other Works by
Mary Ann Mason

From Father's Property to Children's Rights:
A History of Child Custody in the United States

The Equality Trap

The Custody Wars

Why Children Are Losing
the Legal Battle, and
What We Can Do About It

Mary Ann Mason

BASIC
B
BOOKS

A Member of the Perseus Books Group

When I have related the stories of my clients or other persons who have confided in me, I have carefully changed identifying facts to protest their anonymity.

Published by Basic Books,
A Member of the Perseus Books Group

Library of Congress Cataloging-in-Publication Data
    The custody wars: why children are losing the legal battle, and what we can do about it / Mary Ann Mason.
    p.   cm.
    ISBN 0-465-01532-8 (cloth); ISBN 0-465-01529-8 (pbk.)
    1. Custody of children—United States.   2. Child support—Law and legislation—United States.   3. Children's rights.   4. Child welfare.   I. Title.
KF547.M368   1999
346.7301'73—dc21   98-47890
                                                                       CIP

The paper used in this publication meets the requirements of the American National Standard for Permanence of Paper for Printed Library Materials Z39.48-1984.

10   9   8   7   6   5   4   3   2

To my mom, Ann Mason

Contents

Acknowledgments

THE IDEAS THAT PROPEL THIS BOOK are based on nearly twenty-five years of experience as a lawyer, researcher, writer, professor, and mother. Each of these hats has provided me with information, insights, a perspective, and, it is hoped, compassion. The writing of my book on the history of child custody, *From Father's Property to Children's Rights* (1994), provoked me to take on contemporary custody issues. It is not easy to be wise about the world you live in; far simpler is to reflect on the strengths and shortcomings of the past. Yet today is the time in which we live and, however imperfect, I have felt obliged to comment, from as wide a perspective as is possible, about the strengths and weaknesses of the present, particularly regarding our lack of support for children's rights in custody matters. Nearly all countries in the developed industrial world are doing a better job of supporting the rights of children than the United States.

Most of those on whom I depended to write this book would be surprised to learn of their contribution. My clients and those who have contacted me over the years first come to mind. I have told some of their stories, but there are dozens more I have not related that have informed my understanding and contributed to my need to take on this project.

The participants at our family dinner table—my husband, Paul Ekman, and my children, Tom and Eve—always offered, often without knowing it, some of the best material and observations. We have very often discussed issues of custody, from the cases I teach to articles in the newspaper. Through my children, as they grew up, I have heard the response of the child to difficult legal and ethical issues at different developmental stages. I continue to be impressed at the basic good sense and wisdom of children at all stages. In addition, Paul, a social scientist, has been a careful editor and critic of early drafts. I also want to give special thanks to my mother, Ann Mason, for carefully clipping and sending to me articles on custody over many years.

At the University of California, Berkeley, where I have taught children and law in the School of Social Welfare for the past ten years, my students' observations have provided a clarifying and enriching voice. Many of my students have had significant work experience in family court, mediation, and custody evaluations. They have greatly expanded my own knowledge of these practice areas. In addition to the hundreds of students in my classes, I owe special thanks to at least a dozen research assistants from the law school, Boalt Hall. For many years I have worked with these very able students on various custody research projects that preceded this book—the solid foundation on which it is built. Most notably I wish to thank Julie Collins, a wonderful researcher and editor, who worked with me on this book, often on short deadlines.

Thanks also to colleagues at the London School of Economics, where I spent a sabbatical learning about children's rights in England and other European countries. And last, but not least, to my many colleagues at Berkeley with whom I have worked on family issues for many years in our family policy seminar, the Berkeley Family Forum.

Introduction

Children: The New Property

In the cloakroom of my daughter's Montessori preschool a large chart was posted every week that listed every child's name and who would pick that child up each evening. Many of these children were shuttling back and forth between two households. Every day a good portion of the cubbies were crammed with overstuffed backpacks or small suitcases, and on Fridays the backpacks and suitcases overflowed onto the floor.

With such complicated schedules, there were bound to be slipups. One afternoon I was delayed at work and raced to the school, convinced I would be the last parent to arrive; but one other child was still waiting. He sat tensely on the floor by the door, a large backpack in his lap. My daughter gathered her drawings and jacket and we started out the door. She waved at him and he waved back. He said in a small, worried voice, "Bye Eve, I don't remember who I belong to tonight."

It is not surprising that this child thought of himself as a belonging. Many children are exchanged like chattel between parents who insist on their right to them. Not that these parents don't love their children; they love them more than anyone else.

For many adults the parent–child relationship has replaced marriage as their primary social and emotional connection. Children provide the link to neighbors and school activities that tie adults to the community. Without children many adults risk social and emotional isolation.

Perhaps because children are so important to adults, mothers and fathers tend to think of them as their right, as an entitlement. Child custody has become a right for which men and women fight. Unfortunately, this right has become an extension of the battlefield of gender politics.

Mothers and fathers believe that custody disputes are a personal matter, unique to them. They are not wholly correct. When adults negotiate the custody of children today it is not only an individual matter but also part of a greater contest. When men and women fight over the custody of children they are engaging in gender wars that have occurred in the workplace, in the home, and in the bedroom over the past quarter century—and it is in this quarter century that the child's needs have been eclipsed by the needs of their parents.

Mothers and fathers got divorced in previous generations, albeit in lesser numbers, but their children were not held hostage in the same way as they are today. For more than a century the "tender years" doctrine dictated that small children needed the nurture and stability of a primary parent, and that parent was most likely to be the mother. The child then was assigned a single primary residence and a single primary parent—nearly always the mother. While this rule undoubtedly caused some unfairness, it did focus on the child's need for nurture and stability rather than on the parents' rights to access. It also discouraged dispute, since society's attitudes were aligned with the law's judgment about what was best for children.

As a society, we no longer agree on what is good for children. We are more focused instead on the political rights of parents. In my California family law teaching and practice I have witnessed the laws governing custody disputes swing wildly over the past two (nearly three) decades. None of these radical swings in the law was prompted by new research findings about what is good for children. Each emerged from a skirmish in the larger arena of gender politics.

At first the law favored mothers as custodians for young children, presuming that children of "tender years" were best cared for by their mothers. This rule, in place for more than a century, was swept away largely as a consequence of the feminist drive for equal treatment in the 1970s. Men and women, they believed, must be treated equally in this and all other matters before the law. Many feminists feared that the motherhood connection would restrict their opportunities for equal treatment in the workplace. Asking for special consideration for motherhood could shut the door to the male professions even tighter.

The next round was won by men. In the eighties, fathers' rights groups pushed for and won laws favoring joint physical custody, replacing the tradition of a primary custodian and a single residence for the child. The California legislature determined that courts should favor joint custody, even when the parents didn't.[1] Fathers went on to win child support concessions based on a concept of shared custody. According to this view, more time spent with the child lessened support obligations.

The current round is being fought with some success by women. Women's advocacy groups argue that a parent with a history of domestic violence should not have custodial rights. Fathers protest that this offers an easy way for mothers to make false claims and withhold access.

These issues are far more complex than this broad-brush view, and each will be examined in further detail throughout this book. Nonetheless, it has occurred to me, observing these shifts in the law over the years, that "mothering" has been systematically cut out of the law. The abolition of a maternal preference has turned the law away from the caretaking and nurture of children to the rights of parents. Women's rights and men's rights have replaced children's needs, as gender politics have spilled over into custody law.

The tender years doctrine was never a mothers' right; it was a child-centered rule. It forced the courts to move away from treating children as a property right of their fathers to focusing on the child's need for nurture. In my history of child custody, *From Father's Property to Children's Rights*, I trace the evolution of this radical new notion of child nurture.[2] The tender years rule reflected a dramatic transformation in social attitudes toward children in the nineteenth century. Children were no longer viewed primarily as economic assets, laborers under the absolute control of their fathers; they came to be seen as individuals with their own needs that commanded protection by the law. The tender years concept respected the developmental requirements of children, recognizing that very young children have special needs for nurture, normally satisfied by a mother.[3] And in the first part of the twentieth century courts looked to the wishes and feelings of older children as a primary consideration in their decision.[4]

Current laws do not focus on child nurture, nor do they acknowledge developmental stages. Children two years of age are treated the same as children of twelve. Most states simply offer a gender-neutral law requiring judges to apply an elusive "best interests of the child" standard, or they mandate a preference for joint custody, asking judges to divide the child's life. The wishes of the child are not given critical hearing. Rarely are the children, the most important party, allowed to reveal their feelings. Even teenagers have a steadily shrinking voice.[5]

The worth of children has shifted from that of an economic asset to an emotional asset, but one that is still extremely coveted. Once again children of every age are treated as a property right, this time an emotional property right, to be claimed by both mothers and fathers in their custody battles. In most instances the children have no rights and no voices.

Not only custody and child support following divorce have been affected by gender politics. Today nearly a third of our children are born outside of marriage. As a result of the swings in custody laws, fathers now can claim children simply by virtue of their blood tie. In a two-year-long Michigan dispute that commanded front page attention, two couples, the DeBoers and the Schmidts, fought bitterly over custody of a little girl, Jessica. In this case the issue was the biological father's right to block an adoption agreed on by the mother. The father was not married to the mother at the time of Jessica's birth, and had never seen the child. This became a fathers' rights case, with little regard to the fact that twenty years earlier most unwed fathers would have had no claim at all to that child. Before the termination of the "mothering" standard an unwed father who had not raised the child would have had no right to seek custody. Now the law acknowledges the rights of fathers who have in no way participated in nurturing. Fathers' rights have become defined as strictly biological rights, unrelated to actual parenting or even marriage.

Biologism has been newly and vigorously asserted in other contexts as well. Biological rights prevail over nurture in nearly all situations, regardless of who provides the actual parenting. Stepfathers or stepmothers, who may have raised a child for years, typically have no claim to custody or visitation if the marriage ends. About a fourth of all children will spend part of their life in a stepfamily, yet that parenting role is unrecognized by the courts. Stepparents have neither rights nor obligations toward their stepchildren under the law. Other family arrangements include lesbian partners who play a full parental role, often from birth, but are barred in most states from making a legal claim to custody. In all these circumstances the act of nurturing, the "mothering" role, is mostly disregarded by the law.

The latest battle in the custody wars is being waged in the tangled thicket of medically assisted reproduction. The urgent desire to parent has created a rich industry of technological interventions that allow the infertile to circumvent each stage of the traditional procedures of insemination, conception, pregnancy, and childbirth. Such processes raise fundamental questions about the biological essence of motherhood and fatherhood. They also provoke practical concerns about rights over the products of each discrete stage in the cycle of reproduction: ova, semen, pre-embryo, embryo, fetus, and, finally, baby. Are these property rights or custody rights? The effects of the rejection of "mothering" are most evident in this arena in our treatment of surrogate mothers. There is ambivalence and confusion, but most lawmakers essentially believe that the nurturing acts of pregnancy and childbirth are little different from manufacturing a car. A baby, like a car, must be delivered to the buyer who contracted for its production.

Custody issues are not likely to become simpler. They will only grow in variety and complexity as technology advances and marriage retreats from its role as the central child-raising institution. Nearly half of children born today will be subject to a custody negotiation or dispute before they reach adulthood, often under the jurisdiction of a court.[6] In most cases divorce is the triggering event, and it is the biological mothers and fathers (in the traditional sense) who are negotiating custody. Increasingly, however, as children are born and raised outside the confines of marriage, unwed fathers and nonbiological parents (including stepparents, adopting parents, and grandparents) fight for the right to hold on to the children they are raising.

Can we find a better framework to deal with these disputes, in which children are *not* treated as property to be divided? I believe we must. We cannot ignore the needs of our children. Custody is not just someone else's problem, it is a central concern for the majority of Americans. How and with whom children are raised determines much about our society's future.

The end of the mothering standard has created a new battlefield, but returning to a maternal preference is no longer a viable solution. In some families the mother is no longer the principal nurturer of small children. Women have had to make hard choices; some have chosen to leave the primary mothering role to the father or another parental figure. More important, more and more children are raised outside the institution of marriage, and old custody rules do not fit new families.

It is time to completely rethink child custody and support. We need a new vision, a new vocabulary, and uniformity among our states, which now offer a dizzying patchwork of contradictory laws and procedures. Most custody disputes do not reach the courtroom. They are settled around kitchen tables, in lawyer's offices, or in mediators' conference rooms. Still, we depend on the state to tell us what is expected of us as parents—what the society believes is best for children, how the courts will decide if we do not. Laws influence how decisions are made, whether or not the conflicts are raised in court.

This book offers a new framework that focuses on the rights of children, not on those who claim them. Simply put, this framework is based on the following principles, inspired by the 1989 United Nations Convention on the Rights of the Child:[7] children have the right to a nurturing environment in accordance with their developmental needs; the right to have their voices heard in accordance with their ages; the right to legal representation; and the right to economic and emotional support from their parents and from the state.[8]

Fashioning these general principles into specific rules and procedures that apply to child custody is a challenge, but not an impossibility. We have a great deal of knowledge from social and behavioral science as well as our own experience about what works for children at different developmental stages. We know how to listen to children and how to provide legal representation for them; and we understand that children need support— including economic support—and what it takes to provide that.

This book will develop five simple ideas that offer the basis of a child-centered custody policy that could apply in almost all circumstances in which adults fight for custody:

- ◆ Children's needs are not one-size-fits-all. They change over time. Children of tender years should live with their primary parent. As children develop their needs should be reviewed.
- ◆ Actual parenting should receive attention over biology.
- ◆ Children have been silenced. Their wishes and feelings must be listened to. All children should

have a voice, both in court and out; an adolescent's voice should be the deciding voice.

- Children have no place in which their voices are heard and their needs attended to. We must provide them a place.
- Child support is not rent-a-child. Support must not be tied to visitation.

There are principles and there are practices, but first there are human beings whose lives are being torn apart. In this book I approach current disputes through the stories of those who live them. Many of these stories are found in court reports; some are from my own practice. The histories are personal, but they reflect the larger political landscape in which the rights of men and women are in contest. The court reports also reveal the complexity of these disputes; rarely can they be seen as black and white. Perhaps the most striking feature of the court cases is that children are rarely mentioned by name, and sometimes even their ages are omitted, which illustrates the absence of their wishes and feelings from the proceedings. The party with most at stake has no voice.

In the course of writing this book I often have thought of Eve's young friend who couldn't remember who he belonged to. That child, like my daughter, must be approaching adulthood. It is likely, in the light of statistical projections, that one or both of his parents have remarried, creating still more complex parenting relationships and even more parents. I do not know what became of him. Knowing how we deal with such situations in California, however, he probably continued to shuttle back and forth between households unless one parent moved away, which most likely would bring everyone back to the courtroom, where the biological parents would fight for their rights once again. The one thing I can be fairly certain of is that as a young child his wishes and feelings were given little consideration, and becoming an adolescent would not be considered a sufficient reason to review his living arrrangements. No one would want to listen to him.

1

Are Mothers Losing
the Custody Wars?

For many years I had a recurring nightmare. My ex-husband has kept our five-year-old son beyond his weekend visit and is now in court asking for permanent custody. I have not seen my son for several weeks. The nightmare takes different turns. Sometimes I am searching for my son in his school playground, or on the streets; he is never there. In another version I am in court. The judge is questioning me about my work habits as a lawyer and asks how I can be a good mother when I work such long hours. Sometimes he questions my ex-husband as well, impressed that his university job gives him a flexible schedule. The judge disapproves of me. I know I am going to lose my son.

Whichever direction the dream takes, when I wake up I am always greatly relieved. The real-life incident on which the nightmare is based did not end that badly. My ex-husband, in the wake of a bitter argument in which threats were exchanged, kept our son for several days but then relented and returned him to me. My son smiled at me as I picked him up at his dad's house, unaware of my inner terror.

The recurrence of this nightmare long after my son was a toddler attests to the heavy burden of guilt and anxiety I carried as a working single parent. I deeply feared that I would lose what was most important, yet I was uncertain that I was properly fulfilling my role as a mother.

Motherhood is the central dilemma in feminist thinking. Some feminists argue that the family contributes as much to women's subordination in society as discrimination in the workplace. The stereotype of women as "natural" mothers, they claim, has shackled women to the family and prevented their rise in the outside world. Other feminists, however, point out that mothers still perform the great bulk of child-raising duties both within marriage and increasingly outside of it, and they need support in that effort. To deny their motherhood, these feminists believe, is to disadvantage them and their children.[1]

Nowhere is this dilemma more evident than in cases involving child custody. As a result of the rejection of maternal preference in family law, mothers have lost the special protection the law afforded them in their "natural" role as custodians of young children. Many feminists are reluctant to challenge this new direction in the law; they fear that fighting such a trend would encourage the stereotyping of women as "natural mothers," which could be used against them by men in the home and the workplace.

The only arena in which feminists have joined forces and intervened is in working mother cases, where the courts appear to punish mothers who take an active role in the workplace. Working mother cases—where mothers' rights are pitted directly against fathers' rights—are at the very core of the gender wars; they reveal the skein of competing parental rights that characterize modern custody disputes. Above all, they illustrate the failure of our system to put children first.

A well-publicized dispute in Michigan appears at first glance to support claims that working mothers who leave the home are losing custody unfairly. The facts of the case also raise the volatile issues of unwed teen motherhood, domestic violence, and child support blackmail. Yet these critical issues are ignored by the court and the press, who focus only on the day care issue.

Jennifer Ireland gave birth to Maranda when she was a sixteen-year-old high school student. The father, Steven Smith, was also a sixteen-year-old student at the time. They never married. According to Jennifer, Steven at first wanted her to have an abortion. Later, when the baby was born, he encouraged adoption. Jennifer was undecided. She put the baby in foster care for three weeks, contemplating adoption, but could not go through with it. She brought Maranda home and continued high school while her mother took over a large share of the child care.

Steven did not see Maranda very much that first year. He claimed later that "Jenny's parents told me to stay away from Maranda, because Jenny was deciding on adoption."[2] He did begin to see Maranda regularly as she grew older, and she had a room in his parents' house for her weekend visits.

When Maranda was two years old Jennifer graduated from high school with honors and won a scholarship to the University of Michigan. She moved from Detroit to Ann Arbor and enrolled Maranda in a home care facility, operated by a mother with two children who looked after other children. For the first time Jennifer asked Steven for child support. He objected to the amount requested, and the hostility between the two young parents intensified. Jennifer filed a complaint against Steven for assault. At around the same time Steven filed a petition for custody. He claimed that he was better able to care for Maranda since his mother was a full-time homemaker and would care for her at home. Steven would be living with his parents and attending the local community college.

On June 27, following Jennifer's first year at the University of Michigan, Judge Cashen of Macomb County Circuit Court ordered her to give up Maranda to her father. In his order Judge Cashen held that both parents were competent. However, he went on to say, while living with her mother Maranda would be "in essence raised and supervised a great part of the time by strangers." While living with her father, the judge said, Maranda would be "raised and supervised by blood relatives."[3]

The story immediately was labeled the Day Care Case and picked up by the wire services as a hot women's rights issue. Jacquie Steingold, a board member of the National Organization for Women, said, "It illustrates an attitude toward women about where they should be—the bedroom, kitchen and those kind of places, not at college."[4] Many saw the judge's ruling as a punishment for modern women who dare to work, or become educated to work, outside the home. Jennifer's own remark was repeated by many commentators: "It's just unfair. It's a decision based on the 1950s."[5]

Jennifer was wrong, however. This ruling could not have occurred in the 1950s. In all the fuss about day care no one noted the recent revolution in legal rules that made such a decision possible. In the 1950s, and in many states well into the 1980s, mothers like Jennifer were protected in custody disputes by two separate but well-established rules: the tender years doctrine, which favored mothers, and the complete lack of legal standing of unwed fathers to sue for custody. In the 1950s Steven could not have brought his claim for custody before the court.

The tender years doctrine (or maternal presumption, as it was often called) was well established by the 1920s. By the 1950s in Michigan and all other states it was the law. The rule of maternal presumption reflected a universally held belief in the early part of this century that mothers by nature were the more nurturing parent for very young children. In their drive for equal rights in the seventies, many feminists spurned this very assumption, believing it fixed women as second-class citizens in a patriarchal structure.

Feminists have not always been so ambivalent about motherhood. The pioneering feminists of the nineteenth century fought hard to establish custody rights for mothers in the face of a common law tradition that gave fathers paramount rights of custody and control. At the very first women's rights gathering in 1848, the newly drafted Declaration of Rights and Sentiments presented custodial rights for mothers as one of the primary demands:

> He [the legislative and judicial patriarchy][6] has so framed
> the laws of divorce as to what shall be the proper causes,
> and in the case of separation, to whom the guardianship
> of the children shall be given as to be wholly regardless of
> the happiness of women   the law in all cases going upon
> the false supposition of the supremacy of man, and giving
> all power into his hands.[7]

Early feminists struggled to turn the law away from seeing children as the property of their fathers and more toward considering the needs of children. The traditional view of children as helping hands in a labor-scarce economy slowly gave way to a romantic, emotional view of children; they were no longer legally akin to property under the complete control of their fathers, but were finally acknowledged to have interests of their own. Their interests increasingly became identified with the nurturing mother. Feminists strongly applauded the handful of early-nineteenth-century judges who boldly overthrew fathers' property rights in favor of mother nurture. In 1842 a New York judge defied established common law tradition and awarded custody of a three-year-old sickly daughter to her mother, explaining that

> the law of nature has given to her an attachment for her infant offspring which no other relative will be likely to possess in an equal degree, and where no sufficient reasons exist for depriving her of the care and nurture of her child, it would not be a proper exercise of discretion in any court to violate the law of nature in this respect.[8]

By the beginning of the twentieth century most judges concurred with this radical new view of the importance of maternal nurture for children of tender years. The condition of children was greatly advanced as their right to nurture was placed above their fathers' right to their labor.

Ironically, the second wave of feminism—the modern women's rights drive toward equality before the law—helped to abolish this hard-won gain. The modern push for equality has focused mostly on the workplace, but equal rights in the family are of prime concern to second-wave feminists as well. The founding statement of the National Organization of Women (NOW) in 1967 decried "half equality" in the marriage relationship and called for a reexamination of laws governing marriage. "We reject . . . that home and family are primarily woman's world and responsibility—hers, to dominate—his to support. We believe that a true partnership between the sexes demands a different concept of marriage, an equitable sharing of the responsibilities of home and children."[9]

Judges and state legislators have taken seriously the current feminist message that mothers and fathers should be treated equally under the law. Maternal presumption has been largely eliminated from the law and language of child custody. A New York court expressed the new thinking: "The simple fact of being a mother does not, by itself, indicate a capacity or willingness to render a quality of care different from that which the father can provide."[10]

With this simple statement this judge challenged nearly a century of judicial presumption in favor of mothers. To support his thinking the judge invoked the authority of the social scientist Margaret Mead. He quoted her as damning the maternal preference as "a mere and subtle form of anti-feminism in which men—under the guise of exalting the importance of maternity—are tying women more tightly to their children than has been thought necessary since the invention of bottle feeding and baby carriages."[11]

Not all courts are as outspoken in reducing the importance of mothers or in suggesting that maternal presumption is a male conspiracy. Nevertheless, the rule that the interests of a child of tender years are best served in the custody of the mother has been legally abolished or demoted to a "factor to be considered" in nearly all states.[12]

Not only feminists calling for equal treatment under the law, however, have persuaded legislators and judges to abandon the maternal presumption; their arguments are combined with the reality that great numbers of women have abandoned full-time housekeeping for the workplace—most of whom are mothers. In 1970 only 27 percent of women with children under age three were in the workforce; by 1985 this figure was more than 50 percent[13] and has remained so. Though many (if not most) of these women are driven to work by economic necessity in a downward-drifting wage structure, legislators and judges are confused by the new roles mothers are playing. An Illinois court declared, "the 'tender years' doctrine has no application if the mother is working and not in the home full time."[14]

To my knowledge not one of the dozens of commentators and talk-show hosts in the course of the Ireland–Smith dispute mentioned that until recently Judge Cashen would have been obliged to apply the tender years doctrine. He would not have been required to treat Steven and Jennifer as equally appropriate parents of a three-year-old. Instead he would have had to presume that mothers are better suited than fathers to nurture small children. The concept of maternal presumption, which reigned for more than 100 years, appears to have completely disappeared from public discourse.

Also absent from the discussion was any notice that Steven was not married to the mother. As will be discussed in chapter 4, it has been little more than twenty years since the U.S. Supreme Court, in *Stanley v. Illinois,* recognized *any* custodial rights for unwed fathers, much less those equal to the mothers'. This case seems to have given Steven—who never lived with Jennifer and Maranda—the same rights as a recently divorced father who had always lived with them, or, for that matter, the same rights as Jennifer. And no one found this worthy of comment.

Judge Cashen's so-called day care decision was possible because the law and social attitudes have swung dramatically away from favoring either mothers or marriage. Biological parenthood, not marriage or nurture, defines parental rights. The law must treat biological mothers and fathers as equals. Moreover, it gives no special consideration to the needs of infants and toddlers. The rules that Judge Cashen is required to follow in Michigan are the same as in most states: he must consider the biological parents first, and then make a decision in the "best interests of the child." In the vacuum created by the retreat of a maternal presumption, state legislatures have drafted statutes to direct judges left with the task of applying the elusive "best interests" standard.[15] Most states provide only a laundry list of suggestions for the judge to consider. These may include affective factors such as emotional ties, which often favor the mother, but they also usually mention economic stability, more likely to give advantage to the father.[16] In any event they are only suggestions, and by no means determinative. In fact hundreds of family court judges are forced every day to make difficult decisions in the best interests of very young children with no clear rules to guide them. When a mother and father both fight to gain physical custody, judges are frequently at a loss.

A "best interests" rule sounds enlightened and child centered. It appears to have moved beyond gendered stereotypes, to focus only on what is good for a particular child. As well intentioned as it may seem, it is not child centered. It provides no guidance about what we as a society believe is in the child's interest; it offers no recognition of the developmental needs of a child; it leaves no room for the wishes and feelings of the child; and, perhaps most damningly, its vagueness opens the door to almost complete judicial discretion. This allows a judge who doesn't believe in day care to award a child to the other parent. In addition, such a rule encourages parents to fight over custody, because the outcome is unpredictable. Fathers, knowing there is a real opportunity to win, may play the "custody card" to bargain for financial advantage in a divorce settlement. Thereby the door is open for a full-scale battle that pits fathers against mothers and in no way enhances the interests of the child.

In the Ireland–Smith dispute, we don't know for certain why Steven pursued custody. He claimed he did not like the way

Maranda was being raised; Jennifer claimed he did not want to pay child support. We do know that demands for child support are a common trigger of custody disputes.

Once the court battle began the hostility between the two escalated rapidly. Although trial proceedings were closed, later interviews with some of the parties on national talk shows and in the press revealed several nasty details of the confrontation. Jennifer raised the incident of assault in October 1992, when she complained to police that Steven struck her. (Smith was arraigned on that charge the day after Cashen's decision, but the charges were dropped for unexplained reasons.) Jennifer's lawyer claimed that Smith's parents stalked her, driving by her house every day to see whose cars were outside.[17] Domestic violence, common to many custody disputes, appears to have occurred between these two young people as well.

Steven Smith responded to Jennifer's domestic violence allegations with allegations of his own. At a press conference Smith said he had seen Maranda "being pushed by Jennie, pulled by Jennie, slapped on the counter by Jennie and just being rude and yelling." He also claimed that Jennifer handed Maranda off to her friends or her mother and never took care of her. He continued, "Maranda's care is my main concern. I can be a better parent because I am a better person."[18]

In his order Judge Cashen did not rule on these issues of alleged domestic violence and child abuse. He ruled that both the parents were equally competent. His only comment regarding the outstanding assault warrant against Smith was, "The parties in their youthful way apparently crashed or mauled one another. It is superfluous and can have no bearing on the issue of custody."[19] Judge Cashen, like most judges, did not want to enter the dark waters of domestic violence. In most states judges can dismiss domestic violence concerns as irrelevant to child raising.

Ultimately Judge Cashen based his written order on the day care issue. As a family court judge applying a best interests rule this judge was not required to offer a lengthy justification. Typically under these circumstances an appellate court would honor his discretion and stand by his order. It is very difficult to overturn a family court judge's ruling on the facts.

Does Judge Cashen's ruling reflect a trend against mothers? Without doubt the abolition of maternal presumption has caused judges to weigh their decisions differently. While most judges are not likely to say openly what Judge Cashen said about day care, they no longer favor mothers as they once did. An American Bar Association study shows that judges consider the fact of motherhood fairly insignificant in considering the child's best interests. Motherhood is mentioned as a prime factor only 10.6 percent of the time in custody decisions, compared to greater economic stability (46.5 percent) or primary disciplinarian (33.3 percent), traits more often associated with fathers.[20] My own study of historical trends in custody decisions reveals that while motherhood was the most frequently cited factor to be considered in 1960, it is almost *never* mentioned as a consideration in the 1990s.[21]

Most of the legal advances for fathers, however, have come in the growing number of states that encourage or even mandate joint or shared custody. In those states a large percentage of arrangements may be called joint custody, whether or not the child actually splits his or her time jointly. Here the fathers do not have to sue for custody; they are given as much time as they ask for. These cloudy arrangements will be reviewed in the next chapter, as will their first cousins, the "move-away" cases, in which the custodial parent (usually the mother) is threatened with loss of custody if she moves away from the other parent.

Yet the truth of the matter is that fathers typically don't want custody and mothers do. A recent California study of more than 900 divorcing families revealed that when asked their preference 82 percent of mothers wanted custody in contrast to 32 percent of fathers.[22] If these fathers actually take the initiative and sue for custody, they have a very good chance of winning. A Los Angeles study showed they won in court 63 percent of the time, and a similar study in Massachusetts found fathers won custody in 70 percent of the cases.[23]

Fathers may not want custody, but they can use their newly gained rights to influence their support obligations. Although feminists have taken on working mother cases, they have largely ignored the greater threat to all mothers who must fight for custody at the cost of child support.

In most instances child support is the only financial compensation available to custodial mothers and children following divorce. Alarmingly, custody threats can reduce that provision. Recall that Jennifer claimed Steven threatened to demand custody when she tried to force him to pay child support. For many couples custody has become the major bargaining chip in a divorce and in the ensuing years. The law in most states is fairly fixed regarding the purely financial aspects of divorce: child support, spousal support, and even property division. If brought to trial these issues usually are determined by a formula that includes the income of each spouse and the length of the marriage. With the indeterminate best interests standard, however, custody becomes the only issue that cannot be predicted before trial.

The fact that judges are willing to look more favorably on fathers' appeals for custody or joint custody has strongly influenced the private bargaining process before trial. Fathers who may have no real desire for custody threaten mothers with the possible loss of custody under the new rules in order to win concessions in property division and family support.[24] A California attorney who represents mostly men in divorce suits admitted to me that "about sixty percent of my male clients ask for joint custody now, but only ten percent really want it. It's a good bargaining position." On the other hand, it is fair to say that the 10 percent of fathers who do want more time with their children can use the law to bargain for greater access.

I was practicing family law in 1980 when the California legislature introduced the preference for joint custody. This signaled courts that they should encourage a couple to elect joint custody, and if there were resistance they could impose it anyway. Since the law states that custody orders made before 1980 could be reviewed in favor of joint custody, there was a good deal of renegotiating and some severe arm twisting among long-divorced couples.

Gerry, a young woman in her early twenties, came to me for advice. Gerry became pregnant and was married at age fourteen (with her parents' consent) to a young man age nineteen. They lived with her parents for a time after the first child was born, then moved to the southwest, where a second child was born. Her husband was at best an unstable provider. At worst he was violent and sporadically involved in dealing drugs, often bringing home his criminal associates. Gerry finally left him on her twentieth birthday in 1978. "I was afraid he would kill me and the kids. I couldn't sleep for weeks," she recalled.

She returned to her hometown and eventually he followed, demanding to see the children. Since he now seemed to be making money (ostensibly in an auto repair shop), she insisted on child support. He paid for a few months, then stopped. After two years she took him to court and received a judgment for back support of several thousand dollars. He retaliated by threatening to seek joint custody under the new law. His attorney filed a motion for a custody modification hearing.

Gerry was terrified. She was certain he was still involved with criminal activities and feared he could turn his violence against the children. She sought her attorney's advice and was given the harsh news that the judge could well grant joint custody, since her husband appeared financially capable and had remarried, giving the appearance at least of domestic stability. Gerry quickly dropped her claim for back support and moved out of town to escape his demand for joint custody.

When I met Gerry she and her two children were occupying one room of a cousin's apartment in Oakland. She was using a false name and her children had not been to school for several weeks. She told me she was considering leaving the state. "Maybe I can go to Alaska and start a new life," she told me. "Do you think he could find me there? He has lots of connections."

I told her she could not run away from the problem. While her attorney was correct about the court's right to impose joint custody, it might not come to that. Most likely her ex-husband was only threatening her. She arranged for another appointment so that we could contact his attorney for negotiation, but she never appeared. In her mind, she was running away from a system that would not protect her children.

Recently a popular trend toward shared custody—a variation on the joint custody theme—has further weakened mothers' claims for support. In shared custody cases neither parent is considered as primary, even when the child resides for the most part with one parent; the whole structure of child support therefore is considered obsolete. Instead, careful percentages are worked out depending on the number of hours the child ostensibly spends with each parent. It becomes a great economic advantage for a parent to claim that he or she owns a big chunk of the child's time. "Rent a child," as the trend is known among its critics, usually means that the father's time is increased, at least on paper, and accordingly his support obligations are reduced.

Mothers may be losing ground and financial support in the custody wars following the demise of maternal presumption, but is this necessarily bad for children? Custody should not be about mothers' or fathers' rights; it should be about what is best for children. Why should mothers be favored? Isn't it better if each case is treated individually, or perhaps if parents share the child? Let's look at how the decision in the Ireland–Smith case worked for three-year-old Maranda. Judge Cashen's decision to award Maranda to Steven so that Steven's mother could take care of her may have been a blow to women's rights, but was it in fact better for Maranda? We all know day care horror stories; many of our children have lived through them. Isn't it a reasonable argument that a grandmother could do it better?

Or what about the possibility of joint physical custody? This is an increasingly popular notion in many states and is primary on the agenda of most fathers' rights groups. Would Maranda benefit from being raised by both parents, yet in separate homes?

The option of joint physical custody is the easiest to dismiss in this case. Maranda's parents do not live in the same city, much less the same community, and do not get along. This is perhaps the most common situation for children whose parents do not live together. Even if Michigan favored joint custody (which it does not), it would be hard to imagine tiny Maranda traveling back and forth between Ann Arbor and Detroit, every week perhaps, splitting her life in half. It would be even more difficult to imagine her when she entered school—a different school in each city—or a different weekend life. The case for joint custody will be discussed in the next chapter, but Maranda's situation is an unlikely candidate for joint custody by anyone's standards.

Pitting a grandmother against an anonymous day care worker is a more persuasive argument, but not compelling. It ignores the nearly three years of parenting Maranda experienced from her mother, and it belies the fact that most mothers of three-year-olds spend time in the workplace, usually placing their children in and out of home care. We would not like to concede a superior claim to all grandmothers of children with working mothers.

From the point of view of Maranda's needs, in my opinion, Judge Cashen made the wrong decision. More than that, this case should never have been litigated. But in this era of judicial discretion, Steven and his attorney believed they had a chance to win and pursued it. This decision had serious consequences for Maranda. The growing hostility between her parents as they fought their way through trial and afterward could only harm the child. Although social scientists disagree in significant ways about what is best for children, there is consensus that parental conflict, both during and after marriage, is toxic.[25] The trial process inevitably increases hostility between parents who are already angry. A psychologist who interviewed both Jennifer and Steven before the trial commented on the process afterward: "As attorneys are attacking the other parent, we see a level of animosity, hostility and mistrust that grows and grows."[26] Even if Judge Cashen had ruled that Maranda stay with her mother, the full-blown hostility created by the trial would not subside quickly or gracefully.

Domestic violence is a real and continuing issue for many children in contentious custody situations. The effects of this violence on children is reviewed in chapter 6, and the news is not good. Those parents like Steven and Jennifer who introduce domestic violence early in their relationship are likely to have continuing problems, with Maranda caught in the middle. In their case custody and visitation rules should be carefully crafted to reduce contact between the parents.

Almost all the media commentary focused on Jennifer's right to go to school to improve herself versus the allegedly misogynist attitude of Judge Cashen, who believed that women should know their place, and that place is in the kitchen. Shifting focus away from the issue of women's rights, the case for Maranda is altogether different. If both parents are competent (as Judge Cashen said they were), Maranda at age three—a child of tender years—deserves to continue to live with the parent who has raised her. Admittedly in this case it was Jennifer's mother who did a good deal of the child raising, but Jennifer was there for Maranda every day and Steven was not. Even if we discard the nineteenth-century notion that natural law ordains mothers to be the primary nurturers of small children, we still believe that children become attached to whoever takes care of them. It is not hard to imagine the grief Maranda would experience if separated from her mother.

The current standard according to the court's definition of the child's best interests ignores developmental psychology. The tender years doctrine, which preceded modern developmental psychology by about 100 years, viewed a child's first five to six years as a discrete developmental period (as do nearly all present-day human development scientists). When equal rights concerns abolished the maternal preference the concept of "tender years" was abandoned as well, creating the current "one-size-fits-all" standards for custody. These standards offer no guidance that the "best interests" of three-year-old Maranda may be different than those of a ten-year-old.

The social science literature on the issue of attachment and psychological parenthood for infants and very young children is large and contentious. This will be more completely reviewed in chapter 3. Suffice it to say, the concept of attachment introduced by John Bowlby several decades ago[27] has withstood a new generation of researchers, and their findings have direct relevance to legal decision making.

Most experts still believe, as Bowlby did, that the very young child's emotional needs are urgent. Custody arrangements rarely consider an immature sense of time and the anxieties of separation. When a beloved parent leaves the room the infant does not know when and if that parent will return. A baby in a shared custody arrangement may have to wait several days before that return, and after repeated lengthy separations she or he may learn not to expect it. For some children separation from the primary parent may cause permanent damage.[28]

After age five to seven children's increasing cognitive and emotional maturity may allow more complex parent–child relationships. Physical caretaking is no longer the most central and insistent feature of parenting. The child's attachments, more cognitive and less physically based, may change. These years before adolescence offer the possibility of more flexibility and possibly more shared time.

With very young children we therefore should look toward physical acts of parenting to determine custody between parents. No one spoke for Maranda at the trial. She had no legal representative or child advocate to represent her side of the story. If we could put ourselves into the mind of Maranda Smith, however, we would know that her mother—the parent who had taken care of her most consistently for more than three years—is the parent to whom she has grown emotionally attached.

In my opinion a move in the law toward a "primary parent" presumption for young children (at least up to age six) would place the emphasis on actual observed parenting rather than on gender (as with maternal presumption) or on wishful thinking (as with joint custody), where the judge wishes that dividing the child will solve the problem.

A primary parent presumption combines the recent concept of primary caretaker with the traditional idea of psychological parent. Primary caretaker is a functional concept in which emphasis is placed on actual parenting tasks rather than on emotional attachment. The idea has gained popularity with courts in large part because evidence of caregiving can be presented objectively. This differs from the more elusive judgments regarding psychological parenting, which usually require professional evaluation and cannot be clearly measured. To determine a primary caretaker a judge does not have to rely on the testimony of opposing experts. He can count the hours and tasks each party has devoted to parenting or the child's advocate can count them for him. And in most cases with very small children (but not necessarily older ones) the parent who performs the everyday tasks is the one to whom the child is most closely attached. Yet there are cases of emotionally detached caretakers in which this bonding does not take place. If this becomes a serious question, a second-tier psychological examination could focus on the nature of the attachment.

A legal presumption in favor of a primary parent merely means that if both parents are fit, the court will apply a rule which says that society generally believes that very small children deserve nurture and stability, and they will more likely receive that in the custody of their primary parent. This rule, however, is not inflexible and it is not gender biased. Either parent can present evidence that he or she has served as the primary parent. The rule simply means that a judge cannot be arbitrary. It also means that the parties have a good idea of what judgment to expect, since in most families there is a fairly clearly defined primary parent who does most of the essential caretaking and to whom the child is attached. Parents are therefore more likely to settle most disputes without dragging them through the courts or using custody blackmail as a financial bargaining tool, tactics that increase hostility and deplete economic resources.

Fathers' rights advocates may claim that this is a way to reintroduce maternal presumption. Not so. Life has changed for at least some young families, and primary parent presumption would help fathers who do in fact play the role of primary parent. These fathers are also currently at the mercy of open-ended judicial discretion.

Over a period of two years I probably spent nine or ten hours on the telephone with Gary, a graduate student in oriental studies at a southern university. I talked to him because he needed a sympathetic ear; his voice was raw with pain. I could not give him much useful advice. Each state runs its own family law show, with its own rules and procedures. Outsiders are not particularly welcome in other states' courts.

Gary's story, like most custody stories, is familiar yet different. At the time of the divorce his boys were only three and five. He claimed that from their births he had been primary caretaker, since as a student he had a flexible schedule. "I wouldn't crack my books until they were in bed, and I only took classes in the few hours between Marcia's shifts. I knew it would take me a lot longer that way, but it was worth everything," he told me.

His ex-wife, Marcia, was not an uncaring parent, and neither was she feeding her ambition in a fast-track, male-dominated profession of the type judges tend to disfavor. Marcia was a nurse who found that the family could not make ends meet if she did not put in regular overtime. The family situation was complicated by the fact that the younger boy, Jay, had diabetes and other health problems. He needed continuous supervision of both his medications and his activities. Not all of his medications were covered by insurance. "We had a talk about it, and she said she could make more money on overtime than I could with a part-time job in a bookstore or coffee shop. There aren't a lot of job choices in this town."

The details of their divorce are not central to this story; Gary told me he would have done anything to hold on. When they separated, Marcia moved sixty miles away to the largest city in the state. She claimed she could get a better job there. The boys continued to live with Gary until she got settled. Then she asked for custody.

"I just couldn't give them up. They needed me too much. Besides, she was still working long hours. A stranger would be looking after them. She might forget to give Jay his medicine."

They took it to court, and the judge decided in favor of Marcia. According to Gary, he said they were both good parents, but Marcia was a nurse and could better handle Jay's medical condition.

I had little legal advice for Gary. In his state there were no binding guidelines or presumptions; the judge had only to consider the children's "best interests." I didn't advise him to appeal. There had been no change of circumstances since the order, and a judge's decision is very rarely overturned in custody matters. Besides, like most parents Gary did not have the money to pay for an appeal. While a shoplifter who steals a tube of lipstick is entitled to a lawyer free of charge, neither mother, father, nor child is entitled to representation in the matter that most critically affects their lives.

Was Gary a victim of lingering maternal presumption, even after its legal abolition? He thought so, and he may be right. The medical issues on which the judge based his judgment may have been a red herring, since Gary testified that he had performed all the necessary medical care since the child's birth. Many judges still believe that small children belong with their mothers; if Gary's state had enacted a legal preference for a primary parent, however, that judge would have been obliged to give top consideration to the actual parenting relationship in that family. In essence, the judge would have been forced to look at the parents from the children's point of view, and most likely would have decided in Gary's favor.

A primary parent rule is not going to resolve all custody disputes. With both parents working, today there are more families in which much of the caretaking may be done by a third party. And in these families it often is difficult to determine which of the busy parents is more central to the child's life.

In Washington political circles Sharon Prost was considered to be a player, a woman with power. She was chief minority counsel to the conservative senator Orrin Hatch and was best known for badgering Anita Hill during the infamous Clarence Thomas hearings. Prost and Kenneth Greene were married in 1984 and divorced in 1992. At the time, their two sons, Matthew and Jeffrey, were age two and five. Greene's work history was unsteady, and some of the time he was unemployed.

Testimony at the custody trial was conflicting. Prost claimed she picked up her children at the Senate day care before six o'-clock at least half the year when the Senate was not in session, and that she awoke each morning at 5:30 to spend time with her children before she went to work. But the couple's au pair testified that Prost came home from Capitol Hill to cook dinner only once a month and said: "I remember during the Clarence Thomas hearings that she was on the television a lot. She even called me at home to say, 'The kids have not seen me for weeks, so please turn on the TV so they can see me at least on the screen.'" In contrast, the au pair portrayed Greene as the perfect dad. "He had a lot of rules with the children . . . like don't play at the table while you're eating and sit straight," she said.

Greene testified in his own behalf that he had done most of the parenting. "There was only one thing Sharon could do that I couldn't—obviously that was breast-feed the baby. I was willing to do everything. I changed the diapers, put him to sleep, woke in the middle of the night to cradle him and sing to him."[29]

The psychiatrist who interviewed the children claimed that Prost was the psychological parent, and a social worker assigned to the case also agreed that it was in the children's best interests to be with their mother. Nonetheless, Judge Harriet Taylor, a mother herself, described Prost as a workaholic and claimed she was "more devoted to and absorbed by her work and her career than anything else in her life, including her health, her children and her family."[30] She awarded sole custody of the children to Greene, with visitation to Prost.

Protest over this decision invoked the unlikely alliance of the Senate Ethics Committee and the Women's Legal Defense Fund. Waiving its own restrictions, the Senate Ethics Committee authorized a legal defense fund. Fifteen senators signed a letter to the court, stating, in part, "We are concerned primarily because of the inference that women who work in the United States Senate are ipso facto unfit mothers." Feminists claimed that Prost was being held to a double standard. Joan Entmacher of the Women's Legal Defense Fund protested that it was a gender-biased decision, "holding the mother to a much higher standard, expecting much more of the mother than the father."[31]

In response fathers' rights groups defended the decision as a recognition of the new role of fathers in many working families. Michael Pitts, executive director of the Children's Rights Council, which advocates joint custody, asked, "Is it surprising that now women are being held to the same standard?"[32]

In the passionate political diatribes between advocates of women's right to work and fathers' right to parent, few voices spoke directly for the children, Matthew and Jeffrey. Did the legal system do them justice? Like Michigan, home of Maranda Smith, Washington, D.C., has an open-ended best interests standard, allowing the judge almost total discretion. Would a maternal presumption have offered a better result? The facts of this case suggest why a maternal presumption is probably no longer an adequate standard for modern families. In most families mothers still perform the major parenting role for small children. Yet there are a lot of women like Sharon Prost who are trying to make it in a man's world, with a man's career clock. Old presumptions based on old patterns of caretaking may no longer apply. Still, the needs of children have not changed; at least in their tender years they need constant care, nurturing, and supervision. From a child's perspective the parent who provides most of that care is the lifeline.

Would a presumption in favor of a primary parent have worked better? In this case it would be possible to actually measure the hours Prost spent with her children each day, compared with those spent by Greene. Still, I suspect that the au pair could actually claim the largest number of caretaking hours.

As I conceive it, a primary parent presumption emphasizes both caregiving and emotional attachment. It could be a two-tiered test in which the primary caregiver could be established first, and if the other parent objected to the designation he or she could press for an emotional evaluation. In the rare instance where a parent met the first but not the second criteria, other tie-breaking factors would be considered.

The Prost–Greene conflict may be one that would require going to this second tier. Though Greene was deemed more available (although at the time not more involved with parenting), the psychiatrist who interviewed the children claimed that Prost was the psychological parent, and the social worker agreed that she was the preferable parent. This may have given Prost an edge as the primary parent. Or in their case it may simply illustrate that a primary parent presumption will not resolve all cases.

There will be cases in which both parents present evidence that they have served equally as primary caretakers, and the child is emotionally attached to both. Then the judge must look to some other factor to break the tie. Or there may be evidence that the child is not emotionally attached to the primary caretaking parent but rather to the other parent. With very small children this is not usual, but it is possible in the case of a seriously emotionally detached parent. The primary parent preference simply means that a judge cannot be arbitrary and must look first to actual parenting.

Unlike divorce, child custody is not a legal event that can be negotiated or fought over and ultimately settled within a year or two. Legal custody lasts until the child reaches adulthood.

The parties may be back in court many times. Even if they are not, the disagreements and conflict may reignite when one parent moves or remarries, or when the child's developmental needs change. Whether disputes are settled again by a judge on the telephone or on the doorstep when a child is being exchanged, there are few parents who manage the full course of custody without some angry words.

In some cases, though, time does soothe angry feelings, and a smoother course prevails. I was delighted finally to meet Gary, my telephone father, when he came to San Francisco on a vacation trip with his boys, now age six and eight. I had known something of his continuing story. He called me when he left graduate school and went to live in the city where his boys were living. At the time he told me he simply could not bear to be so far from them.

They had just come from a baseball game when I saw them. All three, pink from the sun, grinned happily at me. Gary told me that his life had worked out fairly well after the move. He and Marcia had gradually developed into what amounted to a de facto joint custody arrangement, with the boys going freely to his apartment, only two blocks from their mother's. Marcia had remarried, which had caused some strain, but so far the stepfather had been encouraging the boys to spend time at their dad's.

I didn't bring up his lost graduate school career, but he did.

"Next fall, since the kids are in school all day, I am going to try to finish up my courses; I only have four left before my doctoral exams. I can do it, I think, by spending two nights a week at the university. I have a place to stay. I'll have to quit my job and live on beans, but I know I can make it work. These guys will help me." He gathered them into an affectionate bear hug—the kind the boys clearly were accustomed to.

★   ★   ★

ting, nearly five
nd Steven Smith
e has been heard
ppeal, brought by
ourt" briefs from
.tions. The cast of
.ghts and domestic

en's order based on
his disqualification
eland and "friends"
are not permitted to
can overrule the trial
.rpreted the law. The
.itted a technical legal
error in ... he parties' homes and
child-care arrangements under a statutory guideline . . . exclusively concerned with whether the family unit will remain intact, not an evaluation about whether one custodial home would be more acceptable than the other."[24] They returned the case for retrial on this issue alone. The appellate court also agreed to disqualify Judge Cashen from the retrial, citing the negative media exposure that could bias his future opinion.

Steven Smith and supporters did not accept this defeat. They appealed to the Michigan Supreme Court. While supporting the appellate court's decision to reverse on legal error and send the case back to trial, the Michigan Supreme Court did not allow the day care issue to die.

". . . [W]e need to confirm that actual and proposed child-care arrangements—whether in the custodial home or elsewhere—are a proper consideration in a custody case. Many children spend a significant amount of time in such settings, and no reasonable person would doubt the importance of child-care decisions."[35] Once again, Jennifer and Steven will be back in court. Maranda, now eight, will have spent most of her life with her parents fighting over her, as a case that should never have come before the court refuses to leave.

2

Joint Custody:
Solomon's Solution

Both parents teach school. The mother is in the [father's]
home with the children Monday to Friday from 7:30 A.M.
to 12:30 P.M. The mother has the children in her home
from 4:15 P.M. to 8:00 P.M. Tuesday and on alternate
[weekends] from 10:00 A.M. Saturday until 8:00 P.M. Sunday. The paternal grandmother babysits Monday to Friday
from 12:30 to 4:15 P.M., i.e., from the time the mother
leaves the children until the father gets home.[1]

This is the joint custody arrangement that a Maryland trial
court imposed recently on parents with two young children,
ages four and three, *against* the wishes of the mother, who
claimed it was unworkable and provoked constant conflict. In
making this decision the Maryland court ignored the only
precedent, a 1934 case that claimed joint custody was to be
avoided as "an evil fruitful in the destruction of discipline, in
the creation of distrust, and the production of mental distress in
the child."[2] The court explained that the earlier view of joint
custody required reexamination in light of the "significant

changes that have occurred over the ensuing half century." The court did not specify the nature of these changes.

Joint or shared custody has become the most politically attractive concept of the nineties. It is now allowed in nearly all states, given preference in some, and is sometimes imposed on couples against the will of one or both parties.[3] The concept has been propelled by the rhetoric of fairness to parents, mainly fathers, who believe they have been discriminated against by the courts and excluded from their children's lives. And the idea has grown popular among judges. As New York judge Felicia K. Shea observed: "Joint custody is an appealing concept. It permits the court to escape an agonizing choice, to keep from wounding the self-esteem of either parent and to avoid the appearance of discrimination between the sexes."[4]

Although it also has been presented as a children's rights argument, that is, a child's right to both parents, it is fair to say that the push for joint custody has been initiated more by a concern for the rights of parents, particularly fathers, than it has been for the rights of children. Its introduction was not based on any developmental research, any long-term pilot project, or any historical precedent that indicated the arrangement was in the best interests of the children. When California, the pioneer no-fault state, once again led the nation in 1980 by legislating a preference for joint custody, it was a newly formed fathers' rights group that pushed the bill over the legislative hurdles.[5]

In the American spirit of flexibility, public policy in fact has favored three radically different child-raising attitudes in the past three decades, none of them impelled by an understanding of what is in the best interests of children. In the sixties it was still common wisdom that children were almost always best off in an intact family. Parents, it was believed, must sacrifice their

own happiness and avoid divorce. Divorce laws and social attitudes buttressed this belief. Then in the seventies it became accepted dogma that children were happy only if their parents
were happy, and that divorce was preferable to an unhappy marriage. Still, children were almost always considered better off in
the custody of their mother following divorce. Divorce became
easier, but the maternal preference was still largely intact. In the
eighties joint physical custody was promoted as a way of giving
children access to both parents while allowing the parents the
freedom of divorce. Custody guidelines and public attitudes
turned in this direction.[6]

In truth none of these shifts in the law and social attitudes was
informed by scientific evidence of what is in the best interests of
children. The new laws and judicial opinions creating joint custody did not look to the developmental needs of children, nor
did they allow for a voice for the child. They were instead products of cultural and political shifts—first toward greater individual freedom through divorce, and then toward creating a new
power balance between men and women. There is now, however,
a body of scientific research available on the long-term effects of
divorce and traditional maternal custody, and a more modest offering on joint custody (what we do know will be reviewed later
in this chapter). Although there are few formal studies of long-
term joint custody arrangements (the most comprehensive, the
Stanford study, follows families for two years[7]), those of us who
have been part of the family law system in California have had
nearly two decades, since its introduction into the law as a preference in 1980, to observe joint custody arrangements over the
course of a child's development.

My own observation of custody arrangements began in California in the late 1970s, just before the legal institution of joint

custody. For twenty years I have listened to children and dozens of parents talk about their custody arrangements. I have asked about all aspects of the arrangement: economic division, conflict management, decision making, changes over time, and most of all the feelings of the children. These parents and children have included my clients, mothers and fathers who have written or called about their custody arrangements, and occasionally my friends and those of my children. In some ways I have learned most from the children, who are surprisingly forthcoming about their lives.

While all custody arrangements are problematical in some ways, joint physical custody presents obvious logistical challenges that make it impossible for many parents to consider. In part owing to such difficulties, actual joint physical custody—in which the child spends about 50 percent of his or her time with each parent—is attempted by a minority of divorcing couples in California (about 20 percent, according to the Stanford study).[8] Yet many couples and many courts now favor the concept of shared custody, where neither party is designated as the custodian. This provides an open-ended arrangement with endless potential combinations and permutations. A third popular option is joint legal custody, which usually involves a primary custodian but gives the other parent an equal right to make important life decisions about schools, medical care, and other matters central to a child's life.[9] This latter option is obviously less problematical in terms of demands on the child than the other two.

How does actual joint physical custody work, when the child's residence is more or less equally in two homes? There are a wide variety of solutions to dividing the child's time. Some schedules are half a week at each parent's residence, some a week on, a week off, and others are longer blocks of time. I have observed that the main difference between parents tackling joint custody is not time management but attitude. To my mind it is the attitudes of the parents and the ages of the children that determine success or failure for this difficult venture. I believe there are at least three distinct attitudinal patterns that characterize most joint custody arrangements: the good army, the bitter coalition, and the mediated alliance.

The Good Army

My first experience with joint custody was in 1978, before California promoted the concept to law. Carole became my client, but first she had been a college friend.[10] She asked me to represent both her and George (whom she had married the day following graduation) in their divorce proceedings. I balked at the suggestion—not convinced that one lawyer could fairly represent both party's interests—but Carole persisted. They were certain they wanted a cooperative rather than an adversarial property arrangement, and they also wanted to extend this cooperation to custody arrangements for their two sons, Jacob, six, and Josh, eight.

"I lost my father when my parents divorced," Carole told me, "and I can't let that happen to my boys. You know I think George is a jerk in some departments, but he's good with them."

To achieve this they sold the family house, and each rented an apartment near the school that both boys attended. I helped them draft an elaborate custody plan. The children were to stay at Carole's apartment Wednesday night through Saturday night, and at George's Sunday night through Tuesday night. George picked up an extra Saturday every month to even out the schedule. Holidays were similarly divided. They began with two rules: always keep the boys together, and both parents would try to attend all children's functions.

At that time judges were skeptical of joint custody arrangements and often would not agree to them. To avoid possible rejection we presented a standard custody plan to the court that listed Carole as the custodial parent. This meant, of course, that if there were any difficulty with their arrangement a court would not enforce it. I was also skeptical of their unconventional arrangement and feared it would not last long. I knew Carole and George did not consider themselves friends any longer and had never been happily married.

I did not hear from Carole or George for about two years. I was not sure whether this was good or bad news. Finally Carole called me and asked me to stop by her apartment for a drink after work. When I arrived Carole's younger son Jacob, now eight, greeted me at the door. Carole was smiling. It was good news. She reported that their custody arrangement was going very well. She related with good humor some mishaps of scheduling that had occurred over the past two years—as when the boys were obliged to eat two Thanksgiving dinners at two different grandparents' homes—but overall she seemed pleased with their common venture. She asked Jacob to tell me what he thought of having two homes.

"It's cool, I guess," he said, reluctant to talk at first. Then he began to warm to the subject and confided with a grin, "As long as we don't forget our marching orders."

"What marching orders?" I asked. Clearly he was bursting to tell me.

His grin widened. "Keep time. Truck your stuff and don't tattle!"

With little urging he explained that "keep time" meant that each boy had a watch and was responsible for following "the schedule" without reminders from parents. "Truck your stuff" similarly placed the burden on the boys to keep track of their belongings and transport them back and forth when necessary. "Don't tattle" was a little more complicated. "It means that we can't complain about things at the other house—and—" he paused, "we can't tell about other people—like if Dad's got a girlfriend or something."

Over the next several years I saw Carole occasionally, and she continued to be positive about their joint custody arrangement. Then, at a friend's birthday party about seven years after the divorce, she told me that the boys were now with her permanently and that they saw their father only about once a week, and rarely overnight.

"It didn't end badly," she insisted. "We're all still on good terms, and the boys still love their father." The event that had most influenced the change was the addition to the household of George's longtime girlfriend, Anne, and her six-year-old daughter. "I guess the boys didn't feel they were the center of attention anymore," she said. "But you know, they are at the age when they are mostly with their friends anyway, and they complained it was a drag to worry about 'the schedule'."

Carole and George's plan did not carry through to the boys' adulthood, but for the parents the venture was a success. George did not lose close contact with his sons during critical growing years, and Carole expressed a sense of pride in accomplishing a difficult task; more pride, I suspect, than she felt about her failed marriage.

What about the boys? Was it a success for them? This is a far more difficult question, and one about which I can only guess. I did speak briefly with Jacob again when he was eighteen. I reminded him about the "marching orders" and again a wide grin spread across his face, as it had ten years earlier. "Oh, yes," he told me, "it was a great game."

"Did you resent it?"

"Oh no," he responded quickly. "It was kind of fun, and it taught me to be more responsible. It worked fine until Anne moved in. . . . But she's okay now," he added.

This "good army" enjoyed several important conditions that contributed to its success. The boys were old enough to take responsibility and did not need the constant physical attention that children of "tender years" demand. The housing arrangements allowed the boys to maintain the same school and the same group of friends. And each parent had sufficient resources to provide a suitable home for the boys. Clearly a critical factor was the commitment of parents and children to this venture. For the children, maintaining the schedule became a matter of pride. For the parents, joint custody was not just a goal, it was a mission. Commitment to its success encouraged both to make sacrifices. They had not done well as marriage partners, yet they were determined to succeed in this venture.

And the venture ended when the boys said no. These parents listened to their children throughout the process; they did not treat them as chattel to be exchanged. When the boys ceased to be willing participants, in this case triggered by a remarriage and growing adolescent independence, the parents agreed to accommodate their needs.

The Bitter Coalition

Another pattern that characterizes some joint custody arrangements I call the bitter coalition. These parents have a commitment to joint custody, but one that is not based on a shared desire for children to experience dual parenting. What they share instead is an unwillingness to concede parenting to the other parent. Competition is by no means restricted to joint custody; many arrangements that involve ordinary visitation are characterized by the same bitterness. In such cases, however, the child's life is usually less affected by the discord. With joint custody the child's existence is divided between two hostile camps. All the mundane details that make up a child's everyday life, from junk food to wearing pajamas, can become the focus of conflict.

Since mothers are the traditional custodians, usually the father pursues such a course, sometimes against the wishes of the mother. Beginning in the 1980s, the courts in California could impose joint custody without the agreement of both parties;[11] more frequently (as will be discussed) this arrangement is imposed on a parent by a persuasive mediator. With an unwilling or reluctant parent this is a venture based on resentment. Although these parents genuinely care about their children, they care more about protecting what they perceive as their rights. Because resentment is a great motivator, this type of joint custody arrangement can be very long lived, whether or not the children support it.

I have had experience with several long-lived bitter coalitions. As an attorney I often felt helpless as one party, usually the mother, came to me to complain about the arrangement. In most cases I could do very little. Unless there is a significant change in circumstances, such as a move, the courts most likely will not intervene in a custody arrangement, no matter how difficult the situation becomes for a child. And with a legal system not organized to hear their voices, children are powerless to initiate change of custody arrangements on their own.

Only once did I observe such an arrangement solely from the child's point of view. One of my daughters' closest friends, Lisa, was the child of a joint custody arrangement.[12] From the age of four she and her older sister Anna were equally divided between their parents. I knew Lisa well between the ages of nine and thirteen, when she spent a good deal of time at our home. She was a sweet child with an engaging smile. I knew Lisa's parents also, through school functions, but I was in no way involved with their extended legal battle. As an outsider I did not know the details of their conflict, but I did know that Lisa and her sister had several appointments with the court evaluator, the mediator, and the court over the years. One of the major changes in their physical arrangements occurred when their father remarried and moved out of the city to the suburbs. At that point their schedule changed—but not without a court battle. Eventually they were assigned to their mother's home during the school week and their father's Friday afternoon through Sunday night. Holidays and vacations were carefully apportioned, so that throughout the year each parent claimed a precise 50 percent of the girls' time.

Lisa's parents kept to this schedule rigidly. Lisa did not even ask for special dispensations for parties and other weekend events with her school friends; she knew she would be refused. Instead, as a young child she developed another circle of friends in her father's neighborhood. She invited my daughter to spend the weekend with her several times, but after the first couple of visits my daughter declined.

"I don't know. I just don't feel right at Lisa's dad's house," she told me when she was about ten. "Her dad and stepmom are nice, but Lisa is a different person."

When I asked her what she meant by that, she responded, "You know how Lisa is always joking around; well at his house she is much more—ladylike, I guess. Almost like she was in church."

Still, Lisa appeared good humored at our house. She also seemed popular with the other children and successful as a student—until she was about twelve. In that year I learned from my daughter that her older sister insisted on a boarding school for high school. I asked Lisa about this the next time I saw her. Boarding school was not a popular option for this group of California teens.

She hesitated. "She just wants to get away from my mom and dad."

I did not press the issue, but she volunteered. "She's never been able to handle it like I can; she fights with both of them all the time, and they're always fighting about her."

Lisa visited our home much less frequently in the next two years. When I asked my daughter why I had not seen her she confided to me with the wisdom common to preadolescent girls who have discussed each other's lives in detail. "We all agree that Lisa has a bad deal. She's not part of our crowd anymore because she's always at her dad's on the weekend. I don't think she has any friends there either—she's not at their school. And you know, she hated her sister, but now she's all alone."

When my daughter's class graduated eighth grade I asked where Lisa was going to high school.

"Poor Lisa," my daughter said, sighing. "We really feel sorry for her. She wanted to go to boarding school too, to get away from her parents, but her mom wouldn't let her—she says she already lost one daughter. She also wouldn't let her go to live with her dad. So now she's going to high school in the city and still spending the weekends at her dad's—she'll never make any friends."

Lisa went to a different high school than my daughter, and it was a year before I saw her again. I hardly recognized her. Granted, all children change rapidly at this age, but Lisa had lost the bright engaging smile that had been her signature. Instead she appeared serious, quiet, even a little timid. I asked her about high school and she gave dispirited, noncommittal answers. Only when I asked about her sister Anna did she brighten. "Oh, she's doing great. She has a wonderful room and lots of friends. On the weekends they go skiing or have parties."

When I asked if Anna came home often on weekends, Lisa replied, "She'd never come home at all, if she could help it. Now she has a life."

Virtually all custody arrangements—including those based on sole custody and limited visitation—are questioned by children as they approach adolescence and experience their own needs for independence. Joint custody arrangements obviously demand more constraints and are therefore more likely to be seriously challenged. Unfortunately the law provides little outlet for adolescent discontent. Our custody guidelines are one-size-fits-all, without regard to developmental needs and without reference to the vast body of research that details developmental changes in children as they mature.[13] Children approaching adolescence have a strong need to express their independence and individuality, to begin to make decisions about their own lives. Our legal system does not encourage or permit children to protest their arrangement, no matter how intolerable it may have become to them.

Since most divorces occur in the first seven years of marriage, the children are usually of "tender years" at the time of the original custody agreement.[14] The arrangement becomes fixed in time while the child grows. Although possible, it is not likely that the arrangement will be revisited later in court; even less likely will a child initiate a change.

In my experience it is the good-natured, willing-to-please child like Lisa who most often suffers from regimes completely unsuited to developing adolescent needs. Lisa is not only naturally compliant, she has dealt all her life with her parents' anger and conflict and is unwilling to provoke it further. Her more assertive sister Anna was better able to demand a change in circumstances.

The contrast between the attitudes of Carole and George and those of Lisa's parents is noteworthy. Carole and George allowed their adolescent boys to change their custody arrangement with some grace because their goal was positive parenting, not their own individual needs. In conflict-ridden arrangements like those of Lisa's parents, the needs and resentments of the parents are more likely to prevail over the needs of the children. The joint custody arrangement of the bitter coalition lasted longer, but—at least for Lisa—it can hardly be considered more successful.

These cases point to the need for a voice for the child in the custody process. All custody arrangements, whether joint or sole, should be reviewed when the child reaches age twelve or thirteen. His or her needs, which can be articulated by this time, must be attended to first. While most courts give lip service to the child's preference at this age, less assertive children like Lisa will not be heard without the trained ear of an attentive listener.

The voices of younger children ought to be heeded as well. In all joint custody arrangements, even those agreed on by the parents, the child's needs must be addressed by the court, which gives or withholds its approval of the arrangement. The court, and all those involved in the custody process, needs to be educated about the developmental needs of children in general. Developmental researchers have found, for example, that infants and young children are far more cognitively developed than was previously believed. They are capable of experiencing profound emotional upsets, such as depression, beginning in the first year of life.[15] It is possible for a poorly conceived custody arrangement to have serious traumatic effects on babies as well as on older children.

Increasingly, however, the venue for hammering out custody arrangements is the mediator's office, not the courtroom. Unfortunately in this venue the voice of the child is silenced as well.

The Mediated Alliance

The majority of joint custody ventures are neither cooperative and well-planned nor bitterly determined. Most couples who elect joint custody either do so with some reservations or they do so hastily, without considering long-term implications. In California this decision is most likely to be initiated by a few hours of compulsory mediation. The mediated alliance, however, is at best a volatile venture.

California set the trend in mediation, as it has in most aspects of the divorce and custody revolution, by requiring mediation in all contested custody disputes before a case can be carried forth to trial.[16] This requirement passed as part of a legislative package along with the preference for joint custody. Bargaining in the shadow of California's new legal preferences in the 1980s, a fairly high percentage of divorcing couples chose joint custody. Some chose it because, like Carole and George, they were committed to maintaining dual parenting for their children. Others chose it because they could not agree on any other option, and they were encouraged to take this direction by a mediator. The most extensive study on California child custody, the Stanford Child Custody Study, which examined 908 families, found that joint physical custody was elected by nearly one fifth of all divorcing couples. A large number of these cases involved "intense" parental conflict, however, suggesting that parents could agree on no other arrangement. Nearly all joint custody arrangements were negotiated through a mediator or attorneys, not determined by the courts.[17]

Mediation is different from the legal adversarial process. The goal of a mediator, usually (but not always) a mental health professional, is to achieve agreement between parents. This agreement is based theoretically on the parents' own concept of fairness, not that imposed by state law. A judge, on the other hand, is to apply presumably well-developed principles of law to the facts of a particular family's situation. Mediation sessions are informal and short, with parents representing themselves. In contrast, the adversarial system, weighed down by the burden of due process, requires the lengthy exercise of a formal hearing, including the right of confrontation and cross examination. Most often the parties are represented by counsel in court proceedings; they are not in mediation. In neither model is the child likely to be represented or even present. Children are not welcome in a mediation session, which is considered to be a process of negotiation between the parents, not a democratic family council.

Private mediator Stephen Erickson provides insight into how this process can bring unwilling couples to agree on joint custody in his description of what he views as a successful media-

tion. Don and Linda came to him to deal with issues relating to
the termination of their fifteen-year marriage. Their voluntary
mediation involved support and property division issues in addition to custody. The two main custodial questions to consider
were visitation and what to call the custody arrangement. The
mother claimed that the children, two girls ages nine and thirteen, did not want to visit their father because they feared they
would encounter his girlfriend. Clearly the girlfriend was the
sore point of anger for Linda, who did not want the divorce.
The mediator, though, followed the mediation mantra of looking forward, not backward, and not allowing anger to obstruct a
settlement. Therefore he did not allow Linda to talk about the
girlfriend, insisting instead that they focus on the mechanics of
visitation. Erickson recalled,

> Resorting to my conceptual theory of mediation that says
> people need agreements, not therapy, I asked Linda if she
> wanted a written temporary agreement that states that Don
> will not have his girlfriend stay with him when the chil-
> dren are present. Linda said nothing, and looked at Don.
> He said that he does not live with another woman and that
> such an agreement was unnecessary. After a bit more prod-
> ding, both agreed that such an agreement was acceptable.[18]

As for the legal designation of the custody arrangement, Don
and Linda finally agreed on joint physical and legal custody. According to the mediator Linda initially had resisted joint physical custody: "When I asked her what she understood by her attorney's admonition that she be designated the physical
custodian, she said that she had always been the primary parent,
and even though Don wanted joint custody, it was just not acceptable to her."[19] The mediator argued that these labels be-

come important only in the event that the two of them end up in court and suggested a binding arbitration clause that would eliminate this concern. The couple then both agreed to joint physical and legal custody, and to a binding arbitration clause.

The mediator considered this a successful result because his clients had struck a bargain; but is this a child-centered agreement? Don and Linda have nominally agreed to joint physical custody, but they have not agreed to make it work in any meaningful way. Linda's bitterness is not likely to recede quickly, and it is not clear that Don actually wants the children half the time. As is typical in mediation, the mediator did not consider the interests of the children at all. He did not talk to them, he probably did not meet them; his goal was simply to achieve an agreement between the parents. Don and Linda have reached a nominal agreement, but they have not changed their attitudes toward one another, and the mediator failed to consider how their attitudes might affect working out that agreement.

This agreement will be officially recorded as joint physical custody, but the only likely practical consequence is not wholesome dual parenting but more conflict. Not only is it likely that visitation will continue to be disputed, any significant change in Don and Linda's living arrangements will be disputed as well. If Linda decides to move away, Don could claim custody for himself. Although they have agreed to binding arbitration, the role of the arbitrator will be to enforce the joint custody contract, not to look after the best interests of the children.

A second consequence of Don and Linda's joint custody agreement is that it could lead to less support for the children. Don may insist on lowering child support if they are joint custodians, even if this arrangement exists only on paper. In many states the level of support is determined by the custody arrangement. Research does not support greater child support compliance in joint custody situations; in fact the arrangement can produce the opposite result.[20]

Not long ago I received a letter from Michelle M. She asked me, as do many mothers, if I knew of an attorney who could take her case for a low fee or no fee at all. She told me she found herself in an intolerable financial situation, without money to make her car payment and no way out. She learned, as do thousands of men and women every day, that the legal system will provide an attorney if you steal a candy bar but offers no legal help for critical everyday issues of divorce or custody.

John and Michelle were a typical California couple who experienced a brief fling with joint custody as a result of mediation. At the time they were both living and working in San Francisco's Silicon Valley. Together they had a comfortable income, although John's pay, $60,000, was three times that of Michelle's. Michelle at first resisted joint custody for her two children, then ages two and five, but was urged by the mediator and close friends that this was better for the children. Her lawyer told her that if she went to court the judge would probably grant it. Michelle believed she could not afford to fight a losing battle. The custody arrangement gave each parent approximately 50 percent time, with the children expected to commute between the two households every other week.

Michelle was unprepared for the rest of the arrangement. According to California law both parents are equally responsible for supporting the children, but if the children spend half their time with each, the obligation is essentially fulfilled. For the higher-wage earner (in most cases the noncustodial father) child support payments are reduced proportionate to the time spent with the child.

The joint custody arrangement did not last long; indeed, it never got started. "From the beginning John asked to change his days because of work. He said he was in a traveling phase. I was expected to have the kids ready to go at an hour's notice. His time got less and less. Now (almost two years later) the kids spend only two or three nights a month at his place at most."

Michelle was not complaining about how little time John spent with the children. "I'm happy I don't have to send them away," she wrote. "I just need my fair share of child support. As you can imagine," she continued, "I could not keep the house. I can only afford a small two bedroom apartment. The apartment is 20 miles from my job and I depend on my car. I must get my children to daycare near my work by 7:00. I will have to quit my job if I cannot keep the car."

This well-meaning California law, which tied child support to time spent with children, was intended to promote more even-handed custody—that is, more time with father. In reality, however, this arrangement is likely to be on paper only. The Stanford study found a significant "mother drift" among the 21 percent of families who elected joint custody. Most of the families that chose this arrangement were considered "high conflict." Among those, fewer than half of the children were spending more than three or four nights with their father in a typical two-week period.[21]

The result is that these children do not spend much time with their fathers, and mothers get less child support. This is a hardship for the mothers, but it has serious consequences for the children as well. Michelle did not say much about her children, but we can speculate that their lives mirror those of other children in the same situation—a common story for divorcing mothers whose incomes fall drastically and who receive little or no support from fathers. We know, for instance, that the children must get up at 5:30 to prepare to drive to the day care center near Michelle's work. We know that they will not return home again until at least 6:00, and that their tired mother must then attend to meals and housework, as well as putting them to bed. We know there will not be much money for frills like pizza at a restaurant or new clothes. We may also suppose that the neighborhood into which she moved will have inferior schools, with little opportunity for special lessons or other advantages of a middle-class upbringing.

★   ★   ★

What do experts say about joint custody? Is it helpful or harmful to children? A growing body of research in this area is at best confusing. Social and behavioral science research has been used in varying ways to fit the agendas of opposing camps; and sometimes the same research has been used by both sides.

The psychological authorities most frequently cited by the courts in the seventies and eighties were law professor Joseph Goldstein, child analyst Anna Freud, and psychiatrist Albert Solnit.[22] Their work during those decades was most often enlisted to support the sole custody model, but was applied to nonparent conflicts as well. In their 1973 book *Beyond the Best Interests of the Child* the authors created the concept of the "psychological parent": the one individual, not necessarily the biological parent, with whom the child is most closely attached. In their opinion this person should have total—and if necessary, exclusive—custodial rights, including the right to refuse visitation to noncustodial parents.

> Once it is determined who will be the custodial parent, it
> is that parent, not the court who must decide under what

conditions he or she wishes to raise the child. Thus, the non custodial parent should have no legally enforceable right to visit the child, and the custodial parent should have the right to decide whether it is desirable to have such visits.[23]

This work became the centerpiece for those who objected to joint custody and advocated instead a model favoring a primarily responsible parent. Initially the mother was almost always found to be the "psychological parent." With the systematic abolition of the maternal presumption, however, researchers focused their attention on fathers. Beginning in the 1970s, these studies were promoted by both feminists and fathers' rights groups. Until this time the literature on fatherhood had been scant. Milton Kotelchuck, the Harvard researcher who performed the first laboratory observations of father–child interactions in the early 1970s, said that it took only one half hour to review the literature, and he read "the full articles, not the abstracts!"[24] Most father researchers studied father–infant relationships in a laboratory setting in which fathers were assigned tasks usually performed by mothers. Occasionally, fathers were studied in real-life situations, with the mothers present. The findings from the many studies were ambiguous and produced heated debates among legal scholars regarding their appropriate application to custody standards.[25] Few if any researchers claimed there were no differences between responses of mothers and fathers to children, but they disagreed on the significance of these differences. For example, the psychologist Michael Lamb found that fathers engaged infants in more rough and tumble play and invented new and unusual games. Mothers were more inclined to conventional games such as peek-a-boo and pat-a-cake.[26] Nonetheless, the message heard by lawmakers was that fathers were, on balance, interchangeable with mothers.[27]

Father studies initially promoted father custody. Eventually these same studies also were relied on by advocates of shared or joint parenting. These advocates argued that if mothers and fathers both can serve as nurturers, the child will benefit by having two rather than one nurturing parent. The concept of "frequent and continuing access" to both parents as being in the best interests of the child became a popular catchword and was written into many state laws.[28]

By the late 1980s father studies were complemented with the findings of long-term studies of parenting arrangements. This research, like the father studies, yielded ambiguous findings. One of the most respected of these researchers, Frank Furstenberg, conducted a five-year study of children with a variety of parental arrangements, including two-parent families. Reviewing his own study and the longitudinal research of others, Furstenberg concluded,

> The policy implications of findings reported here are unsettling because they clash with the prevailing practice that attempts to invent policies which increase parental involvement. On the basis of our study we see little strong evidence that children will benefit psychologically from the judicial or legislative interventions that have been designed to promote paternal participation.[29]

Yet inconclusive findings do not dampen the ardor of those convinced that shared parenting is the best custodial arrangement. By the late 1980s courts could choose from a number of studies that supported shared parenting. In *Zummo v. Zummo*, the court addressed a shared custody arrangement that foundered over a conflict of religion between the two parents. The court chose this conflict as a forum to review the scientific literature regarding joint custody. With no individual analysis of any of the literature, the *Zummo* court cited fifteen scientific studies[30] that it claimed justified joint custody, observing,

> The demise of gender stereotypes, and a wide and growing body of research indicating the importance of both parents to healthy child development have caused courts to reconsider the efficacy of the sole custody/visitation concept of post-divorce allocation of parental authority. Current research indicates that, while it may not be appropriate for everyone, in appropriate cases shared custody options may significantly ameliorate the negative consequences of divorce for children, and for their parents.[31]

By the early nineties, however, some of the original cheerleaders of joint custody had changed their minds. Even the California legislature, which had led the nation, reconsidered: it demoted joint custody from a legislative preference to equal footing with sole custody.[32] The wear and tear on children shuttling between two households grew increasingly evident to some researchers.

*   *   *

Parents do not stay in place. Like most Americans, divorced parents often need to relocate for a new job or sometimes a new spouse. Do both parents then still have the right to "frequent and continuous access" and can a moving parent lose custody because the other parent can no longer stop by on a regular basis? A number of "move away" cases in which courts gave conflicting responses to this question forced a reexamination of the presumption in favor of "frequent and continuing basis."

In response to a move-away case that reached the California Supreme Court, noted divorce researcher Judith Wallerstein, whose work had frequently (although not necessarily accurately) been invoked to support joint custody, observed with regard to the value of "frequent and continuing contact" that ". . . the cumulative body of social science research on custody does not support this presumption." Instead, she noted, "a close, sensitive relationship with a psychologically intact, conscientious custodial parent" is one factor that ameliorates the effects of divorce on the child.[33]

The California Supreme Court essentially agreed. They declared that requiring parents to stay in reasonable proximity to the other parent is an unreasonable expectation and that the stability and integrity of the primary custodian is the most important issue for the child.[34]

Where does this shifting body of research leave the judge or well-meaning parents? Do children need the security of one stable household and one reliable parent, or do they fare better with two households and two parents?

In spite of the seeming contradictory nature of the research, two research-based observations regarding the effects of joint custody are compelling. The first is the robust finding that joint custody does not work well in high-conflict families. The second is that infants and small children have greater needs for stability than older children. The Stanford Study found that high-conflict families do not sustain joint custody. Ironically, these are often the kinds of families in which joint custody is either imposed from the outside or adopted because parents cannot agree on any other arrangement and refuse to relinquish their perceived "rights."[35] Other long-term studies have found that children of high-conflict families fare less well in joint custody situations than in sole custody.[36]

Conflict between parents is a major source of stress for children both before and after a divorce. Domestic violence, of course, is at the extreme end of conflict, but angry words and constant tension also negatively affect children.[37] Joint custody demands a very high threshold of cooperation and may increase the tension and conflict between parents who cannot sustain it. Children caught in the middle, like my daughter's friend Lisa and her sister Anna, are likely to suffer greatly from a joint custody arrangement.

The other research finding we have forgotten in our one-size-fits-all-children custody laws is that infants and very small children (children of tender years) have different cognitive and emotional needs than older children. The attachment literature is reviewed in depth in the next chapter; its major message for the purposes of joint custody is that infants and very small children are not infinitely flexible. Cognitively and emotionally they need more stability and continuity than older children might, and they need round-the-clock caretaking. They need a primary parent. This is not news to those who have cared for babies and small children, but it seems to have been forgotten by policy makers. Infants and toddlers who are shuttled back and forth between mom and dad every few days have become commonplace in some states.

Where does this leave joint custody? What are the best interests of children? Continuing contact with children on the part of the noncustodial parent may be desirable for both children and parents. Yet joint physical custody is not likely to be in the best interests of most children, or of most parents for that matter, except under certain limited conditions. The most important factors to consider, in keeping with what we know about what harms children, are (1) that the child be of a sufficient age to understand and cooperate (at least six); and (2) that both parents are completely committed to the idea and are able to deal with one another on a regular basis in a nonconflictual manner. Since divorce and the events leading to it do not usually foster cooperation, this is asking most couples for more than they can deliver. Some families can march together as the good army did, but they are far from the majority. A further condition is that parents live close enough so that children are not forced to divide their lives day by day or even in large periodic chunks. Two grammar schools is unacceptable, but so also may be two sets of friends and activities. Above all the voices of the children should be heard, and the arrangement should change to adjust to their growing needs.

We may know families in which joint physical custody seems to work out well. Those families are to be admired. Yet for the great majority of post-divorce families this is not a realistic option. To encourage or to order an unwilling parent or parents to execute this arrangement is simply to make trouble for them, and may actually cause harm to their children.

3

A Voice for the Child?

CONSIDER THESE FACTS: A child who steals a candy bar at a Seven Eleven can request a lawyer. A child of fourteen whose parents are dead may choose his own guardian. A girl is entitled to an abortion without notifying her parents in most states. Yet a child who is the object of a brutal tug-of-war between adults is powerless.

In the center of most child custody disputes is a large black hole representing the absence of the voice of the child. There are many ways in which the actual child is not attended to. The wishes and feelings of the child, even a teenager, may not be considered or even sought. The developmental requirements of an individual child may not be presented at trial. And in our typical one-size-fits-all-ages custody legislation the developing needs of children in general may not be considered in drafting legislation that determines custody. Toddlers and teens usually are lumped together in laws that either pose a general best interests standard or suggest a presumption in favor of joint custody without regard to the age of the child—and the custody order issued for a toddler will not be modified as the child's needs grow and change.

Finally, the legal rights of the child (such as they are) are usually not represented. Whether the proceeding is a mediation or a judicial hearing, the focus is too often on the rights of the adults rather than on those of the child. In some custody actions the child's best interests are not even a factor. Such an action may be a contempt hearing for the violation of a custody arrangement or a bid for custody by a biological parent against a "biological stranger" who serves as a parent, such as a stepparent. In these instances the only factor considered is whether contact with the biological parent will actually be harmful to the child, not whether it is in the child's best interests.

A recent Illinois court dispute over visitation between Kathy Marshall and Sheldon Nussbaum illustrates the invisibility and powerlessness of children in the legal process.[1] In this case involving two young girls ages eight and twelve, one child was actually ordered to be imprisoned for violating a civil visitation order.[2] Moreover, the children were given no voice to influence the determination of their very lives. The wishes and feelings of the children, expressed directly to the court and to a trained expert, were completely ignored.

Heidi Nussbaum, twelve, and her sister Rachel, eight, refused to visit their father in North Carolina in the summer of 1995, in violation of a court-ordered agreement between Sheldon Nussbaum and Kathy Marshall. When the judge asked the girls if they were going to cooperate and go to North Carolina, both girls responded that they refused to go. The judge found both Rachel and Heidi to be in direct civil contempt.[3] He "grounded" eight-year-old Rachel, ordering that she not leave her mother's home. Rachel was not to be allowed to watch television or have friends over to the house, but she could read and do crafts. He directed her mother, Kathy, to enforce these measures. The judge ordered twelve-year-old Heidi placed in a juvenile detention facility until she agreed to go to North Carolina.[4]

The judge reasoned that no one had proved that the ordered visitation would endanger the welfare of the children. Further, he held that because the girls' mother was a party bound by the terms of the visitation order, the girls were in contempt of court. Although the judge conceded the girls were not actually parties to the agreement between the parents, he ruled that since they were the subject of it, they were therefore governed by it.[5]

A great deal of expert testimony was introduced at the several hearings preceding the contempt hearing. The psychologist, Dr. Ryan, appeared in behalf of the girls. She had interviewed both girls many times over the period of a year. According to facts later recited by the appellate court, Heidi told Dr. Ryan that "during the recent Christmas visitation in North Carolina, her father woke her up every night and said that it was father/daughter time."[6] For Christmas, she reported, she had received a rifle from her father and they went hunting; her father forced her to shoot a bird. She said she began hearing voices after this visit with her father.[7] In addition, she claimed that during the summer visitation in 1993 her father would keep her up until 4:00 in the morning.

Based on sessions with both Heidi and Rachel, Dr. Ryan recommended to their mother, Kathy, that neither child go to North Carolina for the next scheduled visit. Heidi, she said, was seriously disturbed by the visits. She diagnosed the younger daughter, Rachel, as suffering from "adjustment disorder with mixed emotional features."[8] At a hearing prior to the contempt hearing, however, the judge found Dr. Ryan's testimony "nonsensical" and "less than credible."[9] He ordered that Dr. Ryan have no further input with respect to the counseling of the children.[10]

The judge ultimately ignored the recommendation of his own court-appointed psychologist as well. When the parties were unable to agree on a counselor to help facilitate visitation, he appointed Dr. Patricia Miller. Dr. Miller recommended that the girls not leave on their summer visit until a specific plan was fully established and agreed to by the parties. The judge ordered the parties to cooperate with Dr. Miller and obtain additional counseling sessions to facilitate the children's visitation with their father. At the final contempt hearing a few weeks later Dr. Miller recommended further counseling, since no agreement had been reached. The judge, however, ignored this recommendation and placed the girls in contempt, ordering Heidi to a juvenile detention facility.[11]

In this case the only issue the judge considered was whether the mother could prove that the father was endangering the girls' welfare. Since this was technically a contempt hearing for violating a court order, not a custody hearing, the concept of the "best interests" of the child was never introduced. In cases alleging contempt, as with custody disputes involving nonbiological parents, a detriment standard is imposed. This means that a party must prove by the high standard of clear and convincing evidence that the children will actually suffer harm from the contact, not merely that it is against their best interests. The custody agreement is treated like a contract for an exchange of property. The children are the subject of the contract, the property to be exchanged. Like a recalcitrant mule, the property must be forcefully delivered no matter the circumstances. Under these conditions the world-famous due process rights theoretically granted to all Americans under the Constitution are not available to the children.

In the *Nussbaum* case it appeared at first that the children might have a voice. The judge asked them to explain their failure to comply. Initially, too, he permitted their therapist to testify, but ultimately their voices had no bearing on the outcome. Since the children themselves had no legal rights, they became nothing more than the objects of the dispute. The judge could and did choose to ignore them. This is not just an example of one bad judge or one bad jurisdiction; it represents the state of American law in dealing with children's rights.

Adolescents: The Right to Consent

The idea of legal rights for children apart from those of their parents is relatively new and still very controversial for Americans. Thus far progress toward recognizing children's rights has been jagged and uneven. The Supreme Court first introduced children's rights in the 1960s, the decade that celebrated individual liberties. In a 1965 freedom of speech case in which Quaker school children had protested the Vietnam War in the classroom, the Supreme Court boldly proclaimed that children "did not leave their constitutional rights at the school house door."[12] Yet that same court in the more conservative 1970s allowed censorship of school newspapers[13] and gave school authorities wide discretion to search student lockers.[14]

It is in the arena of juvenile justice that courts have most seriously considered rights for children. In 1965 fifteen year-old Gerald Gault allegedly made an anonymous obscene phone call to an elderly neighbor.[15] Without the benefit of a lawyer or trial Gerald was sentenced to incarceration in a Boys' Correctional Institution until age twenty-one. The ensuing landmark Supreme Court decision, *In Re Gault*, expanded by several subsequent decisions, gave children who were defendants in juvenile court criminal actions nearly all the due process protections that adult defendants receive in the regular criminal courts, including lawyers and the right against self-incrimination.

In a vicious, ironic turn of events in the 1990s, however, state legislatures, responding to increased juvenile crime, grew eager to throw juveniles into adult courts at ever younger ages and to apply adult punishments to children. Today in most states a fourteen-year-old can be tried for murder as an adult, and a sixteen-year-old can be sentenced to execution.[16]

While the Supreme Court has been willing to recognize some limited rights for children with regard to schools, courts, and other governmental institutions, it has been reluctant to grant children rights that might interfere with those of their parents. Much of this concern has focused on abortion. Soon after *Roe v. Wade* the Court conceded that an adult woman's right to abortion extended to adolescent girls as well, but it also carved out plenty of room for parents' rights.[17] The Court decided that individual states could pass parental consent laws. However, with the ambivalence typical of its earlier decisions on children's rights issues, the Court also held that a girl could bypass her parents by going to a judge. If the judge declared that she was a mature minor, the decision was hers alone.[18]

A minor's consent to abortion is an agonizing issue for parents, and it crosses dangerous battle lines into the raging abortion wars. States are seriously divided on the issue, and the battles continue. Yet there has been some progress on the somewhat less controversial issue of adolescent consent to other sensitive medical procedures, such as the treatment of sexually transmitted diseases and drug and alcohol abuse.[19] In many states now a doctor who cannot give an adolescent an aspirin without parental consent can treat the minor for a venereal disease.

As a spillover from these medical concerns, there has been a slight movement toward considering the consent of minors in custody disputes. The Supreme Court remains silent on the topic, deferring, as it almost always does in issues of divorce and custody, to the individual states. Some state laws also remain silent on this issue (as do the children in those states), but many states, under a laundry list of factors to consider, now suggest that a judge should listen to the child's preference if the child is fourteen, or, in some cases, if she or he is "of sufficient age and capacity so as to form an intelligent preference."[20]

This is far from a right to consent, since the adolescent is not given the right to make the choice, only to express a preference. The judge is not bound to acknowledge this preference, only to listen to it. Moreover, a child is not able to initiate a change in the custody arrangement. If a child's needs change, as they often do with developing adolescents, he or she does not have the right to reopen the custody issue; that right is reserved for the parents.

Courts impose custodial arrangements typically without regard to the age of the children and without reference to the available developmental research.[21] Although custody orders theoretically can be modified at the request of a parent, this difficult option is rarely exercised and custody arrangements for the most part remain fixed no matter what the child's age. Modification of custody orders requires significantly changed circumstances. The changing needs of the children alone are not considered changed circumstances for modification purposes.

Custody researcher Judith Wallerstein describes the unhappy visiting arrangement of Ellen, age fourteen, whose custody arrangement had been set by the court when she was six.[22] Ellen was forced to follow a rigid schedule of weekend and summer visitation with her father, whom she feared, thereby missing out on social activity with her peers. According to Wallerstein,

> In her quiet way, Ellen raises a question about the long-term psychological and social effect of a court order (whether for visiting or custody), which is out of sync with the changing developmental needs of the child. Arguing her own case, with tears in her eyes, eczema on her hands, and yet with moderation, she conceded that the visiting order may have served her best interests at age six, but it has become detrimental and hurtful to her interests as an adolescent.[23]

Children generally are powerless to initiate a change in their custody or visitation. Currently it seems to take an act of Congress to give adolescents the power to alter their arrangement. In fall 1996 I noticed a small article in the *New York Times* reporting that Congress had passed a special bill, tucked into a massive $37.9 billion transportation bill, that would temporarily change a District of Columbia law and allow children age thirteen or older under certain conditions to choose whether to visit with a noncustodial parent.

I was taken aback. Was Congress growing soft on children's rights? Reading ahead told me otherwise. This turned out to be yet another chapter in the notorious case of Elizabeth Morgan, the plastic surgeon who twelve years earlier accused her ex-husband of abusing their two-year-old daughter, Ellen. The trial judge in his discretion did not agree with Morgan and sentenced her to two years in jail for refusing to allow the father custodial visits.

Time had passed and now Morgan, who had been living in New Zealand with her fourteen-year-old daughter, wanted to bring her home to America. The court that put her in jail continued to stubbornly enforce the old order, which is often the way with most child custody orders in place from infancy until adulthood. In this instance only a special act of Congress can overrule this court. This is the second special act that Congress, in its unique role as local government for the District of Columbia, has passed for Elizabeth Morgan. The first, in 1989, freed her from jail. Yet this bill, the newspaper assures us, will not open the floodgates for adolescents protesting their own custody decisions; the measure is written so that the only child likely to qualify—and therefore benefit—is Ellen.

This unfolding saga highlights a general disregard for the voice of the developing child. Presumably if Morgan had not had good connections in Congress, Ellen would have had to wait until adulthood to return to America and not be subject to the original custody arrangement.

Without doubt, giving a voice to the child is threatening to many parents. This is as true regarding the right of a mature minor to initiate a change in the custody arrangement as it is regarding the right to consent to an abortion or other medical treatment without parental involvement. Of course, the best model to deal with these sensitive issues is the cooperative model of adolescents and parents working through the decision-making process together. In most instances that is probably the normal course of events: parents rally to the predicament of their pregnant teen in an understanding and supportive manner, and divorced parents respond to the changing needs of their mature adolescents, adjusting the living and visitation arrangements accordingly.

This is not the case, however, with all parents or all adolescents. Family breakup and its aftermath may distort priorities for well-meaning parents. Parents are often unable or unwilling to truly consider the needs of their children first, and many parents no longer cooperate with each other. Sometimes they are more concerned with getting out, or perhaps getting even. The facts of the Nussbaum–Marshall case are commonplace; the children were caught in the crossfire of their parents' hostility. Cooperative decision making in that situation is unlikely.

Rather than being treated as emotional weapons to be hurled between two angry parents, children should be able to assert their own rights. Giving a strong voice to the child should be the first priority in a child-centered custody policy. For older children this might be accomplished by limiting judicial discretion with a legislative preference; for example, "In all disputes, the wishes and feelings of the child shall be given preference in accordance with the age and maturity of the child. A mature minor has the right to consent and to bring an action." This simple statement establishes a mature adolescent's right to make a choice and to initiate a change. Judges as well as mediators who practice in the shadow of the law must not simply consider the mature minor's voice, as they are required to do in some states; they must honor it. Only if one of the parents or other parties fighting for custody can prove that the minor's choice is likely to be detrimental to the child will the judge be able to rule otherwise. Power effectively shifts from the parents to the mature child.

Of course such a shift in power unleashes a hornet's nest of potential problems and consequences. For mature children the result would be akin to a veto power in all custody and visitation arrangements. For Heidi Nussbaum this would mean that no *means* no.

There are several obvious objections to such a rule. First, one might argue that adolescents do not know what is in their best interests. They are likely to make choices for the wrong reasons and may not be able to appreciate the negative consequences of their decisions. Another argument might be that leaving custody decisions to the adolescent invites parents to compete with one another to gain custody, thus putting a great deal of pressure on the child. One might also question the wisdom of allowing a child to skip visiting a parent. Finally, if a parent pays support, doesn't he or she deserve access?

Are children truly competent to make these difficult decisions? In fact there is a large body of scientific research regarding children's competence to consent, most of which deals with juvenile delinquency matters, such as the competence to knowingly waive the right to an attorney. Other research focuses on minors' ability to offer informed consent in medical situations. While significant differences exist among children regarding the age of competence (social class is perhaps the most important variable, with more advantaged children demonstrating on average higher levels of competence at younger ages), evidence seems to indicate that children have the cognitive capacity to exercise rational choices at a significantly earlier age than the law assumes. For instance, in one study comparing nine- to fourteen-year-olds with adults, fourteen-year-olds were found to reason as maturely as adults about hypothetical medical and mental-health treatment decisions. Similar findings have emerged in terms of decision making about abortions.[24] On the basis of a wide range of cognitive developmental theory and research, nearly all scientists suggest that children age fourteen and older possess the requisite cognitive and intellectual capacities to render them comparable to adults, as a group, with regard to competency. And most scientists agree that many children reach this level of functioning by age twelve.[25] Preadolescence (ages ten to thirteen) is a period of significant shifts in cognitive capacities. In relevant situations some minors in this group may perform competently as adults, whereas others may not. Individual determinations may be necessary for this group.

Younger children also are found to have better decision-making powers than is commonly believed. Researchers have found that in some instances the understanding and decision-making skills of seven- to nine-year-olds may not be as sophisticated as adults', yet they may be able to arrive at meaningful and logically derived choices and are often eager to become active participants in the decision-making process. Even those under age seven, while not competent by stringent adult standards, may have reasonable preferences and ideas about what they want.[26]

Does this mean that adolescents truly understand the long-range consequences of their actions? A few years ago my son, then fifteen, confronted me with a real-life situation to test my confidence. His friend Harvey, also fifteen, was wild about cars, like most boys his age. He had a calendar on his wall where he marked down the days till his sixteenth birthday, the day, he was confident, that he would receive his driver's license. He lived with his mom in San Francisco and drove with her, as a student driver, when she had the time. I knew that his parents had experienced an unpleasant divorce seven or eight years earlier and that his dad lived in southern California. They were not my clients, so I knew nothing of the custody arrangement except what my son told me. He said Harvey spent the summer with his dad and went back and forth several other times during the year. Harvey, my son said, had good friends in his dad's neighborhood.

Just before his sixteenth birthday my son announced in outrage, "Harvey's moving to southern California! His dad is giving him a car."Then he looked at me squarely and said, "I bet you approve of this.This is the kind of thing you write about."

My son was understandably upset by his friend moving and saw the car as an unfair bribe. Maybe it was. I will never know the whole story. Let's assume those are the facts.What if a fifteen- or sixteen-year-old is encouraged to live with the other parent by the bribe of a car? Certainly the bribe in this circumstance is not appropriate adult behavior.We may not applaud the decision of the child to succumb to such temptation, but neither would we be surprised.The point is, at this time in the child's life he should be able to make such choices if they do not endanger his welfare, and simply living with his other parent is not likely to be harmful to him.This is in fact the kind of material choice that adults must make as well. Should one take a better-paying job that has less social benefit, or choose a friend who could advance one's career? Note that this situation is precisely the opposite from the Nussbaum case, in which the children were forced to visit their father even though there was evidence that the visits did indeed endanger their welfare.

Such circumstances may provoke an instinctive reaction that offering a bribe to the son is unfair to the mother, particularly if she opposes this move.As far as I know she has been the primary parent since the child's birth. It may indeed be a loss for the mother, but the child is the property of neither the mother nor the father and is of an age to competently make choices about his residence.

A different but important point is:What is the alternative? Do we as a society punish the child for doing something that may be at worst unwise? We have decided that we no longer punish so-called status offenders: children who are habitually truant or who run away from home. We have decriminalized these actions; a child who runs away from school or home or is out of parental control can no longer be involuntarily detained for more than a day or two. Can we punish a child for choosing to live with the other parent, or for refusing to visit a parent? And should we punish a parent for offering him or her a car— an offer many parents make to their children?

What if a child refuses to visit a parent who has faithfully paid child support? The argument that a parent who contributes support deserves access has a certain appeal, but access to the child is neither the legal nor moral ground on which support obligations are founded. A parent, whether custodial or not, is obligated to support a child because he or she has assumed that responsibility by the single act of bringing the child into the world. Child support is not "rent-a-child."

I have counseled distressed parents in situations in which the child refused to visit the other parent (usually for good reason), but the custodial parent is forced to insist on it—fearing the loss of the support payment.

Jane Q. was such a parent. Her daughter Melissa was not quite fourteen at this time. An aspiring young actress, Melissa had been accepted as a student in a prestigious acting school. Classes were on Saturday, which was the day she had been spending with her father, John, every other week since her parents divorced nearly ten years earlier. In this case the divorce and custody negotiations had been complicated by ethnic differences. John is Hispanic, and in Jane's mind, authoritarian. She blames their divorce on what she referred to as his "miserable machismo." For his part, John has expressed his disapproval over what he perceives as Jane's permissive style of raising Melissa.

Melissa begged her father to let her come on Sunday, or a week night, but he was adamant. He said that he, too, had other commitments in his life that he could not change. Jane tried to reason with him also, but he became defensive. "My check is always on time; I meet my obligations, you meet yours," he had responded.

She asked me for advice. "I could insist that Melissa drop this class, but it's her dream. He's just as miserably pig-headed as ever, but I can't risk losing child support."

This was a hard issue for me. Clearly Melissa's life had changed. Her expanding adolescent life could no longer be neatly divided. This was not a parenting situation where cooperation and flexibility were possible. I firmly believed that Melissa's wishes should prevail. Her father's rigidity would only make her increasingly resentful of him. Her developmental needs were changing and so should her custody arrangement.

Yet I knew that if the father refused to pay child support it would be a great hardship for Jane and Melissa, and a judge might well agree with him. He could portray Jane as a non-compliant parent and the judge might issue a contempt order against her. Suspension of child support could be the price of failing to comply. As in the Nussbaum case, the law is not set up to respect the wishes of children, and in a contempt action the best interests of the child is not the rule.

In this instance Melissa herself made the decision. She said she couldn't stand being in the middle of this mess and gave up her acting school to resume her visits. There were no winners in this tale. Ultimately the determination as to whose rights prevail is not so much a scientific assessment of competence as an ethical judgment. The child's wishes in a choice so fundamental as to where and with whom he or she will live, at least part of the time, should be left to the mature child. There may be reasons that the child's wishes ultimately cannot be honored—when the adult is clearly a danger to the child or chooses not to accept the child, for example—but where there is a clear, safe choice, it should be the mature child's to make.

The Middling Years: Six to Adolescence

We can feel fairly confident about the competence of a child fourteen or older, but what about younger children? When are they mature enough to make these decisions, and if they are not sufficiently mature, what role should they have? As I have discussed earlier, the middle years are perhaps the most flexible for children. Heidi Nussbaum, almost thirteen, may well be judged mature (although the person to make this assessment should not be the judge), but what about her younger sister? Rachel was only eight at the time she was held guilty of contempt. She was obviously influenced by her older sister, yet she made it clear that she did not want to return to visit her father. In this case Dr. Ryan, her psychologist, agreed with her decision.

Very few states permit younger children to have a voice. Some judges may talk to children in their chambers for a few minutes, and that may be the beginning and the end of it. Clearly, adults trained to listen to children should be involved in the process. If the child's wishes are clearly and consistently expressed, they should be listened to. If a child refuses to express his or her wishes, that silence should be respected as well. It is the job of the trained adult, usually a mental health counselor, not merely to give her own report but to evaluate the child's report as well. There will of course be instances when the child's opinion is unduly influenced by a parent or parental figure, and the trained adult should take that into account as well.

The problem is not a lack of mental health professionals in the courtroom. If a custody case goes to trial, the room is usually bristling with experts: one for the mother, one for the father, and a court-appointed evaluator as well. The lack of objective standards under a best interests rule reduces the confidence of the judge in her own decision-making ability, which encourages reliance on outside authorities. These court evaluations, performed by court social workers or outside appointed psychologists, provide a wide range of information about the parents and children, including social, economic, and "psychodynamic" data.[27] Surveys of judges indicate that the judge is most likely to listen to the court-appointed evaluator rather than those of the mother and father.[28]

Court-appointed custody evaluators then have a great deal of influence—but are they serving as advocates for the child? Are they listening to the voice of the child of middle years? Not always. The evaluation of Ramona X by a California custody evaluator illustrates the ambiguous role of these court-appointed experts.[29] In this case the parents were disputing the custody schedule of their eight-year-old daughter, Ramona. Ramona's mother, Colleen, wanted her home to be Ramona's primary residence, with liberal weekend visits to her father. The father, Ray, wanted a fixed 50–50 schedule—actual joint physical custody. The evaluator, a clinical psychologist, administered a standard personality test, the Minnesota Multiphasic Personality Inventory test, to both parents to determine their psychological fitness. Then she interviewed Ramona with each of her parents and also by herself.[30]

In her final report submitted to the court the evaluator duti-
fully reported her interviews with each parent and with Ramona. She wrote:

> Ramona talked openly about the difficult she has had ad-
> justing to living in two houses. She complained about
> forgetting to bring things from one house to the other,
> and especially about how the transitions interrupt what-
> ever she happens to be doing. Although she says that she
> loves both parents equally, she says that she is more com-
> fortable at her mother's house (she was unable or unwill-
> ing to say why), and that she did not always feel like going
> to her father's house. . . . She was clear about wanting to
> spend more time with her mother than with her father
> and about missing Colleen when she is at Ray's house.[31]

Nonetheless, the evaluator, noting that "Ray and Colleen are
both good responsible caring parents," also claimed that Ray
was correct in his perception that Colleen undervalued and en-
croached on his time with Ramona. Further, she stated that his
request for a custody order that protects his time with his
daughter was reasonable. Therefore, the evaluator recommended
and the court accepted a plan of joint physical custody. The
plan ordered Ramona "live with her father from Wednesday at
5:30 until Sunday at 5:30 (or Monday 5:30 if Monday is a
school holiday) on alternate weekends and on the other week
from Wednesday at 5:30 until Thursday before school, holidays
to be alternated, with Ray on even numbered years and
Colleen on odd numbered years."[32]

The evaluator in this case could not be considered an advocate for the child. We can hear the voice of the child through
the report. Ramona was clearly calling for more stability in her

life. The evaluator instead followed the current trend in California: joint physical custody, whether or not the parties agree or the child feels comfortable. The equal rights of the parents, not the best interests of the child, became the guiding principle.

A few states offer independent legal representation for children in a custody dispute when there is an indication there may be a conflict with the parents' interests. This is going part of the way toward protecting the children's interests; but these representatives, usually attorneys, are neither trained nor prepared to spend the time to discover the wishes and feelings of an individual child.

One attorney commented on his experience as a child's representative: "I have often wondered when I was representing a child in a delinquency or neglect proceeding, what it meant for me to go up to a 9 or 10 year old and say, 'I'm your lawyer. Here I am: tell me what to do. What do you want me to do in representing you?'"[33]

A child advocate must be more than just an attorney. That person must have substantial knowledge of child development and sophisticated tools for communicating with the child. Working with the child alone is not enough. According to the child psychologist James Garbarino, author of *What Children Can Tell Us,*

> To help answer the custody question an assessment of the quality of the parent-child relationship is needed. This assessment is best accomplished by observing the child with each parent and gathering information from significant adults such as grandparents, teachers and baby-sitters. The psychologist's report and testimony are best used as additional information, rather than as a final recommendation. Some psychologists have recommended that personality

tests not be used to determine custody in court, largely on the basis of the difficulty of interpreting these tests.[34]

English courts, following the Children Act of 1989, provide children with two advocates in any court appearance concerning custody: a legal representative and a personal representative, in most cases a social worker. This may seem a great deal of support at high cost, but the philosophy of the Children Act is that children are the least powerful party in any dispute and need the greatest protection. There are ways in the American system, which I shall discuss in chapter 9, that such support could be provided with mostly volunteer help.

A second critical way by which the voices of children of middling years could be respected is with periodic review of custody arrangements. Most custody orders are fixed at the time of the divorce, with no built-in acknowledgment of the changing developmental needs of children. As with Ellen, whose weekend schedule was determined at age six, most agreements can be modified only on the application of a parent based on a significant change in circumstances—in the parent's life.

All theories of developmental psychology suggest discrete stages of development in a child's life. Jean Piaget, who carefully detailed the development of the child's thought processes, believed that children do not consistently differentiate between the subjective and objective until age seven or eight; before that the separation is not clear.[35] He called the period from about seven to twelve years the "concrete operation stage" of cognitive development, where children begin to reason abstractly, are able to focus for longer periods of time, and can carry through a plan.[36] Similarly, most other modern developmental theorists also mark this middle period as distinct from both the infant years and adolescence. Erik Erickson, in his division of psychosocial development into "the eight ages of man," also recognized the sixth year through maturity as a distinct stage.[37] The most important influences during this period, he claimed, were school and the neighborhood. Children learn industry during this period, and they learn how to plan their own lives.[38] More recently, John Bowlby and the attachment research industry he inspired also make a clear separation between the urgent emotional needs of the earliest years and the more cognitively modulated needs of the middle years.[39]

How can this knowledge of the middling years as a discrete stage of life, with growing cognitive and planning skills, be integrated into our mainly one-size-fits-all custody policies? Parents do not conveniently divorce at the child's developmental watersheds. The custody arrangement may be put into place at nine months or at nine years. A mandatory review at about age seven and again at about age twelve would allow the voice of the developing child to be heard at critical junctures in his or her development. For instance, an arrangement that gave the mother custody and father only limited visitation at nine months could be reconsidered at age seven, when the child requires less physical care and could perhaps benefit from more time with the father. For some families joint custody could become a realistic option at this age. Later, at age twelve, the child's preferences and needs may have shifted. Visitation or residence may shift also, depending on the needs and wishes of the growing child.

If routine reviews and readjustments dependent on the child's developing needs were an expectation of parents rather than an exceptional situation, there might be less stress for all parties. If Heidi and Rachel's father expected that the arrangement could well change when Rachel reached age seven or eight and Heidi age twelve or thirteen, he may have considered a more flexible alternative. He would have realized that he could not perpetually enforce the existing arrangement by means of a contempt hearing. Regular reviews at critical developmental junctures would in fact shift the power balance away from the parents and toward the best interests of the children—supposedly already the letter of the law.

Children of Tender Years

What about infants and children too young to express their wishes and feelings? Most custody disputes begin, at least, with small children. More than 50 percent of all divorces occur by the seventh year of marriage.[40] Therefore the typical custody case is initiated with children who are of "tender years."

Do we know what is in the best interests of very small children from birth to, say, seven years of age? Or put differently, if a very young child had a clear voice, what would the child say? This is a tangled arena where science and politics have continued to wage war for the past two decades.

In dealing with disputes between two biological parents following divorce, the conflict has been framed as one between those favoring a single parent and those favoring joint custody. Both sides claim that their viewpoint represents the best interests of the child, and both sides ardently enlist scientific authorities for support.

The most influential authorities have been Joseph Goldstein, Anna Freud, and Albert Solnit, authors of *Beyond the Best Interests of the Child* (1973), at about the time state legislatures began to knock down the maternal preference.[41] Goldstein and his colleagues insisted that courts focus on the child's psychological and developmental needs and introduced the term *psychological parent* to designate the adult who "filled the child's psychological needs for a parent through day-to-day interaction, companionship, interplay and mutuality."[42] Above all, they stressed, the young child's sense of time and his or her need for steady caretaking and continuity in relationships should govern decision making rather than the rights of parents or biological bonds. They maintained that a best interests standard is unrealistic. The child has already suffered the trauma of divorce, and the best the courts can do is to prevent further harm.

Goldstein and his colleagues built their argument in part on the developmental theories of attachment introduced by Bowlby and his colleagues, who studied mother–infant interaction and catalogued the damage done by "maternal deprivation" when children were separated from their mothers for long periods of time. Bowlby claimed that this loss affected the developing personality; early insecurity could lead to a lifelong sense of unworthiness and difficulty in relationships across the life course, especially with one's own children.[43]

A corollary of the "psychological parent" concept introduced by Goldstein and colleagues is their assertion that there is only one psychological parent. That parent should have sole custody of the child along with sole authority, including the authority to eliminate the visits of the other parent:

> Children have difficulty in relating positively to, profiting from, and maintaining the contact with two psychological parents who are not in positive contact with each other. Loyalty conflicts are common and normal under such conditions and may have devastating consequences by destroying the child's positive relationships to both parents.[44]

These are fighting words to many, especially fathers' rights groups, who believe the psychological parent theory is simply a replacement for maternal preference. In reaction an upsurge of father studies were begun in the 1970s. Until this date father–infant relationships had not been considered an important issue for study.[45] The message to lawmakers—that fathers are, on balance, interchangeable with mothers—supports a gender-neutral custody standard, since fathers can fill this role as well as mothers. As the New York family court concluded in *Watts v. Watts,* "The simple fact of being a mother does not, by itself, indicate a willingness or capacity to render a quality of care different from that which the father can provide."[46] The court further explained that scientific studies show that "[t]he essential experience for the child is that of mothering—the warmth, consistency and continuity of the relationship rather than the sex of the individual who is performing the mothering."[47]

These same studies are also relied upon by advocates of shared or joint parenting. These advocates argue that if mothers and fathers can both serve as nurturers, the child will benefit by having two rather than one nurturing parent.

Given contradictory advice from the scientific establishment and the political pressure of those engaged in gender concerns, it is not surprising that both judges and legislatures have see-sawed on which standard to apply. Most developmental psychologists, though, have held firm over these turbulent decades. They have not thrown the baby out with the cloudy bath water. While scientists are now more cautious about predicting the dire consequences of maternal deprivation and speak of "mothering" in gender-neutral terms, the fundamental concept of attachment introduced by Bowlby has withstood a new generation of researchers—and their findings have direct relevance to legal decision making.

It is still believed, for example, that very young children's emotional needs are urgent. Custody arrangements should accommodate an immature sense of time and the anxieties of separation, as we have seen. Children raised in two-parent families can be assumed to be attached to both parents, yet not all attachments are equal. The give and take, the touching, the focus on the child's concerns are what produce adult–child bonds, and children are likely to benefit from some kind of continuing contact with anyone with whom they have established an emotional bond. For very young children, however, the distinction between a primary and secondary attachment may be an important one.[48]

All of these findings favor the continuity and security of a primary attachment during the first years of a child's life. This attachment takes on even greater importance in the so-called blood wars, in which a biological mother or father who has never parented the child challenges the adult to whom the child is attached, as in the famous adoption cases such as Baby Jessica and Baby Richard, and in the less famous (but far more common) cases of stepparents and other legal "strangers" who find they have absolutely no claim to the children they have raised. They are strangers in the eyes of the law. In these cases, again, the attention is focused on the rights of the adults; the issue of loss for the child is generally dismissed.

Researchers still believe that the early loss of a parent through death or separation increases the risk of emotional and social trauma later in life. An apparent lack of distress in the child at the time may be misleading; but emotional numbing and denial are common responses to death and separation at all ages, and not all children will be affected the same way. Some children are more resilient than others and may resist permanent damage.[49]

What rule would work better for protecting the rights of those children too young to express their wishes and feelings?

As we have seen in the cases of Maranda Smith or Baby Jessica, with very young children we should examine the acts of parenting to determine custody between parents. A move in the law toward a primary parent for young children (at least up to age six), as described in chapter 1, would place the emphasis on actual observed parenting.

The concept of primary caretaker, not primary parent, is already familiar to courts. In West Virginia, one of only two states which have adopted a preference in favor of a primary caretaker, the legislature defines the primary caretaker as the parent who prepares the meals; changes diapers and bathes the child; chauffeurs the child to school, church, friends' homes, and the like; provides medical attention, monitors the child's health, and is responsible for taking the child to the doctor; interacts with the child's friends, school authorities, and other parents engaged in activities that involve the child.[50]

There is much to recommend a primary caretaker preference. First, it allows parents the power of factual presentations to support specific legislative criteria. It is a matter of fact who actually changes the diapers and prepares the meals. A judge does not have to depend solely on the testimony of parents or of opposing experts. More important, in most cases with very small children (but not necessarily older ones), the parent who performs everyday tasks is the one to whom the child is most closely attached.

The introduction of a primary parent, as I conceive it, would emphasize both caregiving and emotional attachment—the primary caretaker and the psychological parent—and it would free us from the battles and alliances that have grown up around the old terms. It could be a two-tiered test: first, the primary caregiver could be established. Then, if the other parent objected to the designation, he or she could press for an emotional evaluation. In rare instances where a parent met the first, but not the second, criteria, other tie-breaking factors would be considered.

Such a preference could also help defuse the blood wars that are waged between biological parents against those who have taken parental roles in the child's life. The automatic preference given to biological parents—such as absentee unwed fathers seeking full rights to custody and birth parents seeking to recover adopted children—would be mitigated by a preference that recognizes the value of actual parenting over the tie of blood.

A primary parent rule would also mitigate the rush to joint custody by emphasizing the importance of continuity and stability in a very young child's life. While fully shared or joint custody may be possible for children of middling years (ages seven to twelve) and may be specifically chosen by adolescents, it does not meet the developmental needs of very young children as we know them.

A reform of custody law that focuses on the voice of the child of tender years then would guide the best interests standard with the preference:

> For children of tender years (under age seven), the parent who has acted as the primary parent shall be given preference in determining custody arrangements.

This preference will not decide all cases, nor should it. A legal preference merely means that if both parents are fit, the court will apply a rule—like the primary parent rule—that says that society generally believes very small children receive better nurture in the custody of the parent who has served as the primary parent.

Critics of a primary parent standard may complain that this rule does not treat fathers equally. I would argue that custody issues should be removed from the gender wars. From a child's point of view, gender is not the issue; rather, it is the need for assurance of the continuity of a nurturing parent.

Returning to Rachel and Heidi Nussbaum: the good news is that they were released from the sentence of juvenile detention and house arrest. The bad news is that their voices are still not heard. The Illinois Court of Appeals ultimately reviewed the Nussbaum case and found that the trial court judge was within his discretion both when he ordered the two girls to visit their father and when he ruled them in contempt when they refused.[51] The appellate court did reverse the sanctions he imposed (juvenile detention for Heidi and house arrest for Rachel) and ordered that the court attempt to find a less restrictive alternative. However, the appellate court explained in its ruling,

> ... this should not be construed as a criticism of the manner in which the trial judge conducted himself. Heidi and Rachel's words and conduct were disrespectful to the court, and the judge demonstrated patience and an even temperament throughout the proceedings. Hopefully, during the pendency of this appeal, the parties have come to realize that noncompliance with visitation orders can carry grave legal and emotional consequences for parents and their children.[52]

Once again, the appeals court said not a word about the best interests of the children and gave no credence to their voices except to say they were disrespecful to the court. Neither the trial court judge nor the appeals court judge in this case are particularly unjust individuals; they are simply enforcing the rules of a system that focuses on the rights of parents rather than the wishes or feelings of the children.

4

Enter the Unwed Father

CALIFORNIA RECENTLY PUT INTO ACTION a statutory rape initiative for the purpose of jailing older men who had fathered babies with underage girls. Technically statutory rape means that one of the partners—even if consenting—is a minor. These men were over twenty and the girls were under eighteen, often by many years.

Initially there was a loud libertarian hue and cry. And tearful teen girls appeared on TV news shows begging judges to save their man. At first I sympathized with this point of view. I viewed the initiative as a clumsy and punitive effort in the overall government campaign to get "deadbeat dads." Then I spoke with a friend, an assistant district attorney charged with carrying out this initiative in one California county, who told me he had originally agreed with my point of view and now saw the matter differently.

"You don't know how vulnerable these girls are," he said. "It's not consent, it's child abuse." He told me the story of Jacquie, who grew up in a large Hispanic family with an alcoholic, abusive father. From the time she was thirteen one of her older brother's friends, Raymond, then twenty, began to hang around her and eventually got her pregnant. She had her first child by him at fourteen and her second at sixteen. She continued to live at home because she had nowhere to go and she would not leave her babies. She said her father and brothers would not protect her in any way; that in fact they supported Raymond. Finally she got the courage to leave for her aunt's house after the birth of her second child, but Raymond followed her. He told her he was the father and had a right to be with his children. After a nasty incident in which she was slightly injured, the police got involved. My friend, the assistant district attorney, decided to charge statutory rape, which can carry a serious jail term, whereas domestic violence without serious injuries usually does not.

A significant fact of Jacquie's case—and in all the statutory rape cases pursued in this initiative—is that none of these older fathers were paying child support. My guess is that if they were paying child support, not only would the legal system refuse to pursue a statutory rape charge, they would insist that the father have as much access to the child as he wished, regardless of the concerns of the mother. The statutory rape initiative had been impelled by the greater drive to get deadbeat dads, not by a desire to protect teen mothers or their children. More prominent in this multifaceted drive is the government's efforts to promote involvement of fathers with their children, regardless of the age or the wishes of the mother.

As the end of the twentieth century approaches, nearly a third of all babies are born to unwed parents.[1] This fact more than any other in recent history has changed the nature of the family and provoked a serious national debate. The vigorous crusade for fathers' rights following divorce has been taken up by a few unwed fathers; but the rights of unwed fathers to their children has been pursued far more forcefully by the federal government in its relentless campaign to wrest child support from unwed fathers, most of whom do not pay child support.

Almost 70 percent of women on welfare were unmarried when they had their first child.[2] In a conscious effort to tie the obligation of support to the right to custody of the child, courts and legislatures increasingly have promoted the rights of unwed fathers. Once again there is no real consideration for the best interests of the child in introducing this trend. Unwed fathers, who only twenty-five years ago held no legal rights and were only sporadically pursued for child support, now claim the same rights as wed fathers, and increasingly are held to support obligations. This newly recognized biological right has exploded onto the custody battlefield with tremendous force.

The biological rights of unwed fathers are often asserted in visitation and custody cases, but the most public disputes have occured in the context of adoption. Adoption cases catch public attention because they offer human drama and touch our most intimate emotions. They typically involve a very young child and pit adoptive parents who have nurtured the child against an unwed father who may never have seen him or her. The public is incensed to witness on television a child torn away from parents to whom she or he is clearly attached. They wonder how the law can be so unfeeling to children. These adoption cases are perhaps the clearest example of how law and public policy have focused on biological rights at the expense of children's interests. The public has seen up close that the best interests of the child is not the standard used when pitting the rights of a biological parent— even when not married to the mother—against the rights of those who have served as parents but who can offer no blood tie.

★   ★   ★

In the typical unwed father/adoption case the mother makes the decision to relinquish the baby for adoption. The father may or may not know about this decision. Sometimes, as in the celebrated Baby Jessica case, the mother may deceive him about who the father is, and he may learn the truth only after the baby is in the arms of new parents. In the Baby Jessica story, after nearly two and a half years of legal wrangling the child was removed from the home of her adoptive parents and returned to her biological father, whom she had never seen. The law in this instance considered the biological rights of the father paramount to the fact that Baby Jessica had spent all but a few days of her life in the home of her adopting parents. The legal argument was complex, based on federal constitutional rights and state legislation, but the result was that the blood tie was chosen over actual parenting history.

This is not always the result, however. Some courts have struggled over when to restrict the rights of unwed fathers in adoption situations, and a few have attempted to set clearly defined limits. There is a realization by a few courts that children's interests are being ignored by poorly thought out public policy. In a recent case the California Supreme Court, which often sets the trend for the nation, tried to reconsider this policy.[3] Stephanie H. met Mark K. when she was fifteen and he twenty, a typical scenario for unwed parents. He said he wanted to marry her but she declined, saying she wanted to wait until she finished high school and he quit drinking and using drugs; but they considered themselves engaged. Two years later Stephanie learned she was pregnant. Mark suggested an abortion, but she would not consider it. They talked briefly about keeping the baby, but decided on adoption.

They began attending birthing classes together and Mark accompanied Stephanie to a yard sale to buy baby clothes. He bought a trailer for them to live in together, although they never did. As the pregnancy progressed, their relationship began to deteriorate. Stephanie excluded him from birthing classes. Mark assaulted Stephanie, and after the second incident he was arrested for aggravated assault. He then quit his job, and two days later, on Stephanie's sixteenth birthday, went into the trailer and tried to kill himself.

After that episode Mark and Stephanie had almost no contact. Stephanie completed her pregnancy in the home of John and Margaret, the adopting parents. Meanwhile Mark entered a rehabilitation hospital and decided to give up drugs and seek stable employment. He also decided to try to obtain custody of his child and sought the help of a lawyer. As soon as he learned the baby had been born he sent out birth announcements, bought a car seat, a crib, some baby clothes, and filed his action.

As with so many cases in our clogged legal system, this case bounced among courts for years. By the time it worked its way up to the California Supreme Court, baby Michael had been living with his adoptive parents for four and a half years. The trial court and appeals court both had ruled that Mark had a constitutional right to preserve his opportunity to develop a relationship with his child.

Yet the courts were standing on new and shaky ground. The U.S. Supreme Court, as we shall see, had not given unwed fathers unrestricted constitutional rights; in some cases the Court had insisted that the existence of a biological link alone was not enough,[4] that it must be accompanied by a father "coming forth to participate in the rearing of his child" and "acting as a father."[5]

The California Supreme Court worried over Mark's actions as a would-be father. Although he had shown relentless diligence in pursuing his paternal claim after the birth, initially he had agreed to the adoption. He had not shown the proper intent to commit himself to parenthood. Moreover, he had not adequately attended to the prenatal needs of fifteen-year-old Stephanie. On balance the court decided he had no constitutional right to block the adoption.

Given the facts of this case, the decision to leave four-and-a-half-year-old Michael with his adoptive parents is appropriate by virtually anyone's standard. If there were a jury trial and the jury were asked to decide in the best interests of the child, there is little doubt what they would choose. The decision was made, however, not from a child-centered point of view but rather from careful weighing of a balancing test that leans strongly toward fathers' rights. The majority of the judges gave only brief consideration to the effect of wrenching Michael from devoted parents. They were somewhat more concerned about the contract rights of the adoptive parents who took on the child with the understanding that the father approved the adoption; in other words, they did not get what they bargained for in good faith. They are given little credit for their actual parenting.

A lone dissenting judge (a woman) decided that the majority had made the right decision but for the wrong reasons. This judge asserted that Mark in fact met the very low standard of parental responsibility defined by California courts, but that the child Michael should be the real consideration. The effect of removing a four-and-a-half-year-old from a good and nurturing home should have been the principal consideration of the court, the judge observed.[6]

Child development experts would agree with this dissenting judge. Recent research has shown that the early loss of a parent figure, whether through death or separation, increases the risk of emotional and social dysfunction in later life.[7] This does not mean that all children who experience loss will experience later dysfunction, but it has been shown to increase their odds significantly. Although young children may sometimes appear to recover quickly and be amazingly flexible, emotionally they are more complex than they seem. From a child-centered perspective an abrupt separation from the person or persons to whom she or he is attached does not bode well.[8] These developmental concerns are important in choosing between two parents, as discussed earlier, but they are critical in choosing one who is, in the child's eyes, a parent—and a stranger.

How did we come to value the rights of unwed fathers over the best interests of the child? California, as with most states, no longer recognizes a best interests standard in dealing with an unwed father's right to custody against those who have acted as parents but are not so biologically. If Mark had been given the right to block the adoption, he would have been granted custody unless he was found to be unfit. In choosing between a biological parent and a "biological stranger," as they are referred to (such as a stepparent), it must be shown that it would be *harmful* to the child to live with the biological parent, not merely in that child's best interests. Therefore the adoptive parents would have to prove that Mark's behavior or lifestyle would endanger the child. This is difficult to prove unless he has past convictions of child (but not spousal) abuse or he can be found to be dangerously unstable at the moment of hearing. The fact that Mark has expressed violent and unstable behavior in the recent past would probably not be enough.

What is imperative about the rights of biological parenthood? Why do we automatically presume that living in the custody of the biological parent is best for the child? On some level most Americans and most human beings would acknowledge the importance of biological parenthood. We observe that in most circumstances parents favor their children over others and are likely to make sacrifices for them that other adults are not. One school of sociobiologists claim that adults will only promote the interests of their biological children, and that other family formations, such as stepfamilies, should be discouraged.[9] This group often points to studies that claim that children are far more often physically and sexually abused by their stepfathers (wrongly confusing cohabitors with stepfathers) than by their natural fathers.[10] Yet we also have observed adoptive parents, stepparents, and other "biological strangers" who have lovingly parented the children whom they have come to think of as their own, and we have witnessed biological parents—usually fathers—walk away from their children and never look back.

We have not always recognized the rights of unwed biological parents. For the first two hundred or so years of our history neither the biological father nor the biological mother had any rights over their child if the child was born outside of marriage. Promotion of the institution of marriage and concern for the orderly and proper distribution of inheritance prevailed over the rights of biological parents for most of our history.

The story of the rights of unwed parents is a strange one. In colonial America neither the mother nor the father possessed a legal right to the custody of a child born out of wedlock. English common law defined *bastard* (the legal term for a child born out of wedlock) as "filius nullius," the child and heir of no one, bearing no legally recognized relations with either parent. A bastard had no right to inheritance from either of his parents, and town officials for the most part determined who would raise the child.

Not only were their parental rights unrecognized, but unwed parents (particularly mothers) also were severely punished for their unlawful sexual activities, and fathers were expected to pay support to whoever was caring for the child. If the suspected father denied his fatherhood, evidence could be brought against him. Particularly damning was the accusation of the mother while giving birth; this was considered highly credible by the courts. All the colonies adopted civil laws for support of the child and criminal penalties to discourage fornication.

For example, the records of Prince George County during the years 1696 to 1699 show ten female servants who were found guilty by the court of "bastardizing." The fact that these mothers were all servants is not surprising. Indentured servitude was the principal method of immigration in the Southern colonies. Thousands of teenagers (and sometimes younger children) were shipped over from England to feed the labor-hungry new country. These young servant girls without families were particularly vulnerable to sexual exploitation. They were treated harshly. In seven of the aforementioned cases corporal punishment ranging from ten to thirty lashes (thirty for a third offender, and twenty-six for a servant bearing a mulatto bastard) was imposed on the mother.[11] In no case was a father whipped.

*   *   *

The most noteworthy fact in these cases is that apparently none of the mothers retained custody of their children, and certainly none of the fathers took custody. In several cases the court ordered the offending servant to serve an additional year or half year for the disgrace and trouble to her master's house and ordered the child to be bound out (indentured) until the age of twenty-one. In one such instance the child was only thirteen months old.[12] In most cases the father was not identified, and in all cases the child was apprenticed to another as soon as was feasible. One mother was given a reprieve while nursing: "Ruth Sansbury brought a Child of Stephen Ashbees (who is runneway)" and the court determined "it being not weaned ... that it Continue with her the Said Ruth to have twelve Hundred pounds of Tobacco per year for Nurseing of it."[13]

★   ★   ★

The nineteenth century was kinder to mothers, married and unmarried, and it was certainly kinder to children. In a radical shift in perspective, childhood came to be viewed as a period of nurture rather than of work, and the best interests of the child were put forth as being superior to parents' rights. In most instances the children's best interests became firmly allied with their mothers'. Mothers were considered the natural nurturers of their children and the appropriate custodians for children of tender years. Pushed aside by this new nurturing perception of children and childhood, the common law definition of an illegitimate child as filius nullius, the child and heir of no one, gave way to firm legal recognition of the bond between mother and child. By the end of the nineteenth century almost every state had passed legislation declaring that a child was a member of his or her mother's family, with a right to inherit from the mother the same as a legitimate child.[14] The mother in turn was given the parental prerogatives normally given to the father in a family in which the parents were married. Beyond that the criminal punishment for producing the illegitimate child—the whippings and fines that took up so much of the courts' time and energy in the colonial period—virtually disappeared, leaving only a civil procedure for determining paternity and enforcing support.[15]

Unwed fathers did not fare as well in the nineteenth century. The child now belonged to the family of the mother, and except for the obligation of support, unwed fathers increasingly were treated as strangers to the child. A New Hampshire court in 1836 recited the emerging rule in response to the father of a twenty-two-month-old "bastard" who offered to take the child rather than pay the Town of Hudson 40 cents per week. "It is well settled that the mother of an illegitimate child has right to custody and control against putative father, and is bound to maintain it as its natural guardian. . . . The putative father has no right to the custody and control of the child, except, perhaps, as against a stranger; and his right to this extent is questionable."[16] Even when the mother died courts were unwilling to grant the unwed father custody. They were more likely to give the child to the mothers' relatives or to nonrelatives who were actually caring for the child. As one Minnesota court explained in 1877 when awarding the child to biological strangers who had been caring for the child, the father "has, in law, no better title to its custody, and no more right to ask for it, than any other person."[17]

For a century or so this was the commonly accepted rule. Even a father who lived with the mother and shared in raising the children usually had no legal rights. That was the case of Joan and Peter Stanley, who had lived together intermittently for eighteen years, during which time they had three children. Upon her death in 1969, the children were declared wards of the court under an Illinois statute directing that children of unwed fathers become wards of court on the death of the mother. Stanley objected, claiming that Equal Protection under the Constitution required that he be treated like married fathers, who are presumed fit custodians under Illinois law, whether they are divorced, separated, or widowed.

In 1971 the U.S. Supreme Court partly agreed and determined that Stanley deserved a fitness hearing, as would be the case for all natural parents in this circumstance, before the children could be made wards of the court. If Stanley met the low criteria of parental fitness, he would retain custody of his children. Justice White declared: "The private interest here: that of a man in the children he has sired and raised, undeniably warrants deference and, absent a powerful countervailing interest, protection."[18] For the first time in American history, unwed fathers were given legal recognition.

Peter Stanley had physically lived with his children and acted as a parent, performing all the parental duties of a married father over a number of years. What about the more common case of an unwed father who has neither lived with the child nor acted as a parent? Following *Stanley*, the U.S. Supreme Court struggled further to determine the limits of the rights held by biological fathers who did not cohabit.[19] Did biology alone create a father's right, or was fatherhood a more complex phenomenon?

Jonathan Lehr and Lorraine Robertson had never lived together, and when their daughter Jessica was eight months old Lorraine married Richard Robertson. Jessica was over two years old when Robertson filed a petition to adopt Jessica. There was a factual dispute concerning Lehr's attempts to see his daughter, Lehr claiming that Lorraine tried to hide their whereabouts and that at one point he had hired a private detective to find his daughter. Lorraine claimed he always knew where Jessica was.

Lehr insisted he was denied Equal Protection under the Constitution since he received no notice and opportunity to protest termination of his parental rights, as would a divorced father. The majority of the Supreme Court disagreed. Justice Stevens stated:

> The significance of the biological connection is that it offers the natural father an oppportunity that no other male

possesses to develop a relationship with his offspring. If he grasps that opportunity and accepts some measure of responsibility for the child's future, he may enjoy the blessings of the parent-child relationship and make uniquely valuable contributions to the child's development. If he fails to do so, the Federal constitution will not automatically compel a State to listen to his opinion of where the child's best interests lie. [20]

★   ★   ★

Thus the Supreme Court dragged unwed fathers out of legal limbo and gave them the right at least to be notified if their offspring was going to be adopted or taken as a ward of the state, but only if they met the criteria of having established an "actual family relationship." Exactly what that meant was left up to the states to define.

What the Supreme Court did not do was set a standard for settling a custody dispute. The Court did not insist that a child must be given to an unwed father rather than a biological stranger, unless it could be proven that living with that father would be a detriment or danger to the child. States were still free to apply their own tests, which could include a more child-centered best interests test or even a primary caretaker presumption. Under such child-centered rules stepfather Richard Robertson, who had acted as Jessica's parent since she was nine months old, would probably prevail over Lehr and be allowed to adopt the child; but so too would unwed father Stanley, who had also served in an actual parenting role.

Most states have chosen to go beyond the Supreme Court, giving unwed fathers the full-blown rights of a married father. They have abandoned the child-centered best interests test in favor of a "detriment" test. A detriment test says nothing about a child's best interests; it simply states that the child will be placed with the father, no matter who has done the parenting, unless it can be proven by clear and convincing evidence that it is detrimental to the health, safety, or welfare of the child to live with him. This means that Mark K., the unwed father introduced earlier, would probably prevail against the adoptive family in California and many states—in spite of his violent and unstable history—if he met the minimal requirements of parental intent. Yet the rights of biological strangers who have thought and acted as parents for many years are not considered at all. As Justices Burger and Blackmun predicted in their dissent to the Stanley case, "[The Court] embarks on a novel concept of the natural law for unwed fathers that could well have strange boundaries as yet undiscernible."[21]

Consider another twist of the biological plot: How does one now regard the rights of unwed fathers when the mother is married to another man who is legally presumed to be the father of the child?

In still another California case contemplating the newly gained rights of unwed fathers, Michael M. sought a paternity action to establish his claim as the father of a baby born to his former fiancée, Giovanna. Michael and Giovanna had lived together sporadically and became engaged for a period of time in the fall of 1988. Michael claimed Giovanna was pregnant when they ended their engagement. He said he wrote to her to confirm this fact, but she did not respond. In the spring of 1989 Giovanna married Matthew. Michael did not learn about the marriage until July 1989 when he saw Giovanna, who appeared to be in the last weeks of a full-term pregnancy. Michael tried to speak with her about her pregnancy. She refused to talk to him and eventually obtained an order restraining Michael from further contact with her and her husband. In August Matthew contacted Michael and informed him that Giovanna had given birth, but refused to tell him the birth date or the name of the baby. Michael then sought a declaration of paternity and joint physical and legal custody of Brian.

As the California court admitted (when it finally decided the case four years later), by the standards of common law, constitutional law, and California's own statutory law, Michael should not have a chance. It is well established in common law, they noted, that when a child is born to a married couple the husband is presumed to be the father, unless he is physically unable or is physically absent—away at sea, for example, or war. If he is present, another man is barred from claiming paternity. California's law, based on the Uniform Parentage Act, clearly follows common law rule. A biological father cannot sue for a declaration of paternity if there is a presumed father, and the biological father may not take the child into his home and hold him out as his own.

The rationale behind this time-tested principle is that a stranger should not be able to invade the sanctity of an intact family. If a husband, with the agreement of his wife (only married couples are considered in this tradition), is willing to accept the child of another man, hold himself forward as the father, and raise the child as his own, society and the law should support this decision and protect the integrity of the family. Historically this tradition also protected the child. A child with a married father would not suffer the stigma of illegitimacy or bastardy. For all these reasons the biological connection in this situation was to be strictly ignored.

Only a few years before Michael M. brought his action the U.S. Supreme Court had considered the same issue, but with different facts. In that Supreme Court case a married international model pursued a jet-set life that included several adulterous affairs. She acknowledged that one of her lovers was the father of her daughter, but then returned to live with her husband and denied the lover visitation. The U.S. Supreme Court (in a split decision) denied his rights, claiming that a biological father has no liberty interest strong enough to overcome a state's interest in preserving the integrity of the family.[22]

In spite of the Supreme Court's ruling, the California court decided that Michael M. indeed had the right to establish paternity with a view to gaining joint custody. The court noted that California led the nation in extending the rights of unwed fathers who had made a significant effort to become parents, even when they were thwarted in their attempts. Although Michael M. had not parented Brian—indeed he had never seen him—he had shown good intentions. Moreover, the court reasoned, this was not truly a case of protecting family integrity, since Giovanna was already pregnant by Michael when she married and her husband was aware of this. This was very different from the case of the international model, who was already married, they declared.

While this case, as so many of the unwed father tales, reads like a soap opera, real issues are at stake. All the parties passionately believe they have been seriously wronged. Matthew believes he has acted in all respects as a father and deserves to be legally treated as such. Giovanna believes that Michael has no moral or legal claim and will only cause trouble for her and Brian, and Michael believes he has a biological and legal right to have access to his son.

What about Brian, now age four? As usual, the California court paid little attention to his rights or even to his needs. Brian's best interests were not considered at all in the decision.

By contrast, in the U.S. Supreme Court case involving the international model and her lover, a guardian ad litem (representative for the child) presented the novel argument that the child had a right to be with her biological father. This of course turns conventional wisdom, which strove to protect children from the stain of illegitimacy, on its head. The Court, however, dismissed this argument rather curtly.

What was not said about Brian's rights or needs is his necessity for both stability and lack of familial conflict. While it is difficult and perhaps not desirable to explore the individual wishes and feelings of a four-year-old, we do have clear knowledge about the developmental needs of children generally at this age. They require the stability of a primary caretaker to whom they are attached, and they need to be shielded from familial conflict. Countless studies focusing on both married and divorced families indicate that conflict produces serious negative results in children.[23] Ultimately if Michael's paternity tests bear him out, what is now an argument about who the father is will become a custody dispute. Brian will be subject to a new, additional father who will claim him part or even half of the time. It is unlikely that Giovanna and Matthew will take to this arrangement easily, and Brian will bear the brunt of the adults' conflicts.

This is not to say that children can have only one father. In many stepfamilies, as I shall explore later, both the noncustodial natural father and stepfather play parenting roles in their children's lives. Yet these noncustodial fathers are simply continuing the active parenting role they played during the marriage; they are not being introduced into the child's life as a new father. Other important differences with stepfamilies will be reviewed as well.

What if Giovanna had not married Matthew but was living with him? Or what if she were living alone? Under these circumstances should Michael have full custodial rights? This is a more difficult question. Most courts today would answer yes under certain circumstances: if he is fit and has met a minimum threshold of parental involvement, or if he has shown an intention of parental involvement that has been thwarted through no fault of his own.

This is not a child-centered trend. There may be good reasons why a mother chooses not to share custody voluntarily with the man who fathered her child. She may believe he is unstable, violent, or unable to contribute to family life. Or, like the teen mother, Jacquie, introduced earlier, the mother may be young, exploited by an older man who never intends to marry her but will not leave her alone. Unwed fathers are significantly different from divorced fathers. In the first place they have not married the mother, nor is it likely they have lived with her or the child (only a small percentage of unwed fathers are cohabitors).[24] The reasons for this behavior are varied: their relationships were brief, perhaps, lasting only a week or a night; perhaps they are reluctant to take on responsibility. Whatever the reason, these fathers have not made the same legal and moral commitment as have divorced fathers.

As a group, the fitness of unmarried fathers is problematical as well. It is estimated there are about 1.6 million unwed, nonsupporting fathers. They are young, poor, and most have been in trouble with the law. On average they are twenty-six years old and have just under eleven years of education. Fifty-five percent are African American, 30 percent are white, and 12 percent are Hispanic. The Manpower Demonstration Research Corporation found that in New York, 75 percent of nonsupporting unwed fathers had been arrested and 46 percent had been accused of a crime.[25] Research shows that white unwed fathers are three times more likely to have used drugs and have criminal records than married fathers. African-American unwed fathers do not appear much different from African-American married fathers on these counts, but this is a difficult comparison; proportionately there are many more of them than married African-American fathers.[26]

Unlike married fathers or unwed fathers in other countries, unwed fathers in the United States are not living with their children.[27] Moreover, they have not as a whole proven themselves committed to spending time with the children they father. In one large-scale study the proportion visiting at least *once per year* fell from nearly 60 percent within the first two years of birth to only about 20 percent after the children reached age seven.[28]

In addition, unwed fathers are not good supporters—far worse in fact than divorced fathers. Only about 13 percent of never-married mothers reported to the census bureau in 1985 that they received any support at all from the fathers of their children. Fathers themselves report a much higher rate (35 percent) of contribution, but this may be cash or gifts to the child on a more casual basis than a monthly check.[29]

Frank F. was such a father. Frank, an acquaintance of my son, was seventeen when his girlfriend, Marsha, also seventeen, gave birth to Kevin. They were both seniors in high school and chose to continue living with their own families, the pattern followed by most young teen parents (a generation ago they probably would have married, or chosen not to keep the child). Frank worked part time in a hardware store and he brought Kevin two boxes of diapers and new toys every weekend. He gave Marsha $40 every payday. Marsha encouraged Frank to spend time with Kevin and never obtained a support order. Frank went off to college the following year, while Marsha continued to live at home and attended the local community college. Frank was always loaded with gifts when he came to see Kevin on breaks and holidays, and he would give Marsha a cash present as well, but overall his annual support probably amounted to less than $500.

Such lack of support most strongly fueled the drive for unwed fathers' rights. Beginning in 1975, the federally funded Aid to Families with Dependent Children (AFDC), noting the growing trend in poor single mothers, required all states who participate to locate the fathers of recipient children, married or unmarried. Up until this time social service agencies had attempted only spotty and desultory efforts at collecting child support from absent fathers (and occasionally mothers). The race to get so-called deadbeat dads was on.[30] Once the race was joined, acceptance of unwed fathers as weekend fathers increased dramatically. "If you pay, you get to play" became accepted social policy.

"Pay and play" sounds fair, but is it child-centered? The obligation to support has not historically triggered a right to visitation or custody. The rationale for imposing support obligations (as opposed to that for permitting custody and visitation) was vastly different. Support was considered a moral and legal obligation incurred by the act of bringing a child into the world, an obligation owed to the child and to society. Custody or visitation, however, was based solely on the best interests of the child. It is not always in the best interests of a child to have forced contact with a parent; it may in fact be quite contrary to her or his best interests. Given the overall problematical nature of unwed fathers and the fact that many have had little or no contact with the child (or for that matter with the mother), why should support automatically guarantee custody and visitation rights?

Furthermore, this policy has not produced hoped-for economic results. It has cost far more to identify and track down unwed fathers than has been gained in child support. Large, expensive, private and governmental programs have been launched to try to raise these fathers to the level of employability. One program officer in a large Rockefeller Foundation job-training effort refers to the trainees as "turnips"—as in "you can't get blood from a turnip."[31] Some children actually *lose* support: the government now collects the child support to offset AFDC (now called Temporary Aid to Needy Families, or TANF) rather than to give to the children for whom the support is intended. Many fathers who previously had provided casual under-the-table support no longer do so.

In considering the rights of unwed fathers versus those of unwilling mothers (as opposed to biological strangers, as with adoption), at least three choices are available to the courts. The first is the traditional rule, in effect from the nineteenth century until the recent past, that these children are part of the mother's family and that she is the primary parent and must make the decision about visitation or shared custody. The second is to give unwed fathers rights to visitation or custody against the wishes of unwilling mothers only when they have met certain strict criteria. These criteria must focus not on fitness but on the father's actual relationship with the child and the degree and quality of parenting achieved. If the children are old enough their wishes should also be considered. This is not possible with babies, of course, if the mother has not allowed father participation, but it does cover the situation of a cohabiting couple who have had a falling out. The third choice is the current trend to consider unwed fathers the same as divorced fathers. The second option is the most child centered, since it focuses on the proven parenting involvement of the unwed father; some unwed fathers do take an active role in parenting. Also some may be accepted initially by the mothers as active participants in their children's lives and later rejected through no fault of theirs in their role as parent. Unless a man has held himself out as the father and has significantly involved himself in the life of his child, however, the mother's wishes should predominate—not biology.

What about the unwed father who is barred by the mother at birth from parental involvement? In those instances it can also be argued that the mother's choice should be honored. The unwed father may or may not prove to be a worthy parent, but if the mother does not want him in the child's life, the result will most likely be conflictual. Many young unwed mothers experience domestic violence at the hands of the father of their child. In many cases, particularly with teen mothers, these fathers are older and more powerful than the mothers. Given the demographics of unwed fathers, it is not obvious that the parenting relationship would be in the best interests of the child. In any event the issue of support should not be the determining factor.

We should in fact revisit our now widely accepted deadbeat dad policy. Are we collecting enough support from unwed fathers to justify this huge criminal initiative? What are the effects of this government war plan on children and their mothers? Pushing fathers into the lives of their children without the active cooperation of the mother is not likely to promote a happy childhood.

★   ★   ★

Applying general principles to real-life situations is never easy. Frank and Marsha, who began their young teen parenting with good spirit, eventually began to view one another with hostility.

Frank finished college and obtained a decent job as a salesman in a nearby town. Marsha approached him asking for a regular child support check. She said it was her turn; she needed to move out of her parents' home and finish college. Frank agreed to a very small sum, claiming he still had college loans to repay, a car to buy, an apartment, and all the expenses of a working adult. Marsha threatened to go to court for a support order. She told him the court would back her claim and take it out of his wages if he refused to pay. He countered that he would go for joint custody. If he was going to give up half his pay he wanted something for it.

Marsha came to me for advice. She could not tolerate the idea of five-year-old Kevin being shuttled between two households. "He's a fragile child," she told me. "He hardly knows Frank. His grandfather has raised him, not Frank." I told her it was quite possible that the California court would order shared custody for Kevin; that could be as much as 50 percent time. I suggested they work harder at a better arrangement. Marsha, however, did not approach Frank again, nor did he contact her. Apparently he was just as afraid of paying support as she was of losing Kevin. As far as I know they have severed all contact.

It is difficult to know how better to resolve their situation. The California court may well have imposed joint custody, even though Frank had exhibited minimal parental involvement. Kevin knew Marsha's friends better than he knew his own father. Perhaps because he had not done so before, Frank felt that paying substantial support was not fair to him. In many ways he believed that Kevin was indeed a member of Marsha's family, and her parents could well afford to support him, as they had been all along.

Kevin's best interests probably would have been better served by remaining with his caretaking mother, but spending more time with his father, at least until he was old enough to express his own wishes about the arrangement. His interests also would have been served by receiving regular child support from Frank. With his parents locked in hostility, however, that arrangement does not seem possible, and our legal system is not set up to help them make this decision.

As a nation we are striving to deal with the phenomenon of conflicting parental claims in situations where marriage no longer defines parenthood. Our late but lusty recognition of the rights of unwed fathers partly reflects our confusion over how to deal with the exploding number of births where marriage never occurs. We are no longer willing to apply strict social controls to promote marriage, or to stigmatize unwed mothers and their children as we have during so much of our history. Yet at the same time we are unwilling to assume the responsibility of supporting children when their unwed mothers cannot.

Our recent recognition of the biological rights of unwed fathers is inconsistent and unrealistic. Inconsistent because we refuse to recognize biological rights of fathers in certain circumstances, as when a lover makes a claim to a child when the mother is married to another, or when an anonymous donor in an artificial insemination situation attempts to pierce the secrecy surrounding the identity of his child. Unrealistic because we assume that unwed fathers are like married fathers except for the ceremony. In fact, few unwed fathers live with their children or seriously participate in their upbringing, and as a group unwed fathers exhibit far more socially undesirable characteristics such as criminal records and drug and alcohol addiction than do married fathers.

If our first concern were truly the best interests of children, we would look at unwed fathers in a different light. We would look first of all—as in all custody conflicts—to who is performing the actual parenting, not just the person who cares for the child but the person who thinks and acts as a primary parent. We could make the assumption, unless proven differently, that the unwed mother is the primary parent and support her in her choice of deciding when and under what circumstances she would allow the father into the life of her child. Only fathers with a very strong record of parenting, or the children themselves, would be allowed to challenge this assumption.

If the child were being raised by biological strangers, as in adoption cases, we would look both to their parenting actions and to their parenting intent. Did they reasonably and in good faith expect to become permanent parents? Most adoptive parents do, but foster parents or relatives may not have similar expectations. An unwed father should not be allowed to make a claim at all unless he has shown both involvement and the intent to become a parent. If he can make that showing, an unwed father contesting the rights of biological strangers should be treated as any other contender and the best interests of the child should prevail. If the adoptive parents have demonstrated good parenting over a long period of time, it would most likely be in the best interests of the child to remain with them.

Again, in the best interests of the child, the unwed father's right to protest should be confined to a small window of opportunity. Whether or not he was adequately informed, he should be barred from making a claim after a short time, perhaps a month or less. This rule would resolve most adoption disputes. If the protest is made within that brief window, the courts too must be obliged to make a final decision within a very short time.

In short, the standards governing custody and visitation for unwed fathers should focus less on the rights of the adults involved and more on the potential for serious and long-term harm to the child from familial conflict and upheaval.

A year after Baby Jessica was returned to her biological father, her adoptive mother, Karen DeBoer, still grieving her loss, went on the road to promote legal reform that would prevent such an outcome. "You have to wonder, are children just property, a piece of luggage that can be given back and forth?" she implored. "We keep hearing about the natural family. Well, what is that? Underneath it all, we need to figure out what is a family."[32]

According to their attorney, Marian Faupel, Dan and Cara Schmidt for their part say that the youngster is doing fine and has adjusted to living in their household. "I have talked to family members who believe that they have developed a close and meaningful relationship with her," Ms. Faupel says. "I think the thing that should concern everyone at this point is why is it that the DeBoers and their supporters aren't celebrating this easy transfer."[33]

We can certainly hope that Baby Jessica does do well, and no child development expert could say for certain that she will not. Still, aren't we sending the wrong message as a society that strangers with blood ties count more than nurturing parents?

5

Stepparents and
Other Legal Strangers

CINDERELLA HAD ONE; so did Snow White and Hansel and Gretel. Our traditional cultural myths are filled with the presence of evil stepmothers. We learn from the stories read to us as children that stepparents—particularly stepmothers—are not to be trusted. They may pretend to love us in front of our biological parents, but the moment our real parents are out of sight they will treat us cruelly and shower their own children with kindnesses. Few of our modern children's tales paint stepparents so harshly. Still, the negative image of stepparents lingers; and nowhere is the growing force of the new biologism more striking. Whereas the rights and obligations of biological parents, wed or unwed, have been greatly strengthened in recent times, stepparents have been virtually ignored. They are considered for the most part legal strangers with regard to the stepchildren they are raising.

Custody rights, child support obligations, and inheritance rights exist between children and their natural parents by virtue of a biological tie alone, regardless of the quality of social or emotional bonds between parent and child, and whether or not the parents are married. On the other hand, stepparents in most states have no obligation during the marriage to support their stepchildren, nor do they enjoy any legal authority over them. In fact they are not legally permitted to sign a permission slip for a field trip or authorize the use of an aspirin for their stepchildren. If the marriage terminates through divorce or death, they usually have no right to custody or even visitation, however long-standing their relationship with their stepchildren. If a stepparent dies, the child, no matter how dependent, does not receive any inheritance or survivor's benefits.

There are, as well, other large classes of long-term cohabiting adults who act as parents but are not married to the biological parent. The reasons why couples do not marry are many, and these include couples who are legally forbidden to marry because they are of the same sex. No matter what their reason for not marrying, they are all treated, like stepparents, as legal strangers.

Stepparents are the fastest-growing class of residential parents. Policy makers who spend a great deal of time worrying about the economic and psychological effects of divorce on children rarely consider the fact that about 70 percent of mothers are remarried within six years. In addition, about 28 percent of children are born to unwed mothers, many of whom eventually marry someone who is not the father of their child. It is estimated that one third of the children born in the United States in the early 1980s will live with a stepparent before they reach adulthood.[1]

In my own research with stepfamilies I have found that stepparents often are unaware of their powerlessness until it is revealed by a precipitating event, such as divorce or the death of the custodial parent. Only then do they realize that in most states they have no right to ask for visitation after divorce or to seek custody against a surviving biological parent, even if that parent has virtually disappeared from the child's life. (Ironically, all states have passed laws allowing biological grandparents the right to seek visitation, regardless of their presence in the child's life.)

California is one of the few states to consider the rights of stepparents.[2] It allows a stepparent to seek visitation if the stepparent can prove it is in the best interests of the child. For all nonbiological kin who act as parents, however, this becomes a very tough standard of proof.

Laurie Halpern was born six months after her mother's marriage to Paul Halpern. Paul was not the biological father. He assisted as the Lamaze coach at his stepdaughter's birth, and after the birth worked at home and took care of Laurie during the day while his wife worked to support the family. The little girl called Paul "daddy" from the time she could talk. The Halperns separated when Laurie was eleven months old; thereafter, the mother took over as her primary caretaker. She refused to let Paul see Laurie.

Paul was allowed to plead his case to see Laurie, but he lost. The judge said:

> I have to find the best interests of the child require there be no visitation because [the stepfather] is a non-parent. He absolutely has no relationship to the child bloodwise or otherwise. . . . This child was well under two years of age, so frankly it is just patently almost ridiculous to make the assumption . . . that the child knows there is a father. . . . [T]o try to arrive at any other conclusion based on some psychiatric testimony, frankly, I just do not accept.[3]

The trial judge was obviously not impressed by current psychological thinking in this area. In spite of pleas for fundamental fairness and further expert testimony regarding the attachment needs of very young children, the appeals court upheld the judgment, as appellate courts almost always do in custody cases.

*   *   *

Developmental concerns are important in choosing between two parents. In this instance, however, the judge is not choosing which parent will have greater or lesser access; he is banishing the parent who has served as the primary caregiver. In the majority of states Paul probably never would have not gotten his foot in the courtroom door. Only a few states give stepparents the right to even try to prove their cases. In most it would be up to the judge to decide whether to even consider a stepparent's plea. Many judges believe it interferes with the custodial parent's autonomy and will not consider visitation rights for the stepparent against the wishes of a biological parent. Lawmakers in general believe that recognition of visitation rights for nonparents would make family life too complicated. As an Alaskan judge put it, "We do not intend to open the door to a myriad of unrelated third persons who happen to feel affection for a child."[4]

It is difficult for a stepparent to obtain visitation rights following a divorce,[5] but it is nearly impossible for him or her to gain custody, even when the biological parent to whom the stepparent is married dies. As we have observed with regard to the rights of unwed fathers, the law strongly favors biology over actual parenting. In most states, before being considered for custody a nonbiological parent must prove by clear and convincing evidence that the biological parent is actually unfit. He or she must show that living with that parent would be clearly detrimental to the child. Without such a clear showing, a blood claim eclipses any consideration of the best interests of the child. Actual parenting and the strong attachments it produces are not considered. Upon the death of the biological parent, the surviving biological parent, usually the custodial father, may reenter the scene and claim his children, sometimes after many years' absence.

Such was the case in *Howell v. Gossett.* The Howells had divorced when their daughter was an infant and Billy Howell agreed to forego custodial or visitation rights in exchange for having no child support obligations. For the mother this was a clean break, and she married Frank Gossett a year or two later. For seven years Frank served as the stepfather to the little girl, until the day when her mother was killed instantly in an automobile crash. Billy Howell then returned from a seven-year absence to reclaim his daughter. The trial court first awarded the child to her stepfather, saying the father had abandoned his child. On appeal, the higher court disagreed, stating,

> On the death of the parent who holds custody of a child under a divorce decree, the prima facie right to the custody automatically inures to the surviving parent. In refusing to award the child to her father in this case the trial judge must of necessity have found that the father was not a fit and proper person to have custody of his daughter.

The court maintained that the record contained "no evidence of conduct . . . that would render the [father] unfit to have custody of his daughter."[6]

In the judge's recital of facts the daughter is barely mentioned; neither her age nor her name is recorded. She must have been at least ten years old at the time of the trial, and yet her opinion is not noted. One wonders how she felt about being taken from the only father she had known; but in this case, as with most, the child's voice is not heard.

Only in very unusual circumstances are judges bold enough to circumvent the law, which clearly favors biological parenthood. The circumstances of the *Allen* case are not ordinary. The child in question, Joshua Allen, was born profoundly deaf. Both parents went through a period of depression, emotional trauma, guilt, and almost accusatorial concern about the other's ancestry. They divorced within the first year following his birth. Joshua's mother, Dana, was granted custody but she could not adjust to raising a deaf child and transferred custody to his father, Joe. Joshua was only three years old when his father married Jeannie. As is common in stepfamily situations, the cast of characters expanded greatly with this union: Jeannie had three children of her own from a previous marriage.

Shortly after her marriage to Joe, Jeannie began to help Joshua learn sign language. Her three children also learned sign language in order to communicate with Joshua. At home, sign language became the norm for conversation, so as to include Joshua. Joshua's father also made an attempt to learn sign language, but he did not proceed beyond the most rudimentary signs.

At first Joshua's intellectual development was behind that of other children his age. Jeannie worked to obtain special training for Joshua in the public school, persuading the school district to hire a tutor knowledgeable in sign language. This was the first such effort for a public school in the state of Washington. Jeannie also took special education classes to provide additional tutoring for Joshua at home.

Joshua progressed remarkably. At the time of Joe and Jeannie's divorce four years later his level of intellectual development had caught up to that of his peers. The school specifically credited the home environment with this unusual advance.

In the meantime Joe had adopted Jeannie's three children, their father having abandoned them, in legal terms.[7] Yet stepmother Jeannie could not adopt Josh because his mother, Dana, an occasional presence, refused to relinquish her rights.

At the custody trial following their divorce the judge clearly bent the letter of the law to favor the stepmother, Jeannie. He admitted that the traditional requirement of parental unfitness had not been met. There was no evidence that Joshua's father was an incompetent parent or that it would be detrimental for Joshua to live with him. Yet he found that the circumstances of the stepmother–stepchild relationship were extraordinary and warranted deviating from the explicit rule of law. The appeals court upheld this ruling, adding that Joshua was now part of a family with three siblings who had been adopted by his father. The integrity of the family was at stake, the court said.

This ruling, so clearly in Joshua's best interests, would probably not have been made in most other states (or in the state of Washington for that matter, had the judge interpreted the law more strictly). In some states stepmother Jeannie would not have the right to ask for custody, or even visitation. Only extraordinary circumstances persuaded the judges in Washington to dare reach beyond the letter of the law and consider Jeannie's exemplary parenting as important as Joe's blood claim.

This case also raises the thorny issue of stepparent adoption. Joe adopted Jeannie's children, but Jeannie was not able to adopt Josh. Most states encourage stepparent adoption. Many states reduce, for a stepparent, the arduous requirements normally associated with adopting an infant. Adoption automatically clarifies the shadowy role of stepparents, giving them full parental rights and full parental obligations. At their divorce Joe had all the legal rights to visitation or custody of Jeannie's three children that any divorcing biological father would have. Jeannie, though, had no rights at all with regard to Josh.

Adoption is not possible nor even desirable for many stepparents. Joe was able to adopt Jeannie's three children because their father had moved away and apparently had not objected to the termination of his parental rights. Dana, Josh's mom, did object; she wanted to maintain contact with her son. The hard numbers, as we shall see, are that about 50 percent of parents not living with their children see them at least once a year, and some of these pay child support. This means that the other 50 percent have little or no contact.

We could, as public policy, decide that parents who do not pay support or see their children less than once in six months should lose their parental rights. Would this be in the children's best interests? Completely substituting one parent for another does not match the complex reality of most stepchildren's lives; it might solve some problems, but it could create others. In this case it is not even an available option for Jeannie, since Josh's mom wants to remain connected. A better option, presented later, is to legally recognize multiple parenting roles. This is a concept lawmakers find hard to grasp but one that many children would recognize as the reality of their everyday lives.

The daily life of stepfamilies is complicated and diverse. These cases in which dedicated stepparents struggle to maintain parental contact with their stepchildren against a hostile legal system do not indicate that *all* stepparents are so closely attached to their stepchildren—or that all stepchildren are so attached to their stepparents. Few of us do not count stepparents among our friends or relatives. We know that modern steprelationships are not always easy and that they often involve a large and mixed cast of characters who do not always get along.

The modern stepfamily is clearly different and more complex than family life presented in "Cinderella" or "Snow White" in several important ways. First, the stepparent who lives with the children is far more likely to be a stepfather than a stepmother, and in most cases the children's biological father is still alive and a presence to some degree. Today it is usually divorce rather than death that serves as the background event for the formation of the stepfamily, and it is the custodial mother who remarries, initiating a new family arrangement[8] (86 percent of stepchildren live primarily with a custodial mother and stepfather).[9]

Consider the Jones-Hutchins family. Sara was eight and Josh five when their mother and father, Martha and Ray Jones, divorced. I represented Martha in that action. The divorce was fairly amicable; they agreed that Martha would have sole custody and that the children would visit Ray every other weekend. Three years later Martha married Sam Hutchins, who had no children. They bought a house together and the children received health insurance and other benefits from Sam's job, since Martha was working part-time at a job with no benefits.

Theoretically this new parental arrangement was a triangle, since Ray was still on the scene and initially saw the children every other weekend. In most stepfamilies the noncustodial parent (usually the father) is still alive (only in 25 percent of cases is the noncustodial parent dead or his whereabouts unknown). This creates the phenomenon of the multiple-parent family, a situation that conventional policy makers are not well equipped to address.

In most situations contact between stepchildren and their absent natural fathers is not frequent. Contact falls into four broad patterns: roughly one quarter of all stepchildren have no association at all with their fathers and receive no child support; one

quarter see their fathers only once a year or less often and receive no child support; one quarter have intermittent contact
or receive some child support; and one quarter may or may not
receive child support but have fairly regular contact, seeing their
fathers once a month or more. Using this information to gauge
the quality and intensity of the father–child relationship, it appears that relatively few stepchildren have enough contact with
their fathers to permit them to play a prominent role in the
children's everyday upbringing. Still, at least half of natural fathers do figure in their children's lives to some degree.[10] The
presence of a second biological parent usually precludes the option of stepparent adoption, a solution that would at least solve
the legal ambiguities of the stepparent's role.

In size most stepfamilies resemble modern nondivorced families and single-parent families, with an average of two children
per family. The exception is "the Brady Bunch model": the
rarest type of stepfamily, in which both parents come to the
marriage with custody of children from their previous relationships. These families average 3.4 children per household. In part
because divorce and remarriage take time, children tend to be
older in stepfamilies. The youngest stepchildren are on average
age eleven, while the youngest children in nondivorced families
average six and a half.[11]

There are also nonresidential stepparents (the spouses of parents who no longer live with their children), usually stepmothers. In our case Ray remarried the year after Martha married
Sam. Ray's new wife, Leslie, had a daughter, Audrey, age twelve.
This marriage complicated the weekend visits. The Jones children were resentful of Leslie and Audrey. Ray found it easier to
see his children alone, and his visits became less frequent.

Some children may spend a good deal of time with nonresidential stepparents, and these adults may become significant figures in their lives. This was not so with Leslie, who had little interest in parenting her husband's children. Nonresidential stepparents are generally less likely to be involved in the everyday support and care of their stepchildren.

Like the families of Cinderella and Snow White, the modern stepfamily has stresses and strains. This was certainly true for the Jones-Hutchins family. Sara was eleven and Josh seven when their mother married Sam. At first Sara refused to talk to Sam and turned her face away when he addressed her. Josh was easier. He did not say much, but he was willing to play catch or go on an errand with Sam if encouraged by Sam to do so. Sara grew only slightly more polite as she developed into adolescence. She spoke to Sam only if she needed something; but, as her mother pointed out to Sam, she hardly spoke to her either. Josh continued to be pleasant, if a little distant, as he grew older. He clearly preferred his mother's attention.

Classic longitudinal studies by E. Mavis Heatherington and colleagues[12] spanning the past two decades provide a rich source of information on how stepfamilies function. Heatherington emphasizes that stepchildren have typically experienced several marital transitions. They have usually already experienced the divorce of their parents and a period of life in a single-parent family before the formation of the stepfamily. In the early stages of all marital transitions, including divorce and remarriage, child–parent relations often are disrupted. Parenting tends to be less authoritative than in nondivorced families. These early periods, however, usually give way to parenting situations more similar to nuclear families, although the authority figure is less likely to be the stepparent.[13]

Stepfathers vary in how enthusiastically and effectively they parent their stepchildren, and stepchildren also vary in how willingly they permit a parental relationship to develop. Indeed, many stepfather–stepchild relationships are not emotionally close. Overall, stepfathers in these studies are disengaged and less authoritative compared with nondivorced fathers. The same appears to be true of the smaller class of residential stepmothers.[14] Adolescent children tend to perceive their stepmothers negatively in the early stages of remarriage, but over time they too become disengaged. In an interesting twist on fairy tale lore adolescent children in stepfamilies experience less conflict with their residential stepmothers than do children in nondivorced families with their own mothers.[15]

The age and gender of the child at the time of stepfamily formation are critical in her or his ability to adjust. Remarriage during children's early adolescence results in more sustained difficulties in stepfather–stepchild relations than remarriages when the children are younger. Stepsons who are young are able to develop a closer relationship to their stepfathers after a period of time;[16] this is not as likely with older children, however.[17] Unfortunately, owing to the chronology of divorce and remarriage a large percentage of children are adolescents at the time of the remarriage.

In their lives outside the family stepchildren do not perform as well as children from nondivorced families and more closely resemble children from single-parent families. It seems that divorce and remarriage (or some factors associated with divorce and remarriage) increase the risk of poor academic, behavioral, and psychological outcomes.[18]

The difficulties of the stepfamily relationship are evident in the high divorce rates among such families. About one quarter of all remarrying women separate from their new spouses within five years of the second marriage, and the figure is higher for women with children from prior relationships. A conservative estimate is that between 20 and 30 percent of stepchildren will see their custodial parent and stepparent divorce before they turn eighteen.[19] This is yet another disruptive marital transition for children who have already undergone at least one divorce.

The Jones-Hutchins family unfortunately experienced divorce again shortly after Sara left for college. Josh, fifteen, was still living at home at the time. Martha turned to me once again to represent her but by this time I had become a full-time researcher and could not. To me there seemed to be more sadness than anger in her account of the breakdown of this second marriage. Martha did not blame the dissolution precisely on the difficulty of maintaining a stepfamily; she claimed that Sam seemed to just drift away. "He became extremely busy at work, and joined a senior swim team. There was just less and less time for us."

I asked if the children would continue to see Sam.

"For sure, not Sara, she is mad at him—she claims that she always hated him—but that's not really true. I think she is just feeling protective of me."

I asked about Josh.

"He doesn't say much. He got along pretty well with Sam—they went to games together—and he hardly ever sees his dad. But it's up to them."

Martha's phrase "It's up to them" lingered in my mind. If Sam were the biological father, both society and the law would expect him to continue to participate in their lives. Sam's friends and relatives would ask him about the children and would consider it shameful if he did not spend time with them. Because he is a stepfather, though, the opposite is true. Sam's friends and relatives will not expect continuing contact, and the law certainly does not support it.

What about Josh? Since Josh's biological father has drifted away, preoccupied with his own stepfamily, Sam has been serving as Josh's principal male parental figure. If Sam were Josh's biological father, Josh could expect continuing contact. His adolescent peer group, the most important social authority for him at this stage, also would expect it. The social mores of American adolescents expect shuttling back and forth between mom and dad's house, but not, I have observed, spending the weekend with a former stepparent; most likely this isn't considered cool.

Stepfather Sam and stepson Josh may well miss each other acutely, but it is likely that neither of them will take the initiative to see each other. They have no social support system to encourage continuing contact, and a lingering negative image of the stepparent role precludes any such encouragement.

In truth Martha is far more concerned about money than she is about Josh losing contact with Sam. Sara is a college student and Josh a teenager with the ballooning expenses of adolescence, and Martha holds only a part-time job. The family has depended on Sam's income for seven years; the children were covered by his medical benefits. Over the years Ray paid the small support payments less and less regularly.

No states require stepparents to pay child support following divorce, no matter how long the children have been dependent on them. Most often medical and other benefits the children received through stepparents are cut off at divorce. Though policy makers have struggled to cushion the blow of divorce for children following the breakup of their original families, they have completely ignored the devastation caused by the breakup of their stepfamilies.

Josh and Sara, like many children in stepfamilies, have experienced both the economic and emotional roller coaster of family breakup, reformation, and subsequent dissolution. They are involuntary participants in a modern revolving-door family. When Martha and Ray divorced Martha's income fell sharply, even with child support payments. Stepparents are not legally obliged to support their stepchildren, but it is fair to assume that stepfathers' substantial contributions to family income improves the family's living standard. For many formerly single-parent families a stepfather's added income is essential to prevent or end poverty.[20]

The complications do not end here. Some noncustodial fathers, such as Ray Jones, have remarried and formed stepfamilies themselves. Nearly one quarter of residential stepfathers like Ray have minor children from former relationships living elsewhere.[21] In our case Ray did continue his child support payments, but more and more sporadically. He felt overburdened by the economic obligation of contributing to two households. I think of fathers like Ray as "squeeze box dads," pushed by the demands of two families.

Unless Martha Jones substantially improves her salary she will sink again to the income of a single mother following this divorce. She could try to get Ray to renew his child support payments, but Sara is no longer a minor eligible for support, and obtaining child support for Josh is probably not worth the expense of going back to court.

Children of divorce are almost always economic losers, but children of stepparent divorce fare the worst. There is no mandated safety net of child support or other benefits to cushion the fall. In part because we discourage the continuation of the relationship between stepparents and stepchildren, rarely is there any voluntary support following divorce; resources are suddenly back to the single-parent level. Children financially cushioned after the divorce of their biological parents have no protective support following the breakup of their stepfamilies.

Nor are children protected in the event of the death of a stepparent, clearly another area of vulnerability. If the Hutchins-Jones marriage had been terminated by Sam's death in an auto accident rather than by divorce, the economic impact would have been less drastic but similar. The children would not inherit from him if there were no will, nor would they be considered automatic beneficiaries on his life insurance. Under existing state laws even a dependent stepchild whose stepparent has supported and raised him for many years is not eligible to inherit from the stepparent if there is no will. California provides the most liberal rule for stepchild recovery, but it still poses onerous qualifications. Stepchildren may inherit only if "it is established by clear and convincing evidence that the stepparent would have adopted the person but for a legal barrier."[22] Few stepchildren have been able to pass this test. It is unlikely that the Hutchins children would either, unless Sam had publicly indicated this intention. Similarly, a stepchild cannot bring a negligence suit for the accidental death of a stepparent. The children would not be able to recover if Sam had been negligently killed by another motorist.

Federal policy is, however, more considerate of the actual dependency of minor stepchildren. Federal law provides no relief in the event of divorce, but if Sam had died and were eligible for Social Security, the children would be treated as dependent survivors. In this instance death is kinder than divorce to stepchildren.

What can be done to strengthen the fragile bonds between stepchildren and their stepparents, to make everyday life a little easier, and to protect all parties from the brutal consequences of revolving-door family transitions? As with all matters pertaining to family relations, law and public policy cannot govern the heart, but they can help to shape social expectations. Since a substantial number of these families experience divorce more than once, it makes good public policy sense both to strengthen these stepfamily relationships and cushion the transition for stepchildren should the relationship end.

The reasons why stepparents are less engaged in parenting than natural parents are not clear. Some sociologists have posited that lack of engagement is caused by "incomplete institutionalization."[23] This theory is based on the belief that by and large people act as they are expected to act by society. In the case of stepfamilies societal norms and standards for how to define the remarried family—especially the role of the stepparent in relation to the stepchild—are unclear or absent.

Perhaps it is time to acknowledge the contribution that most residential stepparents make in raising their stepchildren, and to protect stepchildren from economic and psychological loss in the event of termination of the stepfamily by death or divorce. I suggest a whole new legal category that would consider stepparents de facto parents.[24] De facto parents would be defined as "those stepparents legally married to a natural parent who primarily reside with their stepchildren." Stepparents who do not live with their stepchildren would not fall into this category.

For the purposes of federal and state policy a de facto parent would be treated virtually the same as a natural parent during the marriage. The same rights, obligations, and presumptions would attach vis-à-vis their stepchildren, including the obligation of support. These rights and duties would continue in some form, based on the length of the marriage, following divorce or death of either the biological or de facto parent. In the event of divorce the stepparent would have standing to seek custody or visitation, but the stepparent could also be obligated for child support of a limited duration. This support could extend to medical and other benefits on which the stepchildren rely. Upon the death of a stepparent a minor stepchild would be treated for purposes of inheritance and benefits as would a natural child.

Creating a de facto parent category for stepparents would not invalidate the existing rights and obligations of the biological parent who does not live with the child. Rather, this proposal would empower a stepparent as an additional parent.

Multiple parenting is the barrier against which many family law reform schemes have foundered. We seem to be hopelessly stuck on the biological limit of two. Even California, which offers stepparents the right to seek visitation in the best interests of the child, cancels this right if the other parent, typically the noncustodial father, objects.[25] Our resistance to expanding the two-parent limit is one of the reasons why there has been no consistent effort to reformulate the role of stepparents. Working out the details is critical to acceptance. For instance, an important aspect of multiple parenting is legal authority. If stepparents are required to accept support obligations, fairness dictates that they also must be given parental rights. If stepparents were given de facto status, teachers, doctors, camp directors, and other important persons in the stepchild's life could look to the stepparent as well as the biological parents for consultation and approval. The parental role of the stepparent would be recognized as the norm. When the biological parents have shared legal custody, the law could recognize the parental rights of three rather than two parents. While this sounds unusual, in practical terms it is an accurate reflection of how many families now raise their children.

Multiple parenting rights would apply to ongoing custody disputes as well. One stepfamily I interviewed had experienced complicated, but not unusual, stepfamily visitation problems. In this instance both mother and father had children from former marriages living with them, making them both stepparents. The mother's child, a sixteen-year-old girl, lived with them full time. The father's two sons, ages ten and twelve, spent half their time with them early on. Soon the situation soured. The boys' mother decided she did not like the stepmother's influence and began to make excuses about why they could not visit at the appointed times. The visits dwindled to near nothing. The father had no luck reasoning with his ex-wife and took the matter back to court. The court-appointed mediator would not allow the stepmother to be present; she was not considered a party to the conflict. Nor in this instance did the mediator speak with the boys. The mediator agreed with the mother that the situation had changed and the boys needed to spend more time with their mother. The stepmother was resentful.

"I know she tells the mediator that I am the classic wicked stepmother, and I am not able to speak for myself," she confided to me. "John says he doesn't blame me, but he is going crazy without his boys. He is supposed to be their soccer coach and they hardly ever show up for games anymore. We don't need a live-in Nanny anymore, we need a live-in shrink."

It is not clear how this family's custody dispute should be resolved, but it is telling that three of the central figures—the two boys and the stepmother—were not included in the negotiation to determine where the boys should live. Recognition of multiple parenting might have helped resolve the problem, and it would have relieved some of the strain in the couple's marriage.

With the adoption of a de facto parent model the custody situation in the event of divorce would be reconfigured as well. Stepparents would have the right to seek visitation or even custody if it were shown to be in the best interests of the child. This advance would recognize the fact that as a rule, it is in the best interests of children not to be severed from those adults who have, in most important ways, served as parents. This legal stature might encourage the social expectation of ongoing contact with stepchildren, which is not now the case.

Changing the laws, however, will not always change the heart. It is not likely that all stepparent–stepchild relationships will magically become emotionally close with the passage of a new statute. Some stepparents and stepchildren probably would choose not to maintain contact.[26] In stepparent custody disputes, even more than in primary divorce custody disputes, the voice of even the very young child should be heard and respected.

In the Jones-Hutchins divorce a change in the law might have made a difference. If Sam and Martha had known that the law encouraged and supported continuing contact, they might have discussed it themselves. If Josh's adolescent peers expected him to maintain a relationship with his stepfather, he might have welcomed time spent with Sam. The family's expectation of normative behavior would allow them to settle this issue without court intervention.

There would be other advantages for Josh. A de facto model would provide a transitional safety net in the vulnerable period following divorce. For a period of time, based perhaps on the number of years of marriage, Josh would continue to be eligible for medical and other benefits as well as financial support.

This important piece of public policy could protect the children of revolving-door families from falling into poverty.

Critics may argue that adoption, not the creation of the legal status of de facto parent, is the appropriate vehicle for granting a stepparent full parental rights and responsibilities.[27] Termination of parental rights is not an easy matter. Normally the rights of a parent who maintains minimal contact with his or her child cannot be terminated even if that parent is not contributing child support; and when parental rights are terminated, visitation rights are terminated as well in most states. As noted, close to 50 percent of noncustodial parents continue some contact with their children, even when not paying support.[28] Is it in the best interests of children to terminate contact with a natural parent, even if the parent is not meeting his or her financial obligation?[29] Stepparent adoption should strongly be encouraged when it is possible, but this solution will not resolve the problem of defining the role of stepparents who have not adopted.

Thus far we have spoken of the uncertain role of stepparents. There is another large category of legal nonpersons: cohabiting adults, who live with a child's parent but have no legal relationship to that parent or child. The diversity of this category is limited only by the imagination. Cohabitors may include live-in lovers, relatives, or friends who share the household for times ranging from one night to the better part of a lifetime. The cohabitor's degree of involvement with the child is just as varied. Some cohabitors may actively and intentionally assume a parental role, and others may have little interest or contact with the child.

Among those cohabitors who assumed a full parental role was Michele G. The story of her frustrating battle to gain recognition as a parent is another illustration of the inability of our legal system to deal with other-than-biological parents.

Michele G. and Nancy S. began living together in 1969. In November of that year they held a private marriage ceremony. After many years together they decided to have children by artificial insemination. First Nancy gave birth to a daughter. Michele was listed on the birth certificate as the father, and the daughter was given Michele's last name. Four years later Nancy gave birth to a son, and once again Michele was named as father and the son took her family name. Ultimately, the children referred to both Michele and Nancy as "Mom."

Within a year of the birth of their son they separated, agreeing that the daughter, now five, would live with Michele and the infant son with Nancy. They arranged visitation so that the children would be together, at one house or the other, for four days each week. Three years later they had a dispute over the visitation schedule. Nancy then brought an action under the Uniform Parentage Act declaring that Michele had no legal claim to either child. She insisted on full custody with no right of visitation for Michele.

Michele offered several legal arguments as to why she should be recognized as a parent. She proposed that she could be considered in loco parentis, a psychological parent, or a de facto parent. Finally she argued for a new definition of "functional parent" that she defined as "anyone who maintains a functional parental relationship with a child when a legally recognized parent created that relationship with the intent that the relationship be parental in nature."[30]

The court rejected all arguments and denied her any right to custody or visitation. The court claimed that "expanding the definition of a 'parent' in the manner advocated by appellant could expose other natural parents to litigation brought by child-care providers of long standing, relatives, successive sets of stepparents or other close friends of the family."[31]

At first glance this case might seem a clear instance of lesbian discrimination (and indeed discrimination may have played a part); but in fact all cohabitors and most stepparents fall into the same legal category. Homosexuality technically is an issue here only because this couple could not marry, even if they chose to. Although there is some movement toward permitting gay marriage, it will not be a solution in the near future.

In this case the judge suggested as an aside that Michele should have considered adoption to obtain legal parental status. Second-party adoption, in which the biological mother does not relinquish her rights, is becoming an option for cohabitors in some states, but by no means all. As with stepparents, often there is a living natural parent to contend with. If Nancy had chosen a more traditional means of conception than artificial insemination, the adoption option would probably not have existed for Michele.

While the results in this case strike one as patently unfair, and certainly not in the best interests of the children, the court does have a dilemma. Can any adult who takes care of a child over a period of time be granted parental status in custody disputes? Obviously not, although I would argue that any third party who has developed a long-term attachment to the child should have standing to seek continuing contact, particularly if the child expresses that wish.

As for parental status, perhaps it would be possible to extend the model of de facto parent to those cohabitors who actively seek it. This model bestows responsibilities as well as rights and would be pursued only by cohabitors who wish to legally register their intention to take on the full burdens of parenthood.

For the most part it could be employed in place of adoption, with the permission of the cohabiting natural parent, when adoption is not a realistic option. A simple registration would trigger it, just as marriage would for residential stepparents.

The advantage of the de facto model over those proposed by Michele G. is that it deals with actual everyday parenting in modern family configurations. Such a model stresses not just rights but responsibilities as well and offers the vulnerable child support and a safety net in the event of death or divorce.

I have been interviewing stepfamilies for three years now. My goal is to see how these families function on a day-to-day basis, and how their lives could be made easier. A major finding of my study is that stepparents put in almost as much time with regard to caretaking—homework, transportation, and discipline, for example—as do biological parents, and the great majority found stepchildren just as satisfying as natural children.[32] Nearly all consider themselves parental figures, although not necessarily the same kind of parent as a biological parent. One of the questions I ask stepparents is whether they would like continuing contact with the stepchild in the event of divorce. This is a delicate question, but most of these stepparents have been divorced before and with survivor wisdom they have clearly prepared themselves for all future disasters. With only one exception all the stepparents responded quickly that they would definitely like to spend time with the children. These legal strangers do not recognize that they have only an ephemeral hold on the children they parent.

6

Domestic Violence:
The Hot Zone of
the Custody Wars

In 1976 Sergio M. was awarded custody of his four children, even though he had been convicted of murdering his wife by the infliction of twenty-two stab wounds.[1] The court found that the evidence did not prove custody would be harmful to the children and that a crime of second-degree murder did not necessarily prove that the father was unfit.

Could that same decision occur today? Unfortunately, it could.

Spousal abuse is not new to families, and it is no longer hidden from the public. Stories of brutal, repetitive beatings, usually by husbands or male partners and inflicted on wives and girlfriends, are now the standard fare of daytime TV, popular magazines, and other forms of mass culture. The violent face of intimacy has become all too well known. The victims of assault are not always women—women attack men as well—but in the majority of cases where serious damage is inflicted, it is the woman who is damaged.[2]

What is still relatively new and not well thought through is a public consideration of how such violence affects children who witness it. Can a violent parent who batters his partner still be loving and nonviolent with his children? In addition to the usual laundry list of issues that judges must consider in determining the best interests of the child regarding custody and visitation, the ugly fact of spousal battering must be weighed. There is no consensus, however, on what weight it should be given. Moreover, judges and custody evaluators often are hostile to allegations of domestic violence, which almost always come from mothers. They may consider them manipulative or vengeful strategies on the part of mothers to withhold access to the children, and view them with suspicion and mistrust. In addition, many courts invoke a "friendly parent" rule that favors the parent who is not making accusations and not complaining about a child's safety. As a result, ideological battle lines are drawn, with feminists proclaiming that abusive partners are unfit parents while fathers' groups protest that such claims are exaggerated and conniving.

Children are not just hapless pawns in these disputes. One national study estimates that in about 50 percent of all partner abuse cases children also are abused in some way. Children may be injured in an attempt to protect a parent from the batterer; they may be targets of physical attacks themselves, or hurt because they are near the intended victim during an attack. Because the frequency of battering tends to increase during pregnancy, a fetus is at particular risk of injury, and sometimes the uncontrolled rage that causes a batterer to strike a partner may be diverted to the child.[3]

Children also may be the victims of parental sex abuse. Such claims—hard to prove and hard to counter—are regarded with even greater suspicion and mistrust than spousal abuse allegations by the legal community. A parent bringing a claim of sexual abuse runs the great risk of losing custody as an unfriendly or unstable custodian.

Protection of children is perhaps the most basic function that a society must perform, and yet we are confounded as to how to accomplish this task in instances of domestic violence. Our justice system is poorly informed and poorly designed to deal with the complexities of this charged issue. Basic information on the dynamics of domestic violence is lacking, and different agencies within the system divide up domestic violence and disagree on what to do about it. One incident of domestic violence may involve three separate courts. The abuser may be arraigned in a criminal court that is concerned about prosecuting the crime, not protecting the child, while a juvenile court judge, focusing on the protection of the child, may order a batterer out of the home and secure a restraining order from the police. Later on, a family court may award joint custody to the same batterer, now out of jail, because custody law favors equal access to both parents following divorce. The needs of the children often get lost in the shuffle. Rarely are their voices heard.

The confusing and contradictory positions held by the public, mental health professionals, and the legal system were painfully and publicly illustrated in the custody battle that O. J. Simpson fought to gain his children back from their maternal grandparents.

Lou and Juditha Brown cared for their grandchildren, Sydney and Justin, for over two years, from the time of their mother's murder until more than a year following the criminal trial of O. J. Simpson. They resisted giving the children back to their father, claiming that the children would be at risk living with a violent man. The custody trial occurred after Simpson's criminal acquittal for the murder of their mother, Nicole, but during the course of the civil trial for wrongful death. Judge Nancy Stock, the custody judge, would not allow the Browns' lawyer to introduce any evidence regarding the murder of the children's mother into the custody hearing.[4] She did, however, permit evidence regarding O. J.'s alleged spousal battering of Nicole, including Simpson's no-contest plea to a misdemeanor charge of spousal abuse in 1989.[5] At the time, the civil trial against Simpson was in full swing; photographic evidence of Nicole's bruised and beaten face appeared on all the TV networks for several days running.

Judge Stock imposed a strict gag order on all involved, and little is known of the details of the testimony and argument in the courtroom. However, Judge Stock ultimately wrote in her order, "Psychological testing, clinical observations and review of Mr. Simpson's history with the children does not yield a picture of a man who has in the past, or is likely in the future, to lose control of himself in such a manner as to emotionally or physically harm the children."[6]

Whatever one thinks of the judgment, those of us familiar with custody law were not at all surprised. The children's best interests, or even the children's affirmative right to be protected, are not in the language or even the spirit of the law when considering the rights of a biological parent against those who are biological strangers. The court did not consider either the Browns' two years of parenting or O. J.'s parental history. As in most states, the standard in California is that the biological parent is awarded custody unless the other party can prove by clear and convincing evidence that it would be detrimental to the children. As previously noted, clear and convincing evidence requires a high level of proof. The plaintiff must prove to the judge or jury with substantial certainty that the children have been harmed and are likely to be harmed in the future. Although most states, prompted by feminist advocates, have expressed legislative concern about the effects of spousal abuse on children, plaintiffs must still prove harm to the children in each individual case.

Evidence of detriment to individual children based on spousal abuse is very difficult to secure, especially when the victim is no longer available to testify—as was the case with Sergio M., the murderer who stabbed his wife twenty-two times.

The facts of this case are extraordinary, although the decision is not. Judith M. and Sergio were married in 1962. They had four children, two boys and two girls. In July 1971 Sergio went to Texas with his brother to find a job and a new home for his family. A month later he had found both, but Judith refused to join him as they had planned, and he returned to San Diego at once. Subsequently there was a series of unpleasant incidents over several months. At one point Sergio attempted suicide when Judith would not return to him; another time he brandished a knife in front of Judith and their oldest child, James.[7]

On the morning of November 10, 1972, Judith's stepfather called Sergio and told him that he was a fool; that Judith had married Ruben Frederico and that she was taking the children to Alaska to join Ruben there. Judith and Frederico in fact had taken the children to the Canadian border intending to travel to Alaska but were refused admittance into Canada due to a lack of sufficient funds.[8]

Sergio tracked down Judith and tricked her into getting into his car. He pleaded with her to return to him with the children. She refused. They argued. Still in the car, Sergio threatened her with the knife. Sergio later claimed Judith directed the knife to her breast. She may have dared him to use it. Sergio stabbed her over and over. There were twenty-two wounds. A number of people came to the scene, and Sergio gave the knife to one of them.[9]

On June 8, 1973, Sergio pleaded guilty to second-degree murder for this "crime of passion" and was sentenced to five years to life. The trial judge presiding over the criminal case found Sergio to be in need of psychiatric care, and he recommended a minimum term at a facility that would afford treatment, with a long period of parole.[10]

The family court judge in the custody suit clearly exhibited a good deal of sympathy for Sergio, whose wife had jilted him in a humiliating manner. Witnesses at the trial claimed that Sergio's act was totally out of character. The California Institution for Men at Chino had made several evaluations of Sergio. Their witnesses reported his remorse and sense of guilt. They said that he was not violent or delinquently oriented, and that he was genuinely concerned for his children. They noted that his prognosis for success on probation or parole was good.[11]

Testimony about Judith, on the other hand, was uniformly negative. In referring to her behavior in the car, where it was alleged that she goaded him to stab her by pointing to her chest, one of the psychiatrists stated that "it was the expression of a death wish on her part, for whatever that opinion may be worth."[12]

In this case aunts and uncles on both sides of the family had offered to take the children. The children at that time were residing with one set of relatives and presumably would continue to do so until the father was released from jail. No testimony was offered as to the parenting skills of relatives, since they had no rights. The children were not represented at the trial.

While this case is still good law in California, a more recent case indicates there are limits to the court's tolerance of murderer husbands, possibly indicating an increasing awareness of the effects of domestic violence on children. In the 1986 case *In the Matter of Mark G. V.,* the court did find that the father's stabbing murder of the mother constituted a detriment to the two children.[13] The court distinguished this case from the earlier *James M.* case in two regards: first, the two children were in the next room when the stabbing occurred and presumably were directly affected by the event; second, this father received a much longer sentence and the children were establishing a stable relationship with foster parents.[14]

These domestic murder cases raise the serious question of whose interests are being protected. While they represent the extreme end on the continuum of domestic violence, they serve to illustrate a central point: almost no matter what the biological parent does, or to whom, his or her rights are protected against all others, unless it can be shown by clear and convincing evidence that interaction with the biological parent will harm the child.

Ironically, these fathers, O. J. Simpson and Sergio M., received more favorable treatment because their victims were no longer alive. They were fighting for custody against other parent figures, not the biological mothers; and the mothers, of course, were no longer alive to testify about their spouses' violent ways.

In recent years the public and ultimately the legal system have become somewhat more attuned to the prevalence of domestic violence and to the complicated pattern of dependency and violence that make these family breakups more problematical than others. Feminists in particular have pointed out that violence does not necessarily end with separation and divorce;

these events and the continuing efforts to maintain distance may trigger outbursts in the batterer rather than subdue them.

A great deal of controversy surrounds custody decisions in cases involving domestic violence. Spousal battering and its effects on custody disputes have become a nasty side battle in the larger gender wars. Many women argue that since domestic violence is ongoing, custody arrangements force continued contact and therefore constantly renew opportunities for violence against the women and the children themselves. Some men's groups argue, as did the mental health experts in the Simpson and Sergio M. trials, that this is an exaggeration. They claim there is no harm to the children, and that allegations of domestic violence may be used unfairly as a strategy to manipulate custody disputes in favor of mothers.[15]

Judges also take sides in this bitter controversy. Some judges believe a parent can be kind and loving toward his children even if brutal toward his spouse. A Florida court, for example, affirmed that "shared parental responsibility had not been shown to be detrimental to the child,"[16] although the father's acts against the mother included "throwing her to the ground, and beating her when she was four months pregnant and threatening to kill her, her father and himself." The judges in both the Simpson and Sergio M. trials appeared to share this attitude.

Mental health professionals, key players in most custody disputes these days, also are of divided mind about the effect of domestic violence on children. The psychologists who testified in the Simpson trial and the Sergio M. case discounted its importance, emphasizing the positive qualities of the fathers in question and claiming that their violent actions toward their ex-spouses would not affect their relationships with their children. Most psychological experts in *In the Matter of Mark G. V.,* however, emphasized the detrimental effect of domestic violence on the children.

Can a father be kind and loving toward his children yet violent toward their mother? This may be possible for some, but many of these fathers abuse their children as well. As previously noted, research conducted on a large national sample found that at least 50 percent of batterers who assault their wives frequently also physically injure their children.[17] For children who are not physically injured there may be other indirect consequences. A 1994 American Bar Association report on the impact of domestic violence on children estimated that 3.3 million to 10 million American children witness such violence every year, and the immediate impact "can be traumatic, fear for self, fear for their mother's safety and self-blame."[18] Moreover, long-lasting effects may extend to the next generation. Not all children of abusive parents abuse their own children, but they do so more frequently than children in nonviolent families. There is debate over the numbers, but all researchers agree that violence often begets violence in the next generation. No serious researcher claims that domestic violence has no effect on children.[19]

While most states give some recognition to a history of abuse in considering custody, Louisiana takes this consideration furthest. Their custody law states:

> The legislature finds that problems of family violence do not necessarily cease when the victimized family is legally separated or divorced. In fact, the violence often escalates, and child custody and visitation become the new forum for the continuation of the abuse. Because current laws relative to child custody and visitation are based on an assumption that even divorcing parents are in relatively

equal positions of power, and that such parents act in the children's best interest, these laws often work against the protection of the children and abused spouse in families with a history of family violence.[20]

Applying this conceptual framework, Louisiana creates a presumption that no parent who has a history of perpetrating family violence shall be awarded sole or joint custody of children. Like all legal presumptions this one can be overcome by a preponderance of the evidence, but Louisiana is very specific about such evidence. The law insists that a batterer must prove that he or she has successfully completed a treatment program, is not abusing alcohol or illegal drugs, and that the child's best interests require the abuser's participation as a custodian.[21]

Most states, however, do not embrace Louisiana's viewpoint. They do not acknowledge the particular symptomology of domestic violence or its ongoing nature. They may note domestic violence as a factor to be considered, but go no further. To the contrary, most states embrace a "family systems" approach, which views the family unit as enduring following divorce, with both parents continually involved with the children, almost no matter what. This model is widely promoted by the professional corps of psychological evaluators, who do not always separate domestic violence cases from others they are evaluating for recommendations to the court. A family systems model favors both joint custody and a "friendly parent" rule, which directs primary custody to the parent who is most likely to allow access to the other parent. Both approaches work against protecting children from continuing domestic violence.[22]

California offers both a preference for joint custody and a friendly parent rule. In addition, like most other states it lists domestic violence as a factor to be considered in deciding custody.[23] These three factors are sometimes in competition with one another, and, not surprisingly, domestic violence is often the first to fall by the wayside. In a recent Santa Clara case, to be further discussed, the court evaluator recommended that a father who had been convicted of felony domestic violence, served time in prison, and recently had violated his parole by harassing his ex-wife be granted joint custody.

When a court demonstrates such profound lack of consideration of an extraordinary record of proven domestic violence against both mother and children, a case such as this becomes newsworthy. In most cases the violence is not public and its existence may be doubted by the judge, the psychological evaluator, or the mediator. A divorce court in Vermont, for example, openly questioned a woman's assertion of domestic violence by her husband over a period of years simply because she had not left him:

> The marital misdeeds that have been attributed to Stanley, most of them, we don't believe. We do recognize that there was a certain amount of misbehavior; that there may be these temper tantrums and items of misbehavior, but the strangling with the hands and violence and threats that were described by Karen have been blown way out of proportion as evidenced by the fact that she stayed throughout the four years of marriage.[24]

Not all judges would agree with this analysis. Many judges and most mental health professionals are now familiar with the concept of the "battered woman syndrome" pioneered by the psychologist Lenore Walker.[25] A part of this syndrome is a characteristic passivity, a kind of "learned helplessness" developed as a protective stance against the terror of unpredictable violence. Women in this state of mind have lost their sense of identity and self-determination. They are often unable to leave their batterer—or unwilling, for fear of the consequences.[26]

Yet the same learned passivity that makes women unable to leave for many years often makes them unable to assert their rights when a divorce does occur. They may not be able to fight effectively for the safety of their children. This consequence of the battering process has not been addressed by our legal system. For example, mediation, rather than a court hearing, has become a wildly popular alternative form of dispute resolution in most states. Proponents of mediation claim that it promotes negotiation rather than competition, it is cheaper, and its informality allows the individuals to speak up, where they might not in a courtroom.

Mediation has its merits but often works poorly for women who are victims of domestic violence. For women who have been beaten, forced engagement with their husbands or partners without protection of a lawyer and the legal process can be intimidating, replicating their powerless mode in partnership. Batterers, in contrast, are often strong, controlling personalities. They speak decisively and aggressively, giving the impression of supreme self-confidence—and as a consequence may end up with the lion's share in any divorce or custody agreement. [27]

Women who are victims of domestic violence often are powerless within the legal system in other important ways as well. They may not have the means to hire a lawyer. A facet of domestic violence rarely acknowledged, or even outright denied, is that it is not an equal opportunity crime. While domestic violence takes place in middle-class suburbs as well as urban ghettos, the victims are more likely to be poor. The myth of the

1960s that domestic violence did not respect class has been dispelled by studies that demonstrate that poverty, which triggers a number of social problems, is also a major contributor to domestic violence. A recent study of murders in New York City revealed that more women are killed by their husbands or boyfriends than in robberies, disputes, sexual assaults, drug violence, random attacks, or any other crime in cases where the motive for murder is known.[28] In half of all murder cases in which the murderer could be identified it was found to be a husband or boyfriend. Two thirds of these murdered women were from the poorest neighborhoods, and three quarters were African American or Hispanic. In addition, unlike men, who are most often killed by guns, women "are very likely to be punched and hit and burned and thrown out of windows."[29] In one quarter of these cases children were also killed or injured, or they watched the murders or found their mothers' bodies.[30]

Most poor women who are victims of domestic violence are not murdered. In the event of family breakdown or divorce, however, they are less likely than wealthier women to be able to protect themselves or their children from the demands of their batterers. A victim without resources is less likely to leave her abuser, for she may have no place to go with her children. In custody disputes most victims cannot afford to pay a lawyer who will hear their stories and fight their battles if they are incapable of fighting them on their own.

Maria K. was referred to me by a social worker. She had lost primary custody of her eight-year-old son six months earlier. She had had no money to pay for a lawyer and had endured mediation without counsel or support from anyone. Both Maria and her ex-husband, Carl, were born in the Philippines and emigrated as teens. They were married for ten years, and, according to Maria, the beatings had begun when she became pregnant.

"It was only when he was drunk. He really didn't want the baby. He thought I would get fat and lazy. I wouldn't work anymore. I would do anything not to hurt the baby, so I just didn't fight back."

Maria stayed with her husband, she said, partly because she feared what he would do if she left, and partly because she didn't think she could support herself and the baby. "The job I had before, it was piecework. No benefits, no nothing. Not enough to feed a child."

The beatings continued, sometimes once every two weeks, sometimes not for several months. Four times she had to go to the emergency room for treatment of wounds: once, a broken wrist she got when she tried to protect her face—but she never called the police. When I asked her why not she replied that in her country calling the police would bring shame to her whole family.

In Maria's case the event that finally ended the marriage was the intervention of her brother, who had come to live with them when he was out of work. He saw Carl hit Maria when she did not immediately bring him the beer he demanded. Both men were watching a baseball game on television at the time. Her brother, a large man, pulled Carl out of his chair, knocked him down, and then dragged him out the front door. He told him he would kill him if he came back and Carl believed him.

Maria was not certain this had been the right action. "Now I've lost everything, and I hardly ever see my son," she said. According to her, Carl filed for the divorce and demanded custody of his son, Peter.

Maria said,

> The court called me and said I had to come down and
> talk to a mediator. I didn't know what that was. I thought
> it was a judge. It was just me and Carl and this lady in the
> room. I was so scared. Carl said I was living with a man
> who would not let him into the house to see his son. I
> said he was my brother, but Carl laughed, and got the lady
> to believe it was my boyfriend. When she asked me why
> Carl could not enter the house I just said, my brother
> thinks he is a bad man, dangerous. But Carl got her to be-
> lieve that was a lie.

The mediator encouraged them to sign an agreement that
said their son would have primary residence with his father, but
Maria could see him often: every weekend, if she wanted. Maria
sadly packed up Peter's things and sent him to live with his father. It was only a few miles away, but Maria had no car.

> The first weekend I took the bus, but when I got there
> the door was locked. I know Carl was there because I saw
> him staring at me behind a curtain. I went home and
> called Peter. He talked to me on the phone, but he didn't
> have much to say.

I told Maria she could try to change this arrangement. I
would find her a lawyer and they could go directly to court. I
felt confident that we could locate her emergency room medical records and make a strong case for her not freely agreeing
to the mediated arrangement.

I gave her the name of an attorney who did pro bono work
for victims of violence. When I called two weeks later the attorney said that Maria had met with her and that she was opti-

mistic they could change this decision. When next I called I learned that Carl had hired an attorney and a psychologist and was going to fight this action to the end. The last time I spoke to the attorney she said the case had been continued but that Maria now said she wanted to back out.

How could this result have been prevented? Changes in the law that would bar a batterer from obtaining custody might not have made much difference in Maria's case, unless she had been encouraged to tell her story at the mediation. Unfortunately, our legal system has strange priorities: we provide free counsel to anyone accused of the most petty offense but provide no help, legal or otherwise, to parents fighting to keep contact with their own children. In this instance mediation did not work well. The mediator did not ask Maria about her relationship with her husband in her marriage. Indeed, talk of the past is not encouraged in mediation; the focus is on the future. Nor did the mediator or any person speak to the child, Peter. Whatever his fears or concerns, they were ignored.

A trained interviewer should have spent time with the parents and with Peter individually before mediation was imposed. Where there are indications of domestic violence, each of the parties, including the child, should have representation. The hearing process in a courtroom with its legal advocates and neutrally conceived rules, for all of its drawbacks, provides more protection for women and children who are victims of domestic violence than does the free-flowing persuasive model of mediation.

Although Maria's story is a tragic one, at least her abuser ceased to batter her after their breakup. Unfortunately, this is not always the case; in fact, violence against the victim often escalates. The anger and humiliation experienced by many ex-spouses after a breakup can turn into even more uncontrollable rage in those who already could not control their violence when the family was intact. In the New York study of murdered women referred to earlier one third were in the process of trying to end their relationships.[31] When custody involves visitation, picking up and dropping off children provides unlimited opportunities for violent behavior.

One of my first clients, Helene, came to me because she was frightened. I had represented her eighteen months earlier in her divorce from Brian. Her father had insisted that she have representation. He paid the bill. It was the late seventies and joint custody had not yet become popular. She and her ex-husband had agreed to the traditional arrangement: mother had sole custody of their two sons, ages three and six, and father had visitation every other weekend and every other Wednesday. In those days there was little to argue about since the court would have ordered that schedule in nearly every case. Her divorce had been fairly straightforward; there were few assets and nearly as many debts left over from her husband's law school education. Brian, a new Bar admittee, did not have a lawyer. He insisted on saving money—he could do his own paperwork.

At the time of the divorce Helene did not tell me or the judge about the beatings she had endured over the years. She was a small, quiet woman overshadowed by her charming, gregarious husband. The ostensible reason for the divorce was that Brian had fallen in love with a law school classmate. Helene had not demanded the divorce; it seemed to be his idea, and she appeared more fatalistic than distraught.

I would like to say that as a sensitive advocate I recognized the signs of her sad history, but I did not. Spousal abuse was not a public issue then, and even had I known her full story it would have made little difference at that time in the custody determination. Nor did I speak to the children to learn about their concerns. They were very young, and then (as now) it was considered inappropriate and in some instances unethical for a parent's lawyer to question the children.

I did not see Helene again until she appeared in my office eighteen months after the divorce. She had told me on the phone that she needed my help right away; it was about Brian. Something in the tone of her voice made me suspect violence. Standing in my office, she looked nervous and uncertain. I remember the conversation well because it was my first real encounter with domestic violence as an attorney.

I searched her face for bruises. She looked okay. I asked if Brian had hurt her.

"No, not really, but he came to the house when the kids were in school and I refused to let him in. I yelled at him to go away. I thought he had gone and then I heard someone downstairs in the rec room. I was so frightened that I hid in the closet for over an hour. When I finally came out it seemed quiet so I went downstairs."

I asked why she hadn't called the police.

She was apologetic. "Maybe I should have, I shouldn't be bothering you, but he didn't hit me."

I then asked her if she had been hit before and she said it had gone on for years; even last month he had come by to return the boys and slapped her as she tried to get him to leave. Now he had been coming around more often. She thought his romance had gone sour. She continued, "I finally got the courage to go downstairs and he was gone, but he took the stereo with him."

I asked why he would do that.

She said she didn't know. "He always claimed that he bought it before he met me, but he agreed to leave it for the children in the divorce settlement. I don't really care . . . I guess he can have it."

I told her I was going to call the police immediately. She begged me not to—it would only enrage him. She just wanted me to help her somehow. I told her the next time he might have a knife or a gun. She still did not relent.

Two things were apparent to me at once. Helene was in real danger, and the police were unlikely to do anything. In those days police routinely ignored domestic violence calls unless there was a very serious injury. Even today, without an overt threat or fresh physical injury it is difficult to secure a restraining order.

I took three steps to help protect Helene. I told her to take the children for a visit with their grandparents in another state; I called the family court for a hearing on the custody order; and I contacted the police about a restraining order.

Changing the custody order with regard to a no-contact pickup was the easiest. The judge agreed that pickups and drop offs should be at a neutral place, in this instance the school both boys attended. He also agreed to a full hearing on the issue of visitation in a month.

Obtaining the restraining order that would bar Brian from coming near the house or Helene's place of work was more difficult, since there was no physical evidence of violence. Fortunately, we found a neighbor who had seen the slapping incident the previous month that took place on the front porch, and she had seen Brian driving by the house frequently when no one was home. We were able to secure a two-month temporary restraining order.

I had hoped to present the neighbor's testimony and other evidence I could gather, including professional interviews of the children, at the forthcoming custody hearing. I feared the boys were at risk of abuse from their volatile father. I recommended asking for supervised visitation. Helene did not want to pursue this. She claimed that he never touched the boys, and she did not want her own abuse to be investigated at the hearing. "It will only make things worse for me and the boys," she insisted. Since the boys did not have their own attorney, and no report had been made to Children's Protective Services, I had to let it go. The court never heard the voices of these children.

Helene's story turned out as well as one could hope. Brian, a new attorney trying to establish his reputation, was sufficiently intimidated by the restraining order that he stayed away from the house and adhered to the neutral pickup. The family continued in this routine for two years without any contact between Helene and Brian. Then Brian moved across the country and the children visited on holidays.

We know that not all stories go so well. Families experiencing domestic violence need continued supervision and do not get it. Even when the batterers do not get custody or joint custody, even when restraining orders are in place, even when child transfers are on neutral ground with no opportunity of contact, things can go terribly wrong. Courts are reluctant and slow to change custody orders, yet with victims of domestic violence they must be more responsive. Above all, the voices of children should be acknowledged. If a child becomes fearful or if there is evidence of abuse, visitations should be supervised or cut off entirely. Children of families with a history of domestic violence should be assigned a permanent advocate or guardian ad litem who will routinely check on their condition. Current laws and practices do not allow for this responsiveness, nor is family court organized to protect children.

In most states the juvenile court is charged with the responsibility of protecting children. To that end it is equipped with a staff of child protection workers whose business is to investigate the condition of children when abuse or neglect has been reported and to remove them from their home if evidence shows they are in immediate danger. Child protection workers also are prepared to continue supervising children in that home for years if necessary, to ensure that they are safe. Juvenile courts, however, usually are not involved with custody disputes, even those in which domestic violence has occurred, unless a child reportedly has been abused.

One recent California case illustrates the drastic shortcomings of family court in protecting children, even when they have been victims of abuse. Married at sixteen, Kristine Fisher bore two boys and a girl, and endured years of beatings and psychological torture. At times her husband would drive down the wrong side of the street simply to terrify her.

"He threw a knife at me holding our three-week-old son," she said.

Not until he started going after the children did she have the courage to tell him to leave. She was then twenty-two. He was convicted and jailed briefly for misdemeanor battery—the typical domestic violence conviction. She was frightened by his threats that he would kill her and the children and went into hiding. A sheriff's report filed at this time called him dangerous.

Yet two years later a family court assessor recommended that he be granted half-time custody of their children. This despite his having been returned to jail for violating his restraining order and failing to take a domestic violence training program, a condition of his probation.[32] Moreover, the son's therapist had requested that the court take seriously allegations that the husband had stalked and battered Fisher and whipped the oldest son with a wire hanger, among other physical and verbal abuses.

According to Fisher, "I have to force my sons to go; they come home with strange bruises. They come home with pocket knives. I go pick them up and they are playing with lighters unsupervised. The family court says I have to show him to be an unfit parent, but I'm scared to be in the same room as him."[33]

Unfortunately the recommendation of this assessor to grant half-time custody to the father comes as no surprise. Court-appointed custody evaluators often are not responsive to allegations of domestic violence. A recent national survey of psychologists who serve as custody evaluators found that 90.6 percent of psychologists would not consider an allegation of physical abuse of a child by a parent grounds for recommending custody to the other parent. By contrast, 75.6 percent indicated they would recommend against custody to a parent who often attempts to alienate the child from the other parent by negatively interpreting that parent's behavior.[34] In the shadow of this prevailing attitude mothers who fear abuse are better off keeping it to themselves, or they risk losing custody of the children they are trying to protect.

A law in place that presumes that a batterer is an unfit parent unless proven otherwise would have helped to protect the Fisher children. At the very least their father would have had to complete the domestic violence training program ordered by the court as part of his sentence on the earlier assault conviction before gaining unsupervised visitation. Joint custody probably would not have been considered an option under any circumstances.

Such a law, however, is threatening to many. When a version of this law was proposed in California opposition came from the California Judges Association, which sought to preserve judicial discretion; the family law section of the State Bar, which claimed that the current law on domestic violence is sufficient; and from the Coalition of Parent Support (COPS), a fathers' rights group. A spokesman for COPS said, "All someone has to say is, 'He hit me,' and then he has to prove it didn't happen, and that can take months and years, and in the meantime he's separated from his children. Ms. Kuel's [the legislative sponsor] agenda is removing men from the lives of their children."[35]

Other critics point to the history of child sex abuse allegations, which they claim are used falsely by one parent to wrest custody from the other. One may argue that spousal abuse is more likely than child abuse to leave a clear physical evidentiary path. Even if there are no hospital records, almost always witnesses have seen physical damage or have been confided in by the victim.

Yet opponents of more protective legislation see both kinds of allegations as weapons in the arsenals of belligerent parents who work out unresolved conflicts from the marriage in the new arena of custody combat. These allegations are among the primary concerns of fathers' rights groups, who have successfully lobbied for laws favoring the "friendly parent," no matter what his or her relationship is to the child, and without regard for the record of actual parenting.

Is there reason to be concerned about false allegations? Let us examine the claims regarding false allegations of parental sex abuse. In the 1980s child sex abuse first became an issue for public notice and scrutiny. Such cases were highly publicized, such as the McMartin trial in southern California in which a day care owner and six day care workers were accused of abusing hundreds of children over ten years. Most sexual abuse, it was learned in the course of these trials, occurs in the family; often it is the father, or more often the mother's boyfriend or the stepfather, but mothers also could be offenders.

Familial sex abuse touches public fear in a way that other kinds of physical abuse of children does not. Child sexual abuse allegations are treated differently from allegations of neglect or even most physical abuse complaints. Allegations of child sex abuse tend to be taken more seriously by both the police and child protection services, and often trigger the removal of a child, at least temporarily, from the custody of the suspected adult. Criminal convictions of offenders are actively sought, even when the offender is a parent. Even if a jury cannot sustain a criminal conviction beyond a reasonable doubt, a civil action can mandate removal of the child for the child's safety.

Both criminal and civil trials, including custody trials involving allegations of child sexual abuse, are notoriously difficult to win, however. Often the child is under the age of five, with limited language skills, and physical evidence of abuse may be ambiguous or nonexistent. As a result, very few accused sex offenders are actually convicted. One study estimates that fewer than 1 percent of child molestations result in arrest, conviction, and imprisonment of the offender.[36] Similarly, as we shall see, allegations of sexual abuse in the custody arena more often result in punishment of the accuser than the accused.

Owing to the lack of hard evidence in cases alleging molestation, courts commonly rely on sexual abuse experts who have interviewed the child; but each of the parents also may introduce experts, turning the trial into a three-ring circus of experts.

Newsom v. Newsom,[37] a custody trial, is a particularly unfortunate example of such a circus. The Newsoms' tale is a tortured one and illustrates the difficulty of trying to prove sexual abuse with very young children. At the time of the divorce Karen Newsom was awarded custody of Kathryn, then two years and four months old, and Adam, then eight months old. Only a few months later Karen attempted to terminate Eugene Newsom's visitation, charging him with sexual abuse of the children. An extended trial ensued, during which the court heard testimony from four different experts, two of whom were appointed by the court, regarding alleged sexual abuse of the children by the father. The mother's and father's experts supported each of their stories. One court-appointed expert initially decided there was no indication of abuse, but upon speaking with another counselor who had seen the children changed his testimony, based solely on the fact that the mother had provided this counselor with explicit details of abuse that were later determined to be untrue. The court decided to disregard the testimony of this expert and ultimately concluded that there had been no abuse by the father. The judge awarded custody to the father, deeming the mother's actions in pursuing this allegation harmful to the children, in a classic "friendly parent" ruling.[38]

Karen refused to obey the new order and on the advice of her lawyer refused to deliver the children to Eugene, hiding them instead. She was found in contempt and ordered jailed after refusing to reveal the location of her children. While in hiding Karen took her children for examination to yet another doctor, and her lawyer prepared a press release that included reports and statements of the four previous experts as well as the new one. These materials contained detailed and explicit references to the alleged abuse.[39]

Not until after her attorney withdrew from her case did Karen surrender the children to the court. Subsequently, Karen's right to visit the children was severely restricted to an hour and a half each week at Eugene's home, under supervision.

We may never know the truth behind this story of battling experts and angry judges, but the result is that the court punished Karen for bringing forth the allegations. A strong judicial bias against sexual abuse allegations exists among family court judges. The judge in the Newsom case expressed his disapproval forcefully:

> The children of this marriage have been used as a weapon of revenge; victimized by vicious and reputation destroying accusations; and subjected to repeated physical and psychological examinations over a period of many months, intimate details of which were revealed to the press. In addition, Karen Newsom openly defied the authority of the law of the state in refusing to surrender the children in accordance with the order of the court.[40]

The fact that Karen Newsom hid her children from their father was an important consideration for the court. Parental kidnapping is a serious national problem, and state and federal legislation, most notably the Parental Kidnapping Prevention Act of 1980 (PKPA),[41] have attempted to treat it as a serious crime deserving tough law enforcement; but the issue is not always that straightforward. Many parents, including Karen, would claim it is the only way they can protect their children from an abusive parent. They consider it an act of desperation, not revenge—and some states agree that this act cannot always be considered a crime. California, for instance, exempts from the definition of felony kidnapping any person whose intent is "to protect the child from danger of imminent harm."[42] In the Newsom case it is not clear that the children had been abducted since they were remaining with their primary parent, not snatched away from one parent by the other. From the children's point of view they are not suffering the trauma of kidnap.

The decision in the Newsom case to remove the children from the complaining parent is not unusual. As noted earlier, courts tend to favor the "friendly parent," that is, the parent who is not making the accusation or withholding access, and often will transfer custody on that basis. Popular wisdom holds that allegations of sexual abuse in child custody cases are typically a strategy of revenge or manipulation, but the truth can be more complicated. In the limited studies available investigators can substantiate fewer of these allegations in custody disputes (around 20 percent) than in other situations (40–60 percent).[43] Failure to substantiate abuse, however, does not prove it did not occur; and there are possibilities to explain such accusations other than vindictiveness. For instance, parents faced with loss of emotional support during the divorce process may become abusers; former partners inflamed by the dynamics of an adversarial divorce may distort their perceptions of the other and sincerely believe the worst.

Nonetheless, allegations of sexual abuse nearly always distort the process and the children may become the victims. The transfer of custody to the "friendly parent" more often is done to punish the other parent than to meet the needs of the child. In the Newsom case, for instance, there is no evidence that the mother, who had served as the primary parent for these very small children since their birth, functioned poorly as a parent. Subjecting the children to physical exams in and of itself does not indicate bad parenting.

Other problems occur in such cases with older children who are able to testify to allegations of abuse on their own. Here the court tends to suspect that one parent has put them up to it, and the accuracy of children's testimony becomes another area of heated debate among experts. Some experts believe that children as young as four have very accurate recall for incidents of sexual abuse, and others believe that memory in young children is easily influenced.[44]

False accusations of sexual or other abuse, intentionally delivered, can have devastating consequences for the innocent accused and for the children as well. Yet how can one be sure that an accusation is true or false? Some experts claim to know when a child is telling the truth; these experts often rely on some version of the child sexual abuse accommodation syndrome (CSAAS), originally formulated by the psychiatrist Roland Summit in 1983.[45] While there are variations on this theme, indications of abuse most often looked for in children include recantation, secrecy, inappropriate sexual behavior for their age, nightmares, and bedwetting.[46]

Other experts believe they can tell when a child is *not* telling the truth. One of the most prominent among them is Richard Gardner, whose testimony and publications frequently are referred to in custody cases. Gardner claims that he can determine when a parent—usually the mother—has filled the child with false notions about the other parent. Such children, he believes, exhibit what he calls "parental alienation syndrome" (PAS), which can include, but is not limited to, allegations of sexual abuse.[47] He describes PAS as manifesting itself in several primary symptoms: children so afflicted may carry on a campaign of denigration of the alienated parent, show a lack of ambivalence and guilt about it, and reflexively support the loved parent in the conflict. They are likely to spread their animosity to the entire family. Gardner alleges that in its severest form these children refuse to visit their noncustodial parent (almost always the father) and have nothing good to say about him. The child, however, professes that he or she is the sole originator of the feelings and has not been coached by the mother.

In moderate cases, in which the child resists visiting, Gardner first recommends financial sanctions against the mother: for example, reduction of alimony payments. If this does not work, Gardner recommends "house arrest" for periods of time, by means of electronic transmitters on the mother's ankle and random telephone calls to the police. If this fails to cure the recalcitrant mother and child, Gardner calls for actual incarceration of the mother for limited periods.

Gardner suggests that for severe cases of PAS, "where children's blood-curdling shrieks, panicked states and irate outbursts may be so severe that if placed in the father's home they may run away, or become paralyzed with fear," a different legal solution is recommended. He suggests that for these children primary custody should be shifted to the parent they fear, with a "transitional site program" to prepare the child for this new and frightening reality.[48]

With the PAS model the voices of the children are heard, but they are being used against them. The more fear a child expresses about the other parent the more likely the child will be taken away from his or her mother and placed with that parent.

There is no easy way of dealing with these issues of domestic violence and abuse, but a clear rule must be that the child does not become a victim. We have lost sight of this fundamental obligation, too often blinded by the conflicts between mothers and fathers in this highly politicized arena. Feminists may be likely to support nearly all allegations of domestic abuse made by women, including child sex abuse, while many judges, psychologists, and fathers' rights groups are likely to look suspiciously at mothers' claims of violence and abuse and see them as unfair or unscrupulous maneuvers in the custody wars.

In my opinion there are three simple principles that could promote the interests of the child in this tangled battlefield. First, where there is clear evidence of spousal or partner abuse, it must be assumed that the batterer is not an appropriate choice for custody or joint custody. Second, when there is *any* evidence that the child also has been physically abused, only supervised visitation should be allowed and neither parent should have contact with the other. Third, and perhaps most important, whether or not there is clear evidence of physical or sexual abuse of the child, if the child expresses fear or discomfort about spending time with the alleged abuser, visitation or custody should not be forced on the child; this should be true even in cases in which the batterer has completed a rehabilitative course.

The third principle is the most controversial and directly challenges the highly favored "friendly parent" rule. This third principle focuses squarely on the wishes and feelings of the child rather than on the rights of the parent. In some instances the fears of the child indeed may have been unfairly promoted by a vindictive parent, but there will be other cases in which the child has genuine reason to fear physical or sexual abuse that leaves no clear evidentiary trace. In either event the child should be not coerced in a terrifying situation.

What about a parent, in most cases the custodial mother, who makes false allegations purely for vindictive purposes? These are the unscrupulous mothers against whom the friendly parent rule was designed. In practice, however, the truth is less obvious than the rule would indicate. As in the Newsom case, experts can differ in the interpretation of the same facts, and parents may honestly believe their own allegations, even if unfounded. In the rare case in which the allegations clearly are false other sanctions may be imposed on the vindictive parent, including reduction in spousal support or monetary fines. Above all, the child should not be the party to bear the punishment.

In our current confused court structure neither criminal nor family court focuses on protecting children. Only in juvenile court is the protection of the child a main concern. In most cases children enter the juvenile court system only when their parents are not capable of providing a safe home for them. I would argue that children in any family in which there is domestic violence or abuse should be under the jurisdiction of juvenile courts; otherwise a safe haven is not guaranteed (in fact, as will be discussed further, a comprehensive family court based on a juvenile court model is the appropriate venue for *all* custody disputes). In a juvenile court model the child can be talked to, advocated for, and watched over by the court until domestic violence has ceased to be an issue.

7

Fit to Be a Parent?
Gay and Lesbian Parents
Come Out of the
Closet Fighting

WHAT DOES IT MEAN TO BE A FIT PARENT? We have learned that violent criminal behavior—even murder—does not necessarily create a presumption that the perpetrator is an unfit parent in the eyes of the court. Sexual behavior, however, between consenting adults considered deviant for the time and place may do so.

John Ward had served an eight-year prison term for the second-degree murder in 1974 of his first wife, Judy. They were arguing over custody of their children. He shot her six times, reloaded his gun, and shot six more times.[1]

Upon his release Ward found stable employment in a lumberyard, married a woman named Mary, and fathered a daughter, Cassey. The Wards divorced in 1992, and Mary Ward was granted primary custody of their eight-year-old daughter. Three years later Judge Joseph Tarbuck of Escambia County Circuit Court ordered the child to move in with her father after

Mr. Ward told the court that Cassey made statements of a sexual nature, exhibited bad table manners and personal hygiene habits, and preferred to wear men's cologne. Mary Ward was granted limited supervised visitation. Mary, who at the time was a restaurant chef living with a girlfriend and two older daughters—one of whom was a lesbian with a live-in girlfriend—denied that she had exposed the child to any sexual behavior in her home. She noted that she had filed for increased child support shortly before Mr. Ward petitioned for custody.

In a written statement released by his lawyers Mr. Ward described the court's decision as one that held that "growing up in a household with a husband and wife residing together in marriage was more beneficial to an 11-year-old girl than growing up in a household with four adults engaged in homosexual relationships." He said that his daughter "very much loves her mother," but has made new friends and "is not embarrassed to bring them home for a visit or introduce them to her father and stepmother."[2]

Gay rights lawyers said Ms. Ward's case was most disturbing because there was no evidence of any improper conduct at her home. "When a decision like this comes down, it does strike fear into the hearts of lesbian and gay parents around the country because they recognize that if it could happen to a parent like Mary Ward it could happen to them," said Kathryn D. Kendell, the executive director of the National Center for Lesbian Rights, which helped represent Ms. Ward.[3]

The appeals court in the Ward case upheld the trial court's decision. It dismissed as irrelevant a recently passed Florida law creating a presumption that granting custody to a parent who had been convicted of a felony involving domestic violence would be detrimental to the child. The father, the court said, had "reformed."[4]

Domestic violence and lesbianism—two volatile fronts on which women's rights advocates are struggling to advance in the gender wars—are the central issues of this case. On both fronts women believe they are unfairly pitted against a legal system and a society that discredits them. It is true that gay men share the disadvantage of homophobia, which certainly plays a role in thwarting their paternal rights; and some men are victims of violent domestic assaults. Yet women by far fight the majority of these battles in the custody wars.

On its face this case appears to confirm a deeply rooted prejudice against lesbian mothers. It probably does, but an important piece of information is missing: what does eleven-year-old Cassey want? Is she happy to live with her father and stepmother, or is she simply a pawn in this larger politicized battle? No one disputes that her mother has always been her primary parent; but is she, perhaps, genuinely unhappy and embarrassed in her mother's household? If this is the case, while it may not advance the cause of women's rights, her feelings as a developing adolescent should be taken seriously. Yet the court, political supporters, and opponents—and probably even the warring parents—have lost track of the wishes and feelings of this child; the lesbian lifestyle of the mother has blinded all parties to any other consideration.

The sexual lifestyles of mothers is always of great concern to society, and this concern is faithfully reflected in the law. Mothers took a legal leap in the nineteenth century when courts reversed fathers' paramount claims to custody, focusing instead on mothers as the nurturers of small children; but the tender years doctrine offered only a qualified approval of mothers, usually expressed as: "Children of tender years are awarded to the mother unless the mother is unfit."[5] Lack of fitness might include physical neglect or abuse or mental illness, but in most cases for mothers it meant their sexual behavior. The very high moral standards imposed on mothers in the nineteenth century allowed judges to sometimes view them more positively in custody disputes, but it also meant that the system turned harshly against mothers when they strayed from strict, conventional moral standards. Nineteenth-century judges routinely condemned adulterous women, declaring them unfit to have *any* contact with their children, much less sole custody.

Though adultery may have been an inexcusable act for mothers, in the venerable tradition of the double standard it was not so for fathers. Adultery alone was rarely enough to bar a father's custodial rights; an additional factor such as domestic violence was required. In *Lindsay v. Lindsay*, an 1854 case, Mrs. Lindsay claimed that she was not living in an adulterous relationship since she believed her ex-husband had obtained a total divorce.[6] Furthermore, she argued, she left him because he had his adulterous affair while they were still living together. Nevertheless, the court gave their four-year-old daughter to the father, stating,

> [T]here may be no difference in the sin of the man and the woman, who violate the laws of chastity. But we do know, that in the opinion of society, it is otherwise . . . for when she sins after this sort, she sins against society . . . her associations are with the vulgar, the vile and the depraved. If her children are with her, their characters must be, more or less, influenced and formed by the circumstances which surround them.[7]

In the early twentieth century divorce grew more commonplace and courts grew less publicly attached to religious strictures. Judges began to view mothers' extramarital sexual activities more leniently, provided they had clearly mended their ways and their transgressions had occurred in the more or less distant past. The case of *Harmon v. Harmon* provides a glimpse into the Roaring Twenties, but it also reveals that a woman's sexual conduct was no longer a complete bar to custody, and that adultery alone was no longer always valid grounds for divorce.[8] Two married couples in Kansas, Mr. and Mrs. Harmon and an unnamed husband and wife, associated in the same social circles and became good friends, going on late-night rides together and spending much of their free time as a foursome. One day Mr. Harmon found Mrs. Harmon engaged in an act of adultery with the other husband. He insisted that she must go to live with her parents and renounce custody of their five-year-old daughter. Both men made her sign a written agreement admitting her guilt and agreeing to the custody arrangement. Mr. Harmon then sued for divorce on the ground of adultery and sought custody of their daughter. The trial court found that adultery was committed with "the knowledge, connivance and consent of the plaintiff," and denied the divorce. The court was silent on the custody issue.[9]

On appeal a higher court agreed that the adultery was encouraged by the husband. "He must have known the absurd lengths to which extraordinary intimacy, informality, and unconventionality [with the other couple] had grown, [and] was bound to culminate as it did." The court granted temporary custody of the daughter to the mother, reasoning that "except for defendant's temporary infatuation for her paramour, she was a good mother."[10]

Several decades later, in the Swinging Sixties, sexual activity outside the institution of marriage became so commonplace (at least among the young) that the law gradually reflected the more tolerant attitude expressed by large numbers of Americans. The moral indignation of adultery was no longer necessary or important as a ground for ending a marriage as no-fault divorce swept the country in the 1970s. In a separate but related movement the feminist drive for equal rights abolished the distinction between mothers and fathers in custody law as a matter of gender equality. In most states today custody law is drafted in strictly gender-neutral language and excludes specific references to moral fitness as a factor in custody decisions.[11] On paper the old double standard is largely defunct.

Homosexual activity, which in previous eras would have been an automatic and conclusive factor against a parent, is treated with more tolerance, at least superficially. A few states still consider homosexuality evidence of parental unfitness per se,[12] but most states—including Florida, where the Wards fought for custody of Cassey—require proof that homosexual activity or extramarital heterosexual activity has produced an adverse affect on the child.[13] The Ward case, however, demonstrates that official changes in the law do not necessarily mean changes in attitudes. The judicial focus may have shifted from a mother's adultery to a mother's homosexuality, but mothers are still held to a rigid moral standard.

Sometimes the official left and right hand of the law are not in agreement on this sensitive issue. The state of Virginia does not consider homosexuality evidence of parental unfitness per se for purposes of custody,[14] but it is still a designated felony in the criminal code.[15] This apparent contradiction caused great difficulty for Sharon Bottoms, whose mother was awarded custody of her two-year-old son because Sharon was living with another woman.[16] This case received national attention not because Sharon lost custody (not an uncommon experience for gay and lesbian parents) but because it was the child's grandmother rather than his natural parent who triumphed. Virginia, like almost all other states, has a strong presumption in favor of biological parents against all third parties. A third party can only gain advantage if they can prove by clear and convincing evidence that the parent is unfit.

The case dragged on for years, regularly popping up as a lurid headline in national tabloids. During the case Sharon Bottoms and her mother became the focus of the ongoing bitter battle between the activist gay movement and conservative Christian moralists. The facts of the case as related at the trial are straightforward and not refuted by anyone; but as we shall see, filtered through the eyes of their beholders they resulted in three different judgments from three different courts.

Sharon Bottoms was married briefly to Dennis Doustou and was granted custody of their son, an infant, when they divorced. During the three years following her divorce Sharon dated another man, lived with her cousin, lived with two lesbians, and in 1992 began living with April Wade. During this time Sharon had legal custody of her son, but she frequently relied on her mother, Kay, to keep and care for the child. Kay Bottoms testified that she had kept the child most of the time after his birth.

In January 1993 Sharon informed her mother that her son would be spending less time at her mother's house owing to Tommy Conley's presence there. Tommy Conley was Kay's live-in male companion. The two had lived together and reared Sharon from the time she was a child. Sharon explained to her mother that she was taking her son out of the household because while she, Sharon, was growing up, Conley had sexually abused her over 800 times. Kay was initially shocked and upset by the accusations but later decided that they were not altogether unfounded.

Shortly after this conversation Kay filed a petition with the juvenile and domestic relations district court seeking custody of her two-year-old grandson. She asked Conley to move out of the house during the custody dispute because her lawyer "thought it would be best." The circuit court granted Kay Bottoms custody of her grandson.

At the trial Sharon acknowledged that she was a lesbian and that she shared a residence with April Wade, her lesbian companion. Sharon admitted that she and April engaged in consensual sexual acts in the privacy of their residence. Yet she insisted that she and Wade had never engaged in any type of sexual activity in her son's presence, nor had she exposed him to sexual conduct of any type. They had displayed only affection in the child's presence by hugging, kissing, or patting one another on the bottom.

The psychological evaluation ordered by the court related that Sharon Bottoms was "warm" and "responsive" with her son, and that he "behave[s] as if entirely secure and at ease with her."[17] In the closest one might come to presenting the voice of the two-year-old, the evaluator stated that the mother and child have a loving relationship and that Bottoms's open lesbian relationship has had no visible or discernible effect on her son. She had adequately provided him with the basic necessities of life, including food, clothing, and shelter.

Other, more negative evidence was presented at trial, however. On two occasions Sharon spanked the child on the leg "too hard." The evidence did not show that the spankings bruised or injured the child. Testimony also revealed that Sharon had punished the child by making him stand in a corner, and had on occasion cursed in the child's presence. The evidence did not indicate, however, that she physically abused the child, neglected him, or endangered or threatened his life, physical safety, or well-being.

Kay Bottoms testified that on one occasion Sharon left the child at Kay's home for a week without telling her how she could be reached. No evidence showed that Sharon had ever left the child with an irresponsible person or unattended.[18]

The basic facts are uncontested, yet they produced a roller coaster of judicial responses involving a whole cast of organized political and religious advocates on both sides of the incendiary issue. First, the trial court awarded custody to the grandmother, ruling that because Sharon Bottoms lived in a sexually active lesbian relationship and engaged in illegal sexual acts she was an unfit parent as a matter of law.

> Sharon Bottoms has ... admitted ... that she is living in an homosexual relationship.... She is sharing ... her bed with ... her female lover.... Examples given were kissing, patting, all of this in the presence of the child.... I will tell you first that the mother's conduct is illegal.... I will tell you that it is the opinion of the court that her conduct is immoral. And it is the opinion of this court that the conduct of Sharon Bottoms renders her an unfit parent.[19]

Sharon Bottoms appealed this decision to the court of appeals, who reversed the trial court, concluding, "the evidence fails to prove [that the mother] abused or neglected her son, that her lesbian relationship with April Wade has or will have a deleterious effect on her son, or that she is an unfit parent." "To the contrary," said the court, the evidence showed that the mother "is and has been a fit and nurturing parent who has adequately provided and cared for her son. No evidence tended to prove that the child will be harmed by remaining with his mother."[20]

It was the grandmother's turn to appeal, this time to the highest court, the Supreme Court of Virginia.[21] The full attention of gay rights and antigay forces was riveted on this case. Virginia's highest court overturned the appeals court ruling and sided again with the grandmother, granting her custody. Once again a new court's reading of the same facts had produced an entirely different result. Ignoring the custody evaluator's opinion that the mother–child relationship was healthy, the court speculated on what it perceived would be the long-term consequences of being raised by lesbians:

> And, we shall not overlook the mother's relationship with Wade, and the environment in which the child would be raised if custody is awarded the mother. We have previously said that living daily under conditions stemming from active lesbianism practiced in the home may impose a burden upon a child by reason of the "social condemnation" attached to such an arrangement, which will inevitably afflict the child's relationships with its "peers and with the community at large."[22]

Most custody court battles involving a gay or lesbian parent do not become front page news. They are decided by ordinary judges dealing with ordinary people, outside of the political limelight. Even in the majority of states where homosexuality can no longer be considered a controlling issue in custody disputes and no longer constitutes a crime under the criminal code, judicial attitudes may not have changed along with the law. With sexual mores, as with maternal presumption, judges frequently find new reasons within their powers of discretion that allow them to rule as they would have under the old laws.

Such appears to have occurred in the 1985 Indiana case *D. H. v. J. H.*, in which the judge determined the custodial fate of three children, ages eleven, nine, and eight.[23] Much of the testimony at the trial involved the alleged lesbian relationship of the wife with two young women, K. B. and K. R. Both of these young women testified that they had engaged in homosexual activity with the mother, D. H. The father, J. H., testified that he observed his wife and one of the young ladies swimming nude in the parties' pool. This was late at night when the children were in bed. The husband presented photographs he took of his wife and K. R. hugging. The husband also introduced other evidence indicating that the wife left dirty dishes around and that the husband frequently had to prepare meals for the children because their mother was "running around."[24]

The mother presented evidence of her active involvement with all of the children's needs and activities, and, conversely, of the father's lack of concern for his children. She claimed she had been the primary parent since their birth.[25]

As usual, the voices of the children were never heard. No one spoke of their wishes or feelings, or their developmental needs as preadolescents.

The trial court judge awarded all three children to the father, with no real explanation. The mother appealed, claiming the court had not followed the statutory guidelines in Indiana, which does not list homosexuality as indicative of moral fitness.[26] At a loss to find a precedent regarding lesbian mothers, the court decided to treat a lesbian mother as it would an adulterous mother: "[W]e believe the proper rule to be that homosexuality standing alone without evidence of any adverse effect upon the welfare of the child does not render the homosexual parent unfit as a matter of law to have custody of the child."[27] The court then decided there was no evidence of a negative effect on the children.

The legal finding should have allowed the court to overturn the trial judge, but nevertheless it approved the award of all three children to the father. Ignoring the evidence that supported the mother's role as primary caregiver, the court focused instead on her housekeeping. "The evidence concerning wife's lack of proper housekeeping standards, that husband fixed meals for the children because wife was out running around, and that husband assisted children with lessons are all relevant factors which the court could consider and which would support the decision."[28]

Court battles, even those out of the public eye like that between D. H. and J. H., are not the norm. The major conflicts regarding parental fitness, as with all custody disputes, never reach the courtroom. They are played out sometimes in lawyer's offices, sometimes in police stations, and most often on the telephone or in kitchens and doorways when a child is being exchanged from one household to the other. In these disputes the language is not legal; seldom is it polite. Sometimes it is intended to wound, humiliate, or to frighten. When the issue is the fitness of a gay or lesbian parent it can be all three.

My client (I will call her Georgia) called me two years after what I had thought had been a fairly amicable resolution of her divorce from Frank. Georgia had come to America from Guatemala to attend college, where she met Frank. Both seemed to agree that their marriage, hastily entered into when Georgia became pregnant, had not been a mature decision. At the time of the divorce their two girls were two and four. Frank intended to move back east in the near future, so they settled on an arrangement by which the girls would spend Christmas vacation and one summer month with Frank in Connecticut. Frank's parents were very wealthy, so there was no difficulty regarding child support. Georgia had no money, but the child support allowed her to work only part time.

Yet in this phone call, two years after making these arrangements, Georgia's voice was nearly hysterical. "She is not returning my babies," she cried. "She says she won't let a lesbian slut raise her granddaughters."

It took me a while to understand what was going on. The girls had gone to Connecticut for their summer visit at their grandparents' summer house. There the grandmother had learned from the girls that Georgia had a new love interest, a woman. The grandmother swore to Georgia on the telephone that she would fight for their family to have custody and that the girls would be raised decently. She had informed Georgia that she had hired a private detective and she now had "real dirt" on her.

I asked Georgia to come to my office immediately and we would try to find a solution. When Georgia arrived she was clearly frightened, and also reluctant to reveal her story to me. "I am so ashamed," she said. "Now I am being punished. I will lose my babies."

I tried to reassure her, but I needed to know the facts. Georgia haltingly told me her story. About a year after the divorce was final and Frank had moved away she ran into an old friend from college, Helen.

"It was wonderful to reconnect. I was so lonely, I have no family here, and her smile lit up my day. I had never had any feelings, like that, before, when we were in college, but now it was different."

Georgia said she had never thought of herself as gay, although occasionally she had been attracted to women, but this was much stronger than anything she had previously experienced. "We both soon realized that it was serious. But I knew I couldn't or wouldn't do anything about it because of the girls."

Georgia said she continued to see Helen, but thought she was completely discrete. "We would meet often for lunch when the girls were at preschool. Sometime she would do things with us—like go to the zoo or McDonald's or help make dinner, but there was never any touching or anything between us. The girls loved her. She never stayed overnight or anything like that."

It was only this particular summer, when the girls were away for a month, that Georgia allowed herself to spend more time with Helen and to invite her to spend the night.

"That's when that detective must have seen us. I can't believe Flora (her mother-in-law) could do this. She never even let me talk to Frank. I didn't think she hated me, we always got along before. She told me I was a good mother."

Georgia, understandably, could not comprehend the ferocity of her former mother-in-law's actions. In my experience issues relating to sexuality, whether they involve a same-sex lover or a heterosexual affair, can provoke irrationally fierce reactions. Not only are these conflicts suffused with turbulent emotions, they are also the likeliest occasions for physical violence.

I tried to present the problem rationally, pointing out both the strengths and weaknesses of our case. "You will not lose your daughters because of your relationship with Helen," I tried to reassure her and perhaps myself. "The law in California does not allow your sexual behavior to be used against you, unless it is clear that the children are harmed, and I can't see how that can be the case."

I pointed out that since they were not returning the girls as scheduled this was now technically a kidnap case under federal law, the Parental Kidnap Act. We could try to enlist the Connecticut police and, ultimately, the FBI. I also told her there was a law adopted by all states, the Uniform Child Custody Jurisdiction Act, that would force Connecticut to honor her California custody order.

This speech cheered us both, but I felt obliged to point out the downside.

"Georgia," I told her gently, "it could be a while before we get the girls back. Your husband's family has money and probably can at least delay or even block their return. The law is not as good as it should be in automatically enforcing custody decrees. Law enforcement doesn't really consider it kidnap."

What I didn't mention to her was that if the grandmother had gone through the trouble of hiring a private detective, she would also certainly hire a psychologist or two to try to establish that the girls had been harmed by Helen's presence in their life. I also neglected to mention that although I was willing to represent her for nothing, hiring a lawyer in Connecticut to expedite the process as well as additional psychologists to counteract those hired by the grandmother would probably be well beyond her resources.

I advised her to wait at home and told her I would contact the grandmother. In fact, the grandmother's lawyer contacted me first.

"We are going to go for custody," she informed me.

"I was just about to call the Connecticut police," I replied.

We spoke frankly about the legal situation over the phone. There seemed no point in trying to create a smokescreen between us. Finally I said, "I don't think they really want full-time custody of the girls—or at least the father doesn't—he hasn't said a word, and the grandparents are apparently very old."

"You may be right," she said cautiously, "but they cannot tolerate what they consider deviant behavior. Here's their offer. This woman friend totally disappears, and no women replaces her, and they will consider returning the girls."

I called Georgia reluctantly. She clearly had been waiting by the phone. Before I told her of their offer I repeated that I thought we could win this in court; she had done no harm to the children. When I relayed the offer she did not hesitate for a second. "Yes, anything. I promise. Just get them back to me." Then she began to cry with what I imagined could be relief or sadness, or both.

Granted that gay or lesbian behavior provokes irrationally strong responses, yet is there a legitimate concern about the long-term effects on children raised by a homosexual parent or a homosexual couple? Can one peel through layers of modern activist politics and ancient prejudices and focus on what we know or don't know about homosexual parenting?

Until 1975 the American Psychiatric Association included homosexuality among its list of mental disorders. Since that time mental health and social science professionals no longer consider homosexuality a mental disorder. Questions remain, however, voiced by the courts and gay and lesbian parents themselves, about the effects of lesbian or gay parenting on children. The primary concern is that children brought up by gay fathers or lesbian mothers will show disturbance in gender identity or gender role identity, the implication being that children brought up by lesbian mothers or gay fathers will themselves become gay or lesbian. A second, related concern is that these children therefore will be more vulnerable to mental breakdown, will experience more behavior problems, and will be less psychologically healthy than other children. An additional concern is that their social development will be stunted, that these children may be stigmatized, teased, or otherwise traumatized by peers. A darker concern is that they may be more prone to be sexually abused by the parent or by the parent's friends or relationships.

While the volume of research is not yet robust, there is no evidence to support these concerns. In the most comprehensive and professionally respected review of the current literature Charlotte Patterson states,

> Overall, then, the results of research to date suggest that children of lesbian and gay parents have normal relationships with peers and that their relationships with adults of both sexes are also satisfactory. The picture of lesbian mothers' children that emerges from results of existing research is thus one of general engagement in social life with peers, with fathers, and with mothers' adult friends—both male and female, both heterosexual and homosexual.[29]

Still, Patterson acknowledges, the literature is new, relatively sparse, and focused mostly on lesbian rather than gay parents. Owing to a lack of longitudinal studies little is known about the development of the children living with gay or lesbian parents during adolescence or adulthood.

In my opinion there is no legitimate reason for presuming there may be harm to children who live with gay or lesbian parents. In settling disputes between a lesbian mother and a heterosexual father, therefore, the same criteria should apply as with all other parents. For young children, who is the primary parent? For older children, increasing concern for the child's wishes and feelings as they mature is in order. Some teens in this situation may feel acute embarrassment or peer rejection, which may be a wider issue of cultural prejudice that needs to be addressed in the schools and other forums. If an adolescent chooses to live with the other parent for any reason that is not harmful to him- or herself, this should be respected. For some adolescents the social stigma may force them to become more thoughtful, but not judgmental. As the testimony of a fifteen-year-old, the offspring of a lesbian mother and gay father, demonstrates,

> I think I am more open-minded than if I had straight par-
> ents. Sometimes kids at school make a big deal out of
> being gay. They say it's stupid and stuff like that. But they
> don't really know, because they are not around it. I don't
> say anything to them, but they don't know what they're
> talking about.[30]

Choosing between a gay or lesbian and a heterosexual parent is not the only relevant custody decision created by homosexuality. Increasingly, lesbian (and less frequently gay) couples choose to have their own babies. In all states (the issue is currently under litigation in Hawaii) a couple must be of different sexes in order to marry. Since it is still biologically impossible, until cloning is allowed, to reproduce without the contribution of both sexes, same-sex couples must look beyond their union to produce a baby. This means there is a biological parent, usually a sperm-donating father outside the family unit, who may or may not be able to claim parental rights. "Who's your mom?" or "who's your dad?" is not a straightforward question in these households.

A vigorous baby boom has been observed among lesbian couples. By the late 1980s the journalistically labeled "gayby boom" began to swell the ranks of children living with at least one lesbian parent. Since the normal channels of adoption or regulated artificial insemination often are closed to gays and lesbians, these births most likely were arranged privately through a volunteer sperm donor, oftentimes a friend. Even when some legally certified sperm banks opened their doors to lesbian and other unmarried mothers, many women were reluctant to choose this legally safer option, eschewing the anonymity that never would allow their child to discover their biological father.

With private arrangements, the legal structure in place to sort out custody issues—including those of semen donors who contribute through regulated medical providers—is of no use. While the Uniform Parentage Act adopted by all states completely severs the rights and obligations of sperm donors and guards their anonymity, all sperm donors outside this framework may be treated as any other unwed father; they may be awarded full custodial rights and be subject to regular child support.

Fathers recruited under these circumstances clearly understand the limits of their role and agree not to pursue parental rights. They may even sign agreements detailing their rights and obligations, or lack thereof. The law in most states, however, does not recognize these agreements as enforceable contracts. What begins with good intentions and good feeling sometimes degrades into full-scale war. Such was the case when Thomas S., a sperm donor who had agreed to give up his paternal rights, decided to invoke them when the child was eleven.[31]

The story of this family illustrates that good intentions and even written contracts are not enough in nontraditional families. Robin and Sandra became a couple in 1979. Early in their relationship they decided to have children, and also decided that Sandra, the older of the two, would have a child first. They enlisted the help of a gay man, Jack. The three of them agreed that Robin and Sandra would raise, as coparents, a child born of Sandra with Jack's sperm, and that Jack would have no parental rights or obligations.[32]

Cade was born on May 18, 1980. Cade was given the last names of both Sandra and Robin to indicate that they considered her the equal daughter of each of them.

Shortly after Cade's birth, Sandra and Robin decided that Robin should have a child. They again enlisted the help of another gay man, Thomas. They met with him at his office and reached agreement on the principles they intended would govern their future relationship. They agreed that a child born of the insemination would be raised by Sandra and Robin as coparents and as Cade's sister; Thomas would have no parental rights or obligations but he would make himself known to the child if the child asked about her biological origin.

In early 1985 Cade, then almost five years old, began to ask about her biological origins. Robin and Sandra contacted Jack and Thomas, "the men who helped make them," as they referred to them to the children, and asked whether they would meet the children. They agreed, and Robin, Sandra, and the children traveled to San Francisco for the meeting. They spent time together in San Francisco and at a rented beach house near the city. By everyone's account it was a happy encounter that led to a continuing relationship.

Over the next few years Thomas visited with Robin, Sandra, and the girls several times a year. All contacts were at the complete discretion of Robin and Sandra. At first Thomas apparently found it relatively easy to agree to this arrangement. As the years went by, however, he said he found it increasingly burdensome. He felt that he was being forced to follow unreasonable instructions in order to visit with his biological daughter, Ry. He also found it difficult to treat Ry, his biological daughter, as Cade's equal; he was not able to put biology aside, as their mothers demanded. In late 1990 or early 1991 when the girls were ten and eleven he decided to insist on visitation with Ry outside the mothers' presence. He wanted to introduce Ry to his relatives and was not comfortable including Robin and Sandra.

Realizing that a request to visit Ry without seeing Cade would be automatically rejected, and probably also because he did not want to hurt Cade's feelings, he requested that both girls visit with him and his family without their mothers in California in the summer of 1991. The mothers refused, and he brought suit to have his paternal rights recognized.[33]

Thomas had good reason to expect a successful outcome. Informal sperm donors regularly had won paternity rights in many cases, with less parental involvement than Thomas. In a similar parental triangle in California,[34] the donor, Jhordan, had been awarded parental rights of an infant, including regular visitation. The mother's lesbian partner, who had sought joint custody, had been denied any legal status, including that of de facto parent. This partner had participated in the pregnancy, attended the birth, and taken a major nurturing role with the baby. Jhordan had seen the baby only a few times.[35]

In trial court Thomas did not fare so well. The judge dismissed his case, relying on the legal argument of equitable estoppel. This means, essentially, that Thomas had waited too long to make his claim; since Ry was now eleven years old, Thomas was "estopped" from claiming his parental rights at such a late date. More was going on in this case, however. The judge had actually listened to Ry, the child in dispute. Though reluctant to claim this as the basis for the decision, the trial judge clearly heard the voice of the child as told to the child psychiatrist.

The parties had agreed to retain a psychiatrist, Dr. Myles Schneider, to conduct an evaluation and make recommendations to the court. Dr. Schneider reported that Ry understood the biological relationships, but they were not the reality of her life. Her reality was having two mothers who worked together to raise her and her sister. She did not view Thomas as a parent. To her a parent is a person who a child depends on. Furthermore, he warned that she was most anxious about a visit. She would only visit if forced to, kicking and screaming.[36]

The trial judge considered the psychologist's observation and in a rare opinion focused on the voice of the child, attempting to put himself into Ry's mind:

> Thomas apparently believes that Ry, as his biological child, must feel fatherly affection for him. He is incorrect, I think. Ry has been brought up to view Robin and Sandra as equal mothers raising two children and to view Thomas as an important man in her family's life. In her family, there has been no father. Robin and Sandra are deeply committed to this concept of their family, and Ry, who has been raised by them, must also be committed to the concept at this point in her life.[37]

The trial judge denied Thomas's bid for paternal rights. One must applaud this judge's child-centered opinion and cheer for Ry, who was not forced to become a transferable property right.

The voice of this child was soon dismissed, however. Thomas appealed the case to the New York Supreme Court and the decision was reversed. The court, quoting a previous case, declared, "The desires of young children, capable of distortive manipulation by a bitter, or perhaps even well-meaning, parent, do not always reflect the long-term best interest of the children."[38] The court went on to say,

> The apparent manipulation of an innocent child's affections and the obvious damage wreaked upon the once harmonious relationship with her father do not deter the dissent [in previous case] from the view that the child's "haunting fear" of being taken away from "the woman whom she has consistently thought of as her second parent" must have been instilled by petitioner.[39]

This confrontation could have been avoided if the law had simply recognized the contract the parents had entered into at birth. For infants and very young children, who cannot express their wishes, the enforcement of an agreement like this should be respected. A man who enters into such an agreement clearly has rejected the rights and responsibilites of fatherhood and does not meet the minimal level of "actual parental involvement" required by the Supreme Court and most states. While he may, as in the case of Thomas, actually spend time with the child, this may be considered only equal to the involvement of *any* friend of the child.

What about the rights of "the other mother" (or less commonly, "other father"), who considers herself a parent, has actually served, day by day, as a parent, and is considered by the child's biological mother to be a parent? These mothers, like Sandra, are considered legal strangers to the children they raise, with no rights and no responsibilities. No private arrangement or written contract between the biological mother and the "other mother" has any legal force. Even though a sperm donor who has agreed to relinquish any rights to the child and is not actively involved in everyday parenting may change his mind, assert his biological claim, and prevail, the "other mother" will never be allowed in court. She has no standing to request contact with the child.

Recall the case of Nancy S. and Michele G. related in chapter 5.[40] Recall that while Nancy bore the children, they did everything they could by private agreement to give Michele the full rights of parenthood, none of which were respected by the court. Nancy was recognized as the mother with full custody and Michele was completely cut off from the children she had raised.[41]

This case is a classic "other mom" situation, but it applies to all other biological strangers as well. The lesbian nature of their relationship may or may not have disturbed the court, but it probably did not decide the case. Even stepparents who are heterosexual and legally married to the biological parent would receive the same treatment as legal strangers, as the court indeed noted in Michele's case.

There is a growing momentum toward recognizing gay marriages, and perhaps an even stronger counterforce against this policy. Hawaii, the first state to consider legally recognizing such a union under the equal protection clause of the Hawaiian constitution, is still working the issue through the courts and the legislature. Meanwhile Congress, reflecting what it considered to be the will of its constituents, passed the Defense of Marriage Act by a landslide, restricting the definition of marriage to "a legal union between one man and one woman as husband and wife."[42] This legislation allowed all states to avoid the United States Constitution's "full faith and credit" clause and refuse to recognize gay marriages allowed by sister states.

A great deal of hope has been placed on gay marriage as a means to rectify all the legal inequalities suffered by committed gay couples. Medical insurance, tort claims, inheritance issues, and property claims all would be radically affected by legal marriage, but it is not obvious that it would make any difference at all in parental claims. If a lesbian couple such as Nancy and Michele were to marry, the only obvious difference in their situation is that they would have to obtain a legal divorce. The issue of custody would be settled in the same way, as it is with stepparents who divorce. The nonbiological parent still would have no parental claim to the child. Some states might allow nonbiological parents to seek visitation, provided it was in the best interest of the child, but most would not allow a claim at all.

Currently the best route for protection of the "other mom" (or "other dad") is second-party adoption, which is emerging as an option in some states. Second-party adoption, unlike ordinary legal adoption, allows the partner to adopt a biological parent's child without terminating that parent's rights. In typical adoption cases both biological parents' rights are terminated as a condition of adoption. Currently seventeen states have granted second-party adoption petitions. Yet some states, such as Florida, explicitly disallow homosexual adoptions.[43] We also must keep in mind that in twenty states homosexuality is still a criminal offense. Adoption therefore is not a possibility for all "other moms" or "other dads," and it is not likely to be so in all states in the near future.

There are also arrangements in which the biological father (who may be a divorced father or an actively involved sperm donor) does not want to relinquish his biological rights. In these instances the "other mom" (or dad) would be the third parent, a concept for which most states are not yet ready.

For those for whom second-party adoption is not a possibility perhaps the model of de facto parent (described earlier, for stepparents who actively serve a parental role) should be extended to those gay or lesbian partners who actively seek it. A de facto parent, as I describe him or her, acts as a parent, is acknowledged by others (including the child) as a parental figure, and considers her- or himself as a parent, not a temporary caregiver. Most residential stepparents would meet this criteria, as might some cohabitors. The de facto parent model bestows responsibilities as well as rights, including the obligation to support the child during the relationship and, to a limited extent, following its termination. It therefore would be pursued only by cohabitors who wish to take on the full burden of parenthood. A legal registration of this intention to act as de facto parent could be employed in place of adoption, with the permission of the cohabiting natural parent, when adoption is not a realistic option. A simple registration would trigger it, just as marriage would for residential stepparents. If legal registration were not possible, a contract between the partners agreeing on full parental rights could be used as evidence of de facto parenthood.

The advantage of the de facto model, as I conceive it, is that it deals with actual everyday parenting in modern family configurations. It stresses not just rights but responsibilities as well. It offers the vulnerable child a support and a safety net in the event of death or divorce.

Families with two mothers or two fathers challenge our notions of family, of reproduction, and of parenthood. They do not fit into ready-made slots and force us to focus, as we should, on the essential interests of the children involved. Recently I received a letter from a lesbian couple in a state that does not allow second-party adoption. The letter read in part,

> My partner and I want children, but we want to know that
> they will not be taken away from us. What do you think of
> this plan. We will harvest X's egg and plant it in my uterus.
> That way we will both be biological mothers and neither
> of us will fear losing the child. Will this be legal?

I hesitated before replying, imagining the possible consequences for the child. Would a child with two birth mothers
have difficulty dealing with her biological identity? Probably
no different than other "two mom" families. As with all new
technological twists on the "normal" reproductive process,
however, the long-term consequences on children have not yet
been studied or even considered.

Legally the situation is even murkier. I wrote back explaining
that as far as I knew, no court had faced this particular fact situation. The California Supreme Court, however, had declared, in a
two-mother situation in which the gestational mother was the
surrogate mother, that only the egg donor had custody rights.[14]
I told them that this decision was not binding in their state but
that it did not bode well. I suggested that they pursue persuading their state to accept second-party adoptions, or, failing that,
to write a private contract agreeing on full parental rights for
each. While this contract may not be enforceable in their state, it
would provide evidence at least of the parental intentions of
both parties. I gave them a list of gay and lesbian advocacy
groups that could further advise them and wished them well.

Custody disputes stir up the highest levels of emotion: anxiety, fear, anger, depression. Sometimes this takes a permanent
toll on the parent. Mary Ward, the lesbian mother introduced
earlier who lost custody of her daughter to the convicted murderer father, was such a casualty.

Mary Ward had filed a petition for a rehearing after she lost her case on appeal. She was waiting for the response. In the eighteen months of legal wrangling, during which she had only weekly visiting rights with Cassey, Ward unfortunately dealt with the heavy stress in a way many women do: she ate too much.

"Her blood pressure was high; she'd gained about 100 pounds over the last year," remarked Carres, her lawyer. "She'd not been feeling well; she had the flu. Then I got a call early Wednesday. She was dead."[45]

8

Test Tube Troubles:
Custody in the Age of
New Reproductive Technology

NEAR THE END OF THE TWENTIETH CENTURY the world
was alerted to the stunning news that a Scottish laboratory had
cloned a Finn Dorset sheep named Dolly.[1] Scientists accomplished this by removing the nucleus from a sheep ovum, replacing it with the genetic material from the adult sheep to be
cloned (Dolly), then reimplanting the genetically changed
ovum back into the surrogate mother sheep. This effort took
three hundred tries, and scientists assured the world that it was
not being done (yet) with humans. Journalists, however, waved
the possibility of human cloning like a red flag.[2]

The Dolly episode certainly broke through biological frontiers, but it mostly serves as a wake-up call to a public that gradually has been introduced to reproductive novelties from artificial insemination to embryo transplants, and has grown
somewhat complacent about their consequences. Suddenly it is
clear that technology is moving faster than our ability to com-

prehend it, much less control it. Our outdated legal and ethical support systems are lagging behind reproductive breakthroughs.

The development of novel reproductive technology is not a recent phenomenon; breakthrough techniques have been introduced at an astounding rate over the past thirty years or so. Yet we have not matched new thinking with new technology. Reproductive techniques now permit adults to circumvent each stage of the normal procedure of insemination, conception, pregnancy, and childbirth. These technological interventions, often involving a test tube at some juncture, raise basic questions regarding the essence of motherhood and fatherhood; they also raise new issues regarding the custody rights over the product of each discrete stage in the cycle of reproduction from ova to baby. The cast of competing characters goes beyond traditional custody battles. The competitors may include, but are not limited to: the biological (sperm-supplying) father; the biological father's wife; the biological mother's husband; the biological (ovum-supplying) mother; and the surrogate mother who carries either another woman's ovum (the sperm donor's wife's or an ovum donor's) or her own ovum-fetus-child to term under an agreement (possibly for hire) calling for the relinquishment of the child upon birth to one or both biological parent(s) or to adoptive parent(s).

In these disputes gender matters. While one can maintain that parenting is a gender-neutral task, it is not possible to make the same claim for the reproductive process. Pregnancy and childbirth, whether or not there is a genetic connection to the baby, is not an activity shared by both sexes; and harvesting an ovum is a different, more radical procedure than harvesting sperm.

Such complex issues are sometimes confounded further by the separate, volatile legal controversy regarding a woman's right to abortion, another major front of the gender wars. If a biological product not genetically attached to her is planted in a woman's womb, does she have the same rights as other women to an abortion? Conversely, if the biological product, ova or embryo, is not in a womb but in a frozen or preserved state, does a biological mother still have the right to determine its fate, or is this right now equally shared with the biological father? Considered another way, if the biological product (sperm, ova, embryo, fetus) is not attached to a woman's uterus, does it have its own rights?

We may well ask if the child-centered framework for determining custody disputes when children are conceived in the traditional manner—which I have suggested for a variety of parental disputes throughout this book—offers any guidance in this tangled new territory. Or do we need a whole new crew of philosophers and bio-ethicists to make sense of it?

It is my belief that the principles I developed in cases involving traditional reproduction have some value, at least, in sorting out the priorities for settling disputes when conception and birth are separate matters. An emphasis on actual parenting behavior rather than on strict biology and a concern for the wishes and feelings of the child (which in some circumstances must be a forward projection) are clarifying principles. These principles can be applied to a variety of scenarios, allowing one to tease out the interests of the child from the confusing claims of the adults. Each technology presents different issues and requires a separate analysis. Yet a child-centered framework at least may allow us to regard disputes over genetic products as more than ordinary property disputes. As we shall see, however, the mind-boggling possibilities of technology may defy any attempt at imposing a framework developed for parent–child relationships as we know them.

Legal and social thinkers in this rapidly evolving area have addressed a few of the custodial issues, but only piecemeal, after the technological interventions have been well launched. Developed technologies that have provoked thoughtful response (and certain laws) include artificial insemination, surrogate mothers, and frozen embryos. Frontiers yet to be fully explored include cloning, egg transplants in postmenopausal women, and products of the frozen sperm and eggs of men and women who have died, sometimes leaving specific instructions in their wills, or, more often, leaving no written guidance. Other permutations on these themes defy our imaginations—but probably not those of the assisted-reproduction industry.

Artificial insemination, the process by which a woman is artificially inseminated by a donor, was the first and continues to be the most widely established form of reproductive intervention. Hundreds of thousands of women are artificially inseminated each year in the United States alone. There are two forms of artificial insemination: homologous (AIH), in which the sperm is that of the husband; and donor, (AID), in which the donor is not the husband. The second form can give rise to custody disputes. In its early days more than thirty years ago, AID was viewed with grave suspicion. Some considered it adultery (all the mothers were married), and some courts refused to consider the husband as father.[3] Many of the legal wrinkles were ironed out in cases and statutes during the 1960s and 1970s.

One of the earliest AID cases came before the California Supreme Court in 1968.[4] Mr. Sorenson, diagnosed as sterile, in writing reluctantly agreed, after fifteen years of marriage, to his wife's artificial insemination from an unknown donor provided by the doctor. A male child was born to Mrs. Sorenson and the three lived together as a family for four years. When they divorced in 1964, Mrs. Sorenson did not request child support. Two years later, however, she fell ill and requested public assistance. The district attorney then sought support from Mr. Sorenson, who objected on the ground that the child was not legitimate. The California Supreme Court refused to deal with the concept of legitimacy, but insisted that the child had no natural father. For purposes of support, however, Sorenson was clearly the father. The court stated,

> A child conceived through heterologous artificial insemination does not have a "natural father," as that term is commonly used. The anonymous donor of the sperm cannot be considered the "natural father" as he is not more responsible for the use of his sperm than is the donor of blood or a kidney.[5]

This line of reasoning was soon adopted by the Uniform Parentage Act, which provided that a child born of artificial insemination, if the insemination is performed by a licensed physician with the written consent of husband and wife, is legally the husband's child. The donor is specifically "treated in law as if he were not the natural father."[6] In fact the donor is treated, for all practical purposes, as if he never existed.

While the Uniform Parentage Act solved the problem for married couples in states that adopted it or enacted similar legislation (more than half), it did not settle the matter in those states that did not.[7] What if the husband did not consent in writing, or the insemination was not performed by a licensed physician, or perhaps there were no husband? The act failed to address these questions, leaving in doubt the rights and obligations of the donor.

The vigorous new lesbian baby boom and the growing trend of single women adopting or giving birth on their own has forced another look at this abrupt severance policy. Many women prefer their children to know the identity of their biological fathers and make private arrangements to allow for this. Yet as we saw earlier in chapter 7, private arrangements are largely repudiated by courts. They sometimes give the donor full paternal rights and obligations and sometimes deny them, leaving the donor in a sort of paternal limbo and the mother in a state of anxiety.[8]

What would a child-centered framework in these cases look like? Reproduction by donor is different from that accomplished by most other unmarried parents. It must be planned, the mother takes the initiative and for the most part is not interested in giving the donor full paternal rights. Yet there are two distinctly different kinds of donation. In medically regulated circumstances the donor has no contact with the mother and doesn't know the identity of the baby or even if there *is* a baby. The donor often is a student who is paid for his services and signs a consent form insuring his anonymity and guaranteeing neither rights nor responsibilities. In private arrangements the donor most likely is aware of the birth of the child but has agreed, often in writing, to forego paternal claims to custody or visitation, usually in exchange for no obligation to support the child. Depending on the agreement, he may or may not agree to acknowledge his paternity if the child wants to know.

It is in the gray land of private arrangements where custody disputes are most often cultivated. A donor who agreed not to claim paternal rights may change his mind later, particularly if he has contact with the infant. Good intentions and good feelings sometimes sour into out and out war, as in the case of Thomas S. described earlier.[9] In that case, you may recall, the appellate court placed greater weight on biological rights than on the voice of the child and awarded paternal rights to the donor.[10]

At first glance the solution to this dilemma seems obvious. For infants and very young children who cannot give voice to their wishes, an agreement by the donor not to be considered a father should be enforced. For older children the assessment should address first the attitude of the child toward this would-be parent, and second, the actual parenting behavior of the parties in conflict. Even when a child is deeply attached it may not be necessary to grant full paternal status to a donor. Rather, visitation rights as a de facto parent, as one would give to any other family member who had served in a parenting role, would likely be more appropriate.

A child-centered approach raises a more difficult question when the donor does *not* want to claim parenthood. Does the child have the right to know the identity of her or his father? Children who have never known their father may decide at some point that this is important information. With private arrangements the donor and mother could agree to allow this at any point, but what if the donor changes his mind and refuses to come forth? (With anonymous donors covered by the Uniform Parentage Act, revealing the identity of the donor is not an option.) Many mothers and donors still prefer this arrangement, particularly if the mother has a husband. Should a mother be allowed to deny a child the opportunity to know his or her father, and choose complete anonymity with no disclosure at age eighteen? Should a donor be allowed to insist on complete anonymity? Is it the child's right to know?

One of my family law students approached me after class one day and asked if there were any way she could track down her father. Her mother, she said, had told her that she was the product of artificial insemination only after her mother and the man she thought was her father divorced.

"She said she told me," she related, "because he is an alcoholic and a swindler. She didn't want me to fear I was from bad blood."

At the time her mother told her she was ten, too young and confused to ask any more questions. She missed the dad she grew up with, she said. He rarely contacted her, but for many years she didn't want to think about any other father.

"Now I'm older, and I guess frankly curious. I see all these adopted kids on Oprah and other shows. They find their parents and get a whole new family. I love my mom, but she's all I've got. Maybe I've got brothers and sisters somewhere."

Her longing for family was palpable. Like so many other young people she had been swept up by the romanticism of the open adoption movement, which has allowed some children and birth parents to find one another. Sometimes there is a happy ending, with new family and new opportunities; often there is rejection or bitter disappointment.

Yet this was not likely to be a possible journey for her. I told her what I knew about the process of medically regulated artificial insemination at the time she was conceived. The donor, I explained, was most likely a student who probably thought of his contribution as similar to giving blood. Complete anonymity was promised, and as far as I knew there would be no way of learning his identity. I also urged her to consider that even if she learned his name he might resent her contacting him.

Is it fair to the child not to know the identity of her or his father? This threshold question may be addressed to all the complicated variations of the brave new world of reproductive technology. Artificial insemination, however, is perhaps the simplest configuration (one biological mother, one biological father), and the most prevalent. A not entirely satisfactory solution, which attempts to respect the rights of the various parties, is to follow the route taken by the Uniform Adoption Act with regard to adoption.[11] The Uniform Adoption Act maintains anonymous adoption and recommends release only of non-identifying, typically genetic information that could have bearing on the child's health. It also provides a matching registry available to adopted children over eighteen and their former parents. If a birth parent chooses to leave his or her name, after age eighteen the child may choose to locate that parent. If applied to artificial insemination, a donor also might be given that choice so that a child could someday seek him out.

It is difficult to know how many men would choose the option of later contact upon donation—or who would agree to donate were it a requirement; and if the mother were married at the time of the birth, how many would disclose the true facts of conception? Still, such an option could provide more choices for the child, who may or may not choose to exercise it.

The issue of parental identity becomes more problematical as we consider more complicated biological variations. Women, of course, have more donor options available to them: they can donate eggs or embryos, they can offer their nurturing womb for someone else's embryo, or they can carry their own baby, conceived by artificial insemination and under contract, to be relinquished at birth to the father.

The surrogate mother situation, sometimes called "rent-a-womb" technology, has caused the most legal difficulties and provoked the greatest emotional concern. In its simplest form surrogacy may be the oldest of reproductive technologies. Genesis tells of Abraham's servant Haga bearing a child to be raised by the genetic father, Abraham, and his wife, Sarah.[12] In modern versions of surrogacy a woman who is the biological mother carries her own child under contract to the father (or a third party), or a woman who is simply a gestational mother carries another couple's embryo to birth.

It is not as easy for us to dismiss the rights of surrogate mothers as we have those of sperm donors. The acts of pregnancy and childbirth, it seems, are central to our emotional understanding of motherhood; and these acts (at least for now) can only be performed by women. The gendered nature of parenthood is thrust into our public discourse, provoking feminists to openly cross swords. Some feminists decry the potentially exploitative and patriarchal nature of the practice. Rich couples are renting the wombs of poor women, they claim; it is at heart another form of prostitution. Other feminists protest that this stance is misguided paternalism. The state once again attempts to regulate what a woman does with her body. Still others call it baby selling, and blame the surrogate mothers for profiteering.[13] Is the surrogate mother saint, victim, or greedy profiteer?

The practice of surrogate motherhood has been flourishing for more than a decade, and the law has tried to sort out the competing rights. In doing so claims of "biological" surrogate mothers are now distinguished from those of "gestational" surrogate mothers. Biological surrogate mothers arrived on the scene well before the technology for embryo transplantation was perfected. These women, popularly tagged as "surrogate mothers" (although they are the real biological mothers), agree to bear a child for a couple in which the wife is not capable of doing so. The surrogate mother is artificially inseminated with the husband's sperm, carries the baby to term, and is given some payment for her services.

Although the California Supreme Court was able to consider the donor of sperm equivalent to the donor of a kidney in the

Sorenson case mentioned earlier, other courts apparently are unable to treat surrogate mothers in a similar fashion. In one of the first and certainly one of the most highly publicized struggles for custody in this arena, Mr. Stern entered into a surrogacy contract with Mary Beth Whitehead and her husband.[14] Mrs. Whitehead agreed to become impregnated by artificial insemination with Mr. Stern's sperm, carry the child to term, deliver it to the Sterns, and then do what was necessary to terminate her parental rights. Mrs. Whitehead did deliver the baby upon birth but was overcome by an "unbearable sadness" and, threatening suicide, pleaded to have the baby returned to her for only a week. The Sterns complied, but when Mrs. Whitehead failed to return the baby as promised, they began a legal action to enforce the contract. Mrs. Whitehead and her husband fled to Florida, where they evaded the police and the media by staying in roughly twenty different hotels and homes. The media chase became a national obsession, with rumors of Whitehead spottings aired regularly on the evening news. At last police found the child, Melissa, and turned her over to the Sterns. A thirty-two day trial ensued in which the trial court found the surrogate contract valid, ordered Mrs. Whitehead's parental rights be terminated, and granted sole custody of the child to Mr. Stern.[15]

The New Jersey appellate court rejected the trial court's decision to uphold the contract, declaring that under public policy surrogacy contracts were void. The court said these contracts skirted protections afforded by adoption procedures, and were akin to baby selling:

> The evils inherent in baby bartering are loathsome for a
> myriad of reasons. The child is sold without regard to
> whether the purchasers will be suitable parents. The nat-

ural mother does not receive the benefit of counseling and guidance to assist her in making a decision that may affect her for a lifetime. In fact, the monetary incentive to sell her child may, depending on her financial circumstance, make her decision less voluntary.[16]

Treating the surrogacy contract as nonexistent, the appellate court held the legal issue to be custody between a natural mother—Mrs. Whitehead—and a natural father—Mr. Stern. The court determined that the best interests of the child were shown at the trial to reside with the more stable and wholesome father, with some visitation available to Mrs. Whitehead.[17] Ultimately then, Mary Beth Whitehead won the right to be a mother but she lost the right to custody.

Several states do not share the New Jersey court's clear-cut contempt for surrogacy contracts and have enacted statutes that would allow the practice so long as it complies with the state's statutory scheme for adoption.[18] Under these statutes the mother does not relinquish her rights until *after* the birth and is allowed a period of time to revoke her decision. No state has considered treating surrogacy as it does seminal donation. The process of pregnancy and birth clearly separates surrogate mothers from semen donors in the eyes of the law. The New Jersey court struggled with the analogy but could not provide a reasoned distinction. Finally the court stated,

> It is quite obvious that the situations are not parallel. A sperm donor simply cannot be equated with a surrogate mother. The state has more than a sufficient basis to distinguish the two situations—even if the only difference is between the time it takes to provide sperm for artificial insemination and time invested in a nine month preg-

nancy—so as to justify automatically divesting the sperm donor of his parental rights without automatically divesting a surrogate mother.[19]

The Whitehead decision has by no means settled the question. States are still arguing on how to proceed; a few have banned surrogate contracts, one adopted an elaborate rule for regulation, and most have done nothing.[20]

In the meantime another variation on surrogate motherhood has made a dramatic appearance: "gestational motherhood." This variation involves two mothers. In the typical gestational mother situation a couple is capable of conceiving in utero or in vitro (in the womb or in a test tube), but the woman, the biological mother of the embryo, is not able to complete a pregnancy. At some point the embryo is planted in a biological stranger, who becomes the gestational mother.

Mark and Crispina Calvert were a married couple who desired to have a child. Crispina had undergone a hysterectomy but her ovaries remained capable of producing eggs, and the couple eventually considered surrogacy. Anna Johnson heard about Crispina's plight from a coworker and offered to serve as a surrogate for the Calverts.

Mark, Crispina, and Anna signed a contract providing that an embryo created by the sperm of Mark and the egg of Crispina would be implanted in Anna, and the child born would be taken into Mark and Crispina's home as their child. Anna agreed to relinquish all parental rights. Mark and Crispina agreed to pay Anna $10,000 and to take out a $200,000 life insurance policy in case anything should happen to Anna during the pregnancy and childbirth.

Almost as soon as the embryo was implanted, the parties began to fight. The Calverts claimed Anna had not disclosed her history of several stillbirths and miscarriages, and Anna claimed they had not obtained the life insurance. Matters further deteriorated, and a month before delivery Anna demanded full payment or else she would not give up the child. The Calverts sued and Anna countered.[21] The baby was born amid this contention and was assigned temporarily to the Calverts while the court worked out the argument.

As with too many custody cases, by the time the case worked its way through three legal stages to the California Supreme Court, the baby was three years old. No other court had been confronted with such a dilemma. Weighing the claims of the women, the Supreme Court decided that a baby born under these circumstances could not have two mothers.[22] In choosing between them the court did not dwell on the significance of pregnancy and childbirth but instead, borrowing from intellectual property law, developed a new doctrine of "intentional motherhood":

> ... when the two means [genetic tie and giving birth] do not coincide in one woman, she who intended to procreate the child—that is she who intended to bring about the birth of a child that she intended to raise as her own—is the natural mother under California law.[23]

With this reasoning the court awarded the child to Crispina and her husband, the child's genetic father.

The lone dissenter was a woman judge. Recognizing that both women had substantial motherhood claims, the judge asked what had happened to consideration of the best interest of the child? Criticizing the concept of intentional mother-hood, she pointed out,

> The problem with this argument, of course, is that children are not property. Unlike songs or inventions, rights in children cannot be sold for consideration or made freely available to the public.[24]

What are the best interests of the child in this case?[25] If one recognizes both mothers, the dispute becomes like that between a mother and father upon divorce—the choice between two fit parents. In my opinion the fact of actual parenting and the bond between the parent and child then should govern. Pregnancy and childbirth are actual parenting. If they were not, there would not be such an emotional response to the claims of surrogate mothers; and yet, because this case had gone on so long with the Calverts as temporary guardians, the child had experienced more actual parenting with them and became attached to them. Moreover, in this instance (although not always), John Calvert was the biological father, a fact that also influenced the judgment.

What rule would work better to avoid treating children as property, yet not force disputes on a case-by-case basis?

Although there are significant differences between them, it is possible to consider surrogacy arrangements as independent adoptions for purposes of determining custody. In those cases the mother agrees in advance to give up the baby, but has a short period of time to change her mind. Under the guidelines of the Uniform Adoption Act this period would be very short (192 hours after birth).[26] If she did decide to keep the baby during this period, she would prevail. This tiebreaking rule recognizes that at the moment of childbirth it is the surrogate mother who has performed all of the actual parenting. Such a rule would treat the claims of both types of surrogate mothers—genetic and gestational—equally. Mary Beth Whitehead and Anna Johnson each would be considered mothers. Giving birth would define motherhood—as it does in all other countries that have considered this issue.

Where would this leave Crispina Calvert? In what may be considered an odd turn of this multiple-parent story, she would become a stepmother, since the claim of her husband Mark as father would be unchallenged. As we learned earlier, however, as a stepparent she would receive no recognition as a parent, even if she became the primary caregiver. Clearly then, such a policy would not solve all the issues.

Legal invisibility was the fate of Cynthia Moschetta, whose husband left their home with their seven-month-old daughter, Marissa, in tow.[27] The Moschettas hired Elvira Jordan as a surrogate mother because Cynthia was infertile. Like Mary Beth Whitehead, Jordan was the biological mother as well. Jordan relinquished the baby at birth without a problem. Later, however, when Robert Moschetta walked out with the baby after seven months she reasserted her custody rights, claiming she had agreed to give up the child to a stable two-parent family, not a single dad.[28] During the time the dispute initially was being decided the baby lived with her father and a nanny, but was subject to visitation by Cynthia on Tuesdays and Fridays and by Jordan on Mondays, Wednesdays, and Thursdays.

This case illustrates the absurdity of dealing with multiple parenting with no clear rules in place to promote the child's best interests. In the first custody trial the judge decided the three-way custody battle by giving Elvira Jordan and Robert Moschetta joint custody. Cynthia Moschetta was granted no visitation rights. In a public moment of anger Cynthia tore off her ex-husband's toupee in front of television cameras on a national news show.

Robert Moschetta appealed the joint arrangement, arguing that Jordan had already relinquished her rights, but the appellate justices disagreed. In the spirit of the Mary Beth Whitehead decision, the court claimed that Jordan was the biological mother and the contract was not enforceable.[29]

The shared arrangement proved contentious. The parents clashed bitterly over everything, from where Marissa should attend preschool to how she should be disciplined. Jordan related that on one occasion she didn't tell Moschetta that Marissa was infected with head lice because she was afraid he would blame her. A court-appointed psychiatrist testified that shared parenting was creating emotional problems for the child that would likely worsen as she got older.

In a bizarre turn Cynthia Moschetta appeared for the second custody trial, this time to testify to save the right of Elvira Jordan, as against her ex-spouse, to parent the now five-year-old Marissa.

Her testimony was to no avail. "It is in the child's best interests to live in a stable home and environment free from excessive tension with orderly and routine daily activities," declared the judge, granting primary custody to the father. The judge claimed Marissa was better off in the home where she lives with Moschetta, a thirty-nine-year-old occupational safety specialist, and his current wife. He described Jordan's neighborhood as one troubled by sporadic gunfire and gang activity, and noted that Jordan, who is single, was convicted of welfare fraud and has a son in prison.[30]

How could this three-ring circus have been avoided? Is it the best course to ban surrogacy arrangements, as have some states?

Perhaps, but it is unlikely one can reverse the flood of new reproductive technologies that give adults hope for a child to love in an increasingly anonymous world. Some commentators have suggested that all parents be recognized—that a child cannot have too many parents to love her.[31] Yet as the Moschetta case illustrates, a child *can* have too many parents to fight over her.

The interests of Marissa and similar children would be best served, I believe, by a few clear rules that emphasize parenting and attachment and downplay biology. By treating Marissa's case like an independent adoption, Jordan would have been forced to permanently relinquish all custody within a very short time, and Marissa could have been immediately adopted by Cynthia Moschetta. In the event of the Moschetta's divorce, Cynthia then would have had full parental rights, and, as the primary parent of the seven-month-old child, could have been granted primary custody.

If Jordan had refused to relinquish the baby, she would have received primary custody and the father would have received visitation rights, as would be the case with adoption. Joint custody is an inappropriate option for these parents, who have never parented together and, as the judge pointed out, do not agree on anything.

It is more difficult to downplay biology as we move backward in the reproductive cycle toward what most would consider the beginning of human life. Here we confront the contentious custody disputes over frozen embryos. These embryos are the product of in vitro (literally, "in glass") fertilization, a highly technical medical intervention. Unlike artificial insemination it cannot be performed with tools one can find in the kitchen. In the in vitro procedure an ovum ready to be released from the ovary is identified through laparoscopy or ultra sound and removed by surgery or aspiration through a hollow needle. The ovum or ova (in most cases more than one is harvested) is placed in a container with the appropriate amount of semen containing fertile sperm. Between fifty thousand and several hundred thousand sperm are utilized to fertilize one ovum. The entire IVF procedure, which often involves several attempts and expensive drugs to promote ovulation and pregnancy, is costly. This limits the potential pool of recipients to high-income couples.

It takes several attempts to successfully implant the fertilized ovum (sometimes referred to as pre-embryo); therefore the unused fertilized products are frozen for future attempts. These frozen products, stored in a freezer in the IVF clinic, can become the issue if the couple change their minds, divorce, die, or achieve success with other fertilized ova.

One of the first of these disputes caught the public's attention and created a new law in Tennessee.[32] In March 1989 a Tennessee resident, Junior Lewis Davis, sued his wife in a divorce action to restrain her from having any of their seven fertilized eggs implanted. During their ten years of marriage Mrs. Davis had experienced five tubal pregnancies that led to infertility. At an in vitro fertility clinic the doctors harvested her ova and twice attempted, unsuccessfully, to implant the eggs fertilized with her husband's sperm in her uterus. When the couple divorced five frozen pre-embryos were still awaiting implantation.

The court actions that ensued reveal a painful confusion about the respective legal rights of mother, father, and the frozen pre-embryos. Mary Sue Davis originally asked for control of the "frozen embryos" with the intent of having them transferred to her own uterus, in a post-divorce effort to become pregnant. Junior Davis objected, saying that he preferred to leave them in their frozen state until he decided whether or not he wanted to become a parent outside the bounds of marriage. He told the court that he was the fifth of six children. When he was five years old his parents divorced, his mother had a nervous breakdown, and he and three of his brothers went to live at a home for boys. He said he suffered from his lack of opportunity to establish a relationship with his parents, and particularly regretted the absence of his father. Therefore he vehemently opposed fathering a child that would not live with both parents.[33]

In spite of Junior's objections, the trial court awarded custody of the embryos to Mary Sue Davis, that she "be permitted the opportunity to bring these children to term through implantation."[34] However, the court of appeals reversed, finding that Junior Davis has a "constitutionally protected right not to beget a child where no pregnancy has taken place." The court awarded them "joint control . . . and equal voice over their disposition," effectively granting each former spouse veto power.[35]

While the case dragged through the legal system, working its way up to the Tennessee Supreme Court, the facts changed. Each of the parties remarried, and Mary Sue decided she did not want to use the embryos for herself; rather, she would donate them to another needy couple. When the case finally came before the Supreme Court of Tennessee it was carefully watched by lawmakers across the nation. The court entertained extensive scientific testimony before definitively labeling the frozen embryos as pre-embryos, thereby avoiding the growing body of law that gives some rights to the fetus. As pre-embryos the frozen matter has no rights, and the test is not a "best interest of the child" test but rather a contest between the rights of the adults. The court determined that the rights at stake were the right to procreate and the right not to procreate. Upon carefully weighing the interests of each party, the court decided in favor of Junior Davis:

> ... we can only conclude that Mary Sue Davis's interest in donation is not as significant as the interest Junior Davis has in avoiding parenthood. If she were allowed to donate these preembryos, he would face a lifetime of either wondering about his parental status or knowing about his parental status but having no control over it. He testified quite clearly that if these preembryos were brought to term he would fight for custody of his child or children. Donation, if a child came of it, would rob him twice—his procreational autonomy would be defeated and his relationship with his offspring would be prohibited. The case would be closer if Mary Sue Davis were seeking to use the preembryos herself, but only if she could not achieve parenthood by any other reasonable means.[36]

Carefully avoiding creating a clear-cut rule, the court determined that, absent an agreement or a contract, the party wishing to avoid procreation should prevail, assuming that the other party has a reasonable possibility of achieving parenthood by means other than the use of pre-embryos. If not, that party's argument should be considered

This carefully restricted reasoning was not convincing to all states, nor to all ethicists. While avoiding the word *property*, the Tennessee Supreme Court did not give the pre-embryos any legal status. As state legislatures struggled with the issues, Louisiana—the only state to pass a law—declared that disputes between parties should be resolved in the "best interest of the embryo," and that interest would be "adoptive implantation."[37]

What does the best interest of the embryo mean? Is this the appropriate child-centered approach to custody disputes? The American Fertility Society has wrestled with this question and come up with three viewpoints: at one extreme is the view of the pre-embryo as a human subject after fertilization, which requires that it be accorded the rights of a person. At the opposite extreme is the view that the pre-embryo has a status no different from any other human tissue. The third view, most widely held, takes an intermediate position: it holds that the pre-embryo deserves respect greater than that given to human tissue (as in organ donations), but lesser than that of a born human.[38]

While it is a stretch to extend our child-centered framework to pre-embryos, in many circumstances one could acknowledge the future life of this pre-embryo as a factor to be weighed. In adopting the third and most widely held position of the American Fertility Society respect for future human life could become the tiebreaker in some disputes. In the Davis case this vitalist position would weigh in with the mother's vote, and the pre-embryos would be given to a third party for implantation. With this decision both the mother's and father's rights would be relinquished. As with anonymous sperm donors, it could be possible to ship these embryos to another part of the country for anonymous implantation.

The Davis situation represents a family-sized dispute: mother, father, and five pre-embryos; in these circumstances the extension of a model based on other family custody disputes seems conceivable. Unfortunately the pre-embryo problem is much larger than family size. Tens of thousands of pre-embryos are accumulating in tanks of liquid nitrogen across the country, the eerie consequence of successful in vitro fertilization. Infertile women now routinely have eggs harvested from their ovaries, fertilized in a laboratory, and implanted in their wombs. Many of them deliver babies. Just as routinely, many have leftover pre-embryos, which are frozen and stored (unlike sperm, unfertilized eggs cannot be stored by freezing them). The pre-embryos are in a sense a sort of perpetual youth for the couples. As a woman's ovaries age, they cease to produce eggs capable of being fertilized. A woman with frozen pre-embryos, however, can become pregnant in middle age or even beyond. Some women with cancer have stored pre-embryos before undergoing chemotherapy and radiation, which damage the ovaries and cause sterility. The pre-embryos can offer a kind of immortality; some of the women with cancer have died, and their relatives have been selected as surrogates to carry the embryos they left behind.[39]

As the years go by, the people who provided the eggs and sperm often divorce, die, or simply lose contact with the centers where their pre-embryos are stored. How should one treat these pre-embryos? Is the hospital or the state obliged to find host parents for them, or to maintain them in a frozen state indefinitely, perhaps for generations?

There are few host parents for orphan pre-embryos. At a time when couples without viable eggs or sperm can create a sort of custom embryo by carefully picking sperm or egg donors, no one is choosing a donated frozen pre-embryo. Egg and sperm donors offer detailed medical histories and even provide photographs, heights and weights, and descriptions of their education, hobbies, and personality quirks. People who donate pre-embryos provide almost none of this information. Even if the court in the Davis case had decided to spare the pre-embryos, there is no reason to believe they would have found host parents.

We have no national policy on the fate of orphan frozen pre-embryos. England, however, has imposed a five-year rule. If the donor cannot be found or is not willing to pay for continuation for another five years, the pre-embryos are destroyed. The first five-year alarm clock went off in 1996. At that point there were 3,300 abandoned pre-embryos. A few couples bought a re-prieve for their pre-embryos; the rest were destroyed. There was a world-wide protest against this move, and the Vatican newspaper, *L'Osservatore Romano*, condemned the program as a "prenatal massacre."[40]

To my mind, child-centered models based on family-sized disputes do not have anything to offer to solve the problem of thousands, or perhaps hundreds of thousands or more, of orphaned frozen pre-embryos. If there is an opportunity for a host family, that opportunity should be granted. If the choice is unlimited frozen storage for ever-increasing numbers of frozen pre-embryos, however, the prospect of life is dim.

Likewise, moving down the biological ladder there are virtually trillions of frozen sperms suspended in sperm banks all over the world, and a lesser but growing number of frozen eggs. Even the vitalists do not take a stand on these reproductive parts that have not yet joined into an embryo; but some individuals—usually family members in dispute after the donor has died—do care about their fate.

Deborah Hecht, for instance, battled her late husband's children for several years to secure the frozen sperm that he had willed to her. John Hecht, foreseeing the end of his life, deposited a total of fifteen vials of his sperm at the cryobank. He made these deposits in six installments, each requiring a separate trip to the cryobank facility, stretched out over a month. A few weeks later he flew to Las Vegas with $20,000, lost it, and committed suicide.

Along with his will Hecht left a letter for his grown children from his first marriage, and for the child he hoped Deborah would produce after his death:

> I address this to my children, because, although I have only
> two ..., it may be that Deborah will decide—as I hope she
> will—to have a child by me after my death. I've been assid-
> uously generating frozen sperm samples for that eventual-
> ity. If she does, then this letter is for my posthumous off-
> spring, as well, with the thought that I have loved you in
> my dreams, even though I never got to see you born.[41]

A nasty will contest followed his death. Deborah finally settled with his children for 20 percent of Hecht's property. According to the court this meant three out of the fifteen frozen
vials were Deborah's property; the others belonged to his children. Deborah had trouble conceiving with the three vials,
however, and returned to the court to ask for more.

The court was faced with the problem of deciding whether
the sperm were in fact just property or should be treated differently. Wrestling with this issue, the court finally decided there was
a constitutional right at stake; the right of John Hecht to procreate. The court held that neither this court nor decedent's adult
children possessed reason or right to prevent Hecht from imple-
menting decedent's preeminent interest in realizing his "fundamental right" to procreate with the woman of his choice.[42] They
ordered the remaining vials of sperm be turned over to Deborah.

While such thinking may seem to produce satisfactory results
in this case, it would not be of much use in those cases in which
several adults assert their right to procreate and others, such as
Junior Davis, assert their right not to procreate. Yet acknowl-
edging the capacity for future life to billions of sperm is not
satisfactory either.

There is hope that this quagmire of competitive rights for reproductive material and the unborn in various developmental

phases will be clarified in the future. In the post-Dolly era reproduction itself could be greatly simplified. The most significant fact about Dolly is that all of her genetic material came from the cells of one donor sheep. Dolly's type of cloning does not require both a man and a woman; the cells from either one will do. If an artificial womb is perfected in the near future, as some predict, men and women can reproduce themselves—their exact selves—completely on their own. Biological competition for custody as we have come to know it in this technological era may simply fade away.

9

A Place for the Child

THE COURTROOM IS SMALL, with few seats for spectators. The judge's podium is only a step up from ground level, not raised loftily above the participants. The chairs and tables are casually placed and the witness chair faces the judge. The judge herself is not dressed in heavy black robes, but rather wears a black shawl loosely on her shoulders. In fact this looks more like a classroom than a courtroom.

This is a custody hearing. It will determine who takes custody of three children: Annie G., age five, her sister, Leona, age ten, and her brother, Leonard, age twelve. All three children are present, and the judge talks to each in a friendly, direct manner. The judge also talks at some length to each child's court-appointed special advocate. The advocates are volunteer workers who have spent many hours with the children over the past several months. In addition, the judge interviews the social worker in charge of the children's case. The children have court-appointed attorneys as well, but they are not called upon until near the end of the hearing.

The children's mother and father are present, also represented by court-appointed attorneys. The judge calls on each parent to explain their situation in an informal manner. Although many attorneys are in the room, there is no adversarial argument. The attorneys are not allowed to interrupt or object to the judge's interviews.

This is a custody hearing, but the issue at hand is not whether the children's mother or father will gain custody; it is whether the state will take over temporarily or permanently as guardians of the children. The parents of Annie G. and her siblings have failed to protect or nurture their children. Each has a serious substance abuse problem. The father, disabled from a work injury, is a heroin addict and rarely at home; the mother recently has become an alcoholic. Neighbors report that the children are stealing food. This courtroom is part of the juvenile court system. In virtually all states juvenile courts attend to the needs of children whose families abuse or neglect them. The public thinks of juvenile court principally as a place to prosecute teenagers who have gotten into scrapes with the law. A large percentage of juvenile court cases, however, are like Annie G.'s: they involve abuse and neglect on the part of parents. In these cases, the state steps in to protect the children.

In another part of town three other children, roughly the same ages as the siblings in Annie's family, are also the subject of a custody trial. This time, however, the dispute is between the parents. This courtroom is a traditional high-ceilinged room with an elevated judge's bench and strictly organized plaintiffs' and defendants' tables. The judge is dressed in formal black robes. The private attorneys for the mother and father take the lead in questioning the witnesses, often jumping up to object during testimony. In addition to lay witnesses three expert witnesses are called, all psychologists. One has been hired by the mother, a second by the father, and the third is appointed by the court. Each gives opinions based largely on the standardized psychological tests they have administered to the parents and to the children.

Yet where are the children? They are not present in this courtroom. They are not represented by an attorney, or any other advocate. The judge has never laid eyes on them; in most jurisdictions he would not consider it necessary. Nor have the attorneys seen these children; the lawyers would consider it a breach of legal ethics to interview them. It is the parents, not the children, whom the lawyers represent. The decision as to where and with whom the children will live will be made without the children's participation. This is the family law court's trial division, where matters of divorce and custody between parents are heard.

This two-tiered court system today exists in all but a few states. Juvenile courts were established around the turn of the century to acknowledge the need for children in trouble to be treated differently from adults. These courts operate in quite another way. Among many important differences is that the children are at the center of the proceedings, and they receive representation. In family court custody proceedings, by contrast, only a few states require an advocate for the child.

A great deal of variation exists among juvenile courts between states, and even within states. All children in abuse and neglect proceedings, however, by virtue of federal law are entitled to a court-appointed advocate, often called a *guardian ad litem*.[1] This advocate may be a lawyer, or he or she may be a special volunteer. A nationwide volunteer organization, Court-Appointed Special Advocates (CASA), trains lay people to advocate for children. They are trained in basic child development and child interview techniques, and they are expected to spend a good deal of time with children before their appearance in court.[2] In some states the child may have both a CASA advocate and an attorney representing her or his interests.

Juvenile courts also offer support for parents. A well-functioning juvenile court will work with a wide range of social services to provide support to families in crisis, which may include parent education, child care, and counseling. Parents usually receive legal representation at hearings as well. In addition, juvenile court is prepared to monitor families over a long period of time.

In divorce and custody proceedings, although they may be held in what is referred to as family court, little or no support for families is provided. Family courts are better prepared to handle financial issues of property division and child support than they are the social and psychological needs of the family in crisis. In family courts neither parents nor children are entitled to representation, nor is a social service support network available to them.

Children in particular often are ignored in family court cases, both by the court and at home. Parents who are otherwise sensitive to their children's needs may become totally absorbed in their own problems during a painful divorce. Divorce researcher Dr. Judith Wallerstein found that four fifths of the youngest children studied were not provided with an adequate explanation or assurance of continued care. "In effect they woke up one morning to find one parent gone." Moreover, these children received little help from outside sources: relatives, family friends, schools, or churches. Fewer than 10 percent of the children Dr. Wallerstein studied received adult help from their community or family friends. Often their teachers were not even aware of the breakup.[3]

Federal task forces and the American Bar Association have argued for a comprehensive family court that would combine the juvenile court, divorce and custody proceedings, and various bits and pieces of other court actions that focus on the family.[4] These bits and pieces would include domestic violence, adoption, and guardianships. One of the incentives for arguing for a comprehensive court is that a family in crisis may find itself in several different court actions taking place in several different courtrooms. For example, sometimes a charge of domestic violence in a family, which would be prosecuted in criminal court, is the catalyst for a divorce and custody action that would take place in family court. That same crisis may precipitate a delinquent offense on the part of a teen in the family, which would be handled in a juvenile court. The family could get shuttled from courtroom to courtroom, with no one attending to the larger picture.

To my mind the greatest advantage of a comprehensive family court would be to better focus on the best interests of children. The best aspects of juvenile court—social support services, representation, and long-term monitoring of families in crisis—could be offered to all children and their parents.

Yet there is little interest in extending this child-friendly approach to divorce and custody cases. Only six states and the District of Columbia offer statewide comprehensive family courts, and all but two were formed before 1980.[5] Nationwide enthusiasm instead has turned to mediation as the major solution for resolving divorce and custody disputes, which offers less rather than more court involvement.

The trend toward mediation undoubtedly is rooted in what is perceived to be a current avalanche of divorce that in turn has produced an unprecedented number of custody disputes. Courts feel ill-equipped to handle the volume and decision-making burden, and look to mediation as a substitute for adversarial court proceedings. Mediation offers two immediate advantages: it is fast and cheap.

California set the trend in mediation (as it has in most aspects of the divorce and custody revolution) by requiring mediation in all contested custody disputes before a case can be carried forth to trial.[6] The mediation requirement coincided with enactment of a preference for joint custody. The cooperative model of mediation is viewed as facilitating the ideal of joint custody in a manner that the adversarial trial process does not. Other states have followed California's lead enthusiastically, encouraging a wide variety of mediation efforts, both public and private, that often include property and support issues as well as custody arrangements. Although only five other states have made mediation mandatory in all custody disputes, many others permit courts to order divorcing spouses to undergo mediation and it is now a very popular alternative.[7]

When mediation is mandatory, the actual process may vary widely among jurisdictions, but it is always relatively short.[8] In Los Angeles, for instance, a number of interviews are conducted over a four- to five-hour time period. The counselor first meets with the attorneys, then with the parents together without their attorneys. If the parents request it, or if the counselor deems it necessary, the counselor also will meet with each parent individually. On some occasions the children are interviewed as well; this is not to elicit their preference but to determine the effect of the divorce on them.[9]

The informal nature of the proceedings means there is no established recipe. While the mediator's role is supposed to be that of facilitator rather than director, the mediator's personality can heavily influence the course of the session. In theory mediators are not limited by how a court would decide the issues. Working under the shadow of a looming trial, however, court-appointed mediators are likely to be influenced by a trial's potential outcome. This pressure is exacerbated by the fact that in most jurisdictions the mediators' recommendations will be sent to the court; their recommendations, therefore, must adhere to the law.

Voluntary mediation sought by divorcing couples, however, often has a different character. The goal of the parties is to avoid the long-lasting acrimony and exorbitant expense of the adversarial process. Mediation sessions are likely to extend over a longer period of time and to include other issues in addition to custody.[10] Private mediators typically have either a legal or a mental health background. Since the mediator is not appointed by the court nor obliged to forward a recommendation to the court, the parties are not tied to results that a court might reach. This freedom presumably allows the couple, facilitated by the mediator, to reach a solution that reflects their own sense of fairness, not that imposed by the law.

Although initial public response to mediation was almost universally enthusiastic, a strong negative reaction has taken form, led principally by feminists.[11] While most of this criticism has been leveled at mandatory mediation, many of the same points also can be made against voluntary mediation. The essence of the feminist criticism is that mediation favors the party who enters the mediation with the most inherent social power in other words, the man. In general, feminists claim, women are the less powerful partner in the marriage, and mediation exacerbates this differential. Women may have severe grievances, such as spousal or child abuse, and as a result may appear hysterical or uncooperative in mediation sessions as compared to the (generally) more composed behavior of men. This could influence mediators to see the husband's wishes as more rational.

The forward-looking style of mediation also may work to the disadvantage of mothers with other real concerns. The mantra of mediation is to let go of the past and concentrate on the future. One feminist scholar, Trina Grillo, describes the case of a mother named Linda who sought to rescind a joint custody agreement. The father refused to return their son as agreed, at Thanksgiving, and instead placed him until Christmas in a day care center where the teacher frequently relied on corporal punishment. Linda claimed that the child returned manifesting violent and aggressive behavior. Grillo describes the mediator's advice as follows: "The Thanksgiving is past history, and she is sure that they both have complaints about the past. Blaming one another is counterproductive. The mediator goes on to tell Linda that she must recognize the parent who has the child is responsible for choosing daycare. Linda must learn to give up control."[12]

Even more problematical is the battered woman issue. Some social scientists claim that women who have experienced violence in a relationship develop a passive personality.[13] In contrast, the violent husband is often charming and seemingly forthcoming. According to the critics, mediators are too often swayed by the husband, who appears to be the friendly parent, belying the violence of his domestic behavior. Even for women who have not been beaten, forced engagement with their husbands, without the protection of a lawyer and the legal process, can intimidate them, replicating their powerless mode in marriage.[14]

Most of the feminist critics assert that the adversarial court process, warts and all, provides more protection and support for women than does mediation. Even granting the patriarchal nature of the legal process and the almost unlimited discretion afforded individual judges, these critics maintain that the presence of lawyers serves women's rights, and that the authority of rules and precedent, neutrally conceived, provides a more empowering alternative for the powerless. As the legal scholar Martha Fineman observed: "The public nature of the legal process means that the basis for decisions will be explained, debated, and publicly considered. This process may not be foolproof, but it is better than one in which substantive rules and standards evolve and are implemented behind closed office doors without any possibility of checks from the political system."[15]

Other critics of mediation, both mandatory and voluntary, claim that the high percentage of joint physical custody agreements achieved through the process does not fit the reality of familial needs, and is not in the best interests of the child. Very few parents can sustain a sharing arrangement in which the child actually resides with each parent one half of the time. Inevitably the child drifts toward spending most of her or his time with one parent, most often the mother. Child support, however, usually is configured for fifty-fifty joint custody. A mother therefore could find herself with effective sole custody but less child support than a sole custodian might otherwise receive.[16]

Responding to growing criticism, advocates of mandatory mediation have maintained their enthusiasm but have revised the model, making it less mandatory. Some states include exceptions in their statutes exempting cases involving child abuse and spousal abuse.[17] Other states allow the judge to decide whether mediation is appropriate upon presentation of evidence to the contrary. The Wisconsin law advises courts to consider "evidence of child or spousal abuse, evidence of alcohol or drug abuse, and any other evidence indicating that a party's health or safety will be endangered by attending the session."[18]

Mediation has its place. In my opinion that place is in a comprehensive family court that offers this service, among others,

on a voluntary basis. Both private and court-centered mediation should be recommended only for parents capable of con-
fronting one another without fear or intimidation, a condition
rare among divorcing parents. For many routine matters, such
as minor changes in visitation, mediation may be the fast and
efficient solution. For initial custody determinations and reex-
aminations as the child reaches important developmental mile-
stones the child should have his or her own advocate. With
older children, the child should be allowed to represent her- or
himself. In any case, a full hearing should be granted if any of
the parties, including the child's advocate, believes they are not
well served by mediation. In addition, mediation should always
take place in the shadow of well-defined rules that let the parties know what society believes is in the child's best interests.

Our system is overwhelmed by families in crisis. Between
1984 and 1994 juvenile court filings increased 59 percent, and
domestic relations cases—divorce, support–custody, domestic
violence, paternity, interstate child support enforcement, and
adoption—increased 65 percent. A quarter of all civil court
cases now deal with domestic relations issues.[19] Yet for the most
part these issues are given lowest priority in the legal system.
Most judges resist domestic relations or juvenile court assign-
ments, and family law attorneys are accorded low status in the
hierarchy of the bar. Parents who cannot pay are rarely considered worthy of low-cost or free legal representation.

The major federal initiative aimed at handling the crisis has
focused on collecting child support, or going after so-called
deadbeat dads. Because the issue of child support has been im-
properly confounded with that of physical access to the child,
however, support has become one of the major battlefields of
the custody wars. In my opinion child support should be han-

dled completely separately from custody, perhaps by an independent administrative agency, as it is in England. This agency could operate by means of automatic payroll deduction and support its own enforcement mechanism. "Pay and play," which makes the child a commodity of exchange, should not be a method of determining child custody.

There must be a place for children and families—a place where children are heard and their changing needs addressed; a place where judges are educated in child development, and court support systems provide counseling and other services; a place where the rule of law, while flexible, rather than catering to gender politics or treating the children as "biological property" truly promotes the best interests of our children.

Afterword

In 1992 a twelve-year-old boy in Florida, Gregory Kingsley, sought termination of his mother's parental rights so that he might be adopted by his foster family. Assisted by a lawyer, he pursued the suit on his own, since the social service agency that was legally his guardian did not want to cut the parental tie. This despite the fact that he had spent only eight months of his life with his mother, an alcoholic unable to care for him. His foster parents, like almost all other nonbiological parent figures, had no standing to bring a suit for custody, and neither did Gregory for that matter, which is why the suit is so unusual. Like all other children in custodial situations he had no power to change what he considered an intolerable situation.

The story caught the popular imagination for several reasons. Those not familiar with the law were shocked to learn that natural parents, even in extreme cases of neglect, continue to hold rights over their children. Others were heartened that a child had asserted his own rights and did not play the passive role of victim usually assigned to children in custody disputes. A few commentators, rather than cheering Gregory, saw his victory as a dangerous precedent, empowering children to effectively divorce their parents.

The publicity ultimately provoked a response on the part of the social service agency, and Gregory's foster family were allowed to adopt him; but this did not change the law. It did not mean that any other child could seek redress for an intolerable situation, or that other adults were likely to do so for him.

Today there are women's rights advocates, father's rights groups, and grandparents' rights advocates, all pulling in different directions. In addition there are state and federal government agencies whose main concern is collecting child support, at whatever cost to the child. There are children's advocates, but they are small in number and largely concerned with child poverty, a critical cause, but so draining of scant resources that little energy is left for other children's issues. There is no national coalition of feminists, philanthropists, and lawmakers, as there was early in the twentieth century, the Progressive Era, to consider children first. In that era children's advocates established the juvenile court and put in place the structure of the modern system of child welfare. Today family law reforms—even those as drastic and far-reaching as the no-fault divorce revolution and consequent changes in custody—are undertaken with little forethought as to the effects on children. Children, who have no political voice, are too often used as political weapons in others' battles or simply are not considered. Children will never be the first consideration in custody matters unless adults advocate their interests.

The role of social and behavioral sciences in the custody wars is particularly problematic. As I've demonstrated, social science almost always claims that its findings, methodology, and expert practitioners are working for the best interests of the child. We have seen that social scientific concepts and practitioners have gained tremendous influence, sometimes at the expense of established laws and legal procedures. Mental health professionals are frequently called as expert witnesses in custody disputes following divorce, and the model of mediation, a form of dispute resolution developed by the social sciences, has replaced legal proceedings in many custody battles.

Without doubt, social science can inform us about human behavior in a manner that the law cannot. Studies of child development and parent–child relationships could provide important information to decision makers. As we have seen, however, social science sometimes is utilized selectively to promote arrangements, such as joint custody and father custody, that are largely politically inspired. In these instances political advocates do not accurately present the full range of social scientific research. Mother–infant studies and attachment studies, which might have promoted different solutions, are ignored. Also ignored are developmental studies suggesting that different arrangements are more appropriate at different stages of development, and competency studies that support an adolescent's right to choice.

A second pitfall in the application of the social sciences is the risk inherent in taking away the court's ultimate decision-making power. Critics have pointed out that expert witnesses do not have infallible, or even very accurate, rates of predicting which parent will do a better job of raising a child. Most important, these experts are not representing the child. Sometimes they are hired by the parents, and when they represent the court much of their evaluation is devoted to psychological assessments of the parents, not the needs of the child.[1] With mediation, likewise, the court could abandon important procedural safeguards of the trial process for the individuals involved, including the children. The mediator, while assuming a neutral posture, is in fact influencing the couple to make an agreement—almost any agreement—without considering the interests of the children first.

Social science can be a complement to the law without taking away its ultimate responsibility to protect children. Yet the law must set the standard for guarding the rights of children. In this book I have suggested a few simple principles that, if consistently applied, would protect the interests of children in nearly all custody disputes.

Most custody negotiations do not reach full-scale court battles. Parents and other adults decide arrangements in the lawyer's office, in the kitchen, on the phone. Yet they bargain in the shadow of the law, for their agreement must be approved by the court, and they have an idea of how the court would decide if they moved into a full trial. The law must make it clear to these adults that it will protect the voice and interests of the child above theirs. The custody wars are not likely to cease, but giving a voice to children could turn their course.

Notes

Introduction

1. California modified this law again in 1989, demoting joint custody from a preference to an equal status with sole custody. Cal. Family Code, § 3040

2. Mary Ann Mason, *From Father's Property to Children's Rights: A History of Child Custody in the United States* (New York: Columbia University Press, 1994).

3. Ibid.

4. Mary Ann Mason, "Read My Lips: Are Mothers Losing Custody? Trends in Judicial Decision-making in Custody Disputes," *Family Law Quarterly* 31, 2 (Summer 1997): 215–37.

5. Marc J. Ackerman and Melissa C. Ackerman, "Child Custody Evaluation Practices: A 1996 Survey of Psychologists," *Family Law Quarterly* 30 (1997). 565.

6. Nearly half of all couples married today will divorce. All children of divorce are under the jurisdiction of the court, even if they reach a private settlement. In addition, nearly one third of children are born out of wedlock. Unwed fathers may (and increasingly do) press for custodial rights, which the courts will support.

7. The United States alone among the nations of the Western world has failed to sign this convention as of this writing.

8. United Nations Convention on the Rights of the Child, Art. 3, 1; Art. 12, 1; Art. 6, 2.

Chapter One

1. Mary Ann Mason, *The Equality Trap* (New York: Simon and Schuster, 1988).

2. Steven Smith, *Larry King Live*, 5 August 1974.

3. AP, Day Care Costs Mother Custody of Daughter, 3. *New York Times*, 27 July 1994, A14.

4. Ibid.

5. Ibid.

6. Modeled after the Declaration of Independence, the Declaration of Rights and Sentiments used the pronoun *He* to represent a generic legislative and judicial patriarchy rather than *George III*.

7. Seneca Falls Women's Rights Convention of 1848, Declaration of Rights and Sentiments, reprinted in Susan B. Anthony and Ida Hustead Harper, eds., *The History of Women's Suffrage*, 4 vols. (Rochester, NY: Hustings, 1902), 1:70.

8. People v. Mercein, 3 Hill 399, 410 (N.Y. 1842).

9. National Organization of Women, "Statement of Purpose" (1967), in Aileen S. Kraditor, ed., *Up from the Pedestal* (Chicago: University of Chicago Press, 1970), 368.

10. State ex rel. Watts v. Watts, 350 N.Y.S.2d 285 (1973).

11. Margaret Mead, "Some Theoretical Considerations of the Problems of Mother-Child Separation," *American Journal of Orthopsychiatry* 24 (1954): 24, as quoted in State ex rel. Watts v. Watts, 350 N.Y.S.2d 285 (1973).

12. By 1982 only seven remaining states gave mothers a preference over fathers for children of tender years: Alabama, Florida, Kentucky, Louisiana, Mississippi, Utah, and Virginia. Jeff Atkinson, "Criteria for Deciding Custody in the Trial and Appellate Courts," *Family Law Quarterly* 18, 1 (1984): 11.

13. Barbara R. Bergmann, *The Economic Emergence of Women* (New York: Basic Books, 1986), 25, table 2.3.

14. In re Stevens, 183 Ill. App. 3d 160, 538 N.E.2d 1279 (1989).

15. The Uniform Marriage and Divorce Act, put forth by the Commissioners on Uniform State laws, defines the child's best interest as a composite of the following factors: "(1) the wishes of the child's parent or parents as to his custody; (2) the wishes of the child as to his custodian; (3) the interaction and interrelationship of the child with his parent or parents, his siblings and any other person who may significantly affect the child's best interest; (4) the child's adjustment to his home, school and community; (5) the mental and physical health of all individuals involved. The court shall not consider conduct of a present or proposed custodian that does not affect his relationship to the child." UMDA § 402.

16. Mary Ann Mason, *From Fathers' Property to Children's Rights: A History of Child Custody in the United States* (New York: Columbia University Press, 1994), 174.

17. Elizabeth Kastor, "The Maranda Decision," *Washington Post,* 30 July 1994, D1.

18. Gene Schabath and Rebecca Powers, "Custody Case Put on Hold: Mother Accused of Abusing Child," *Detroit News,* 9 August 1994.

19. Ibid.

20. Thomas J. Reidy, Richard M. Silver, and Alan Carlson, "Child Custody Decisions: A Survey of Judges," *Family Law Quarterly* 23 (1991), 75.

21. Mary Ann Mason, "Read My Lips: Are Mothers Losing Custody? Trends in Judicial Decision-making in Custody Disputes," *Family Law Quarterly* 31, 2 (Summer 1997): 215–37.

22. Eleanor Maccoby and Robert Mnookin, *Dividing the Child: Social and Legal Dilemmas of Custody* (Cambridge, MA: Harvard University Press, 1992).

23. Lenore Weitzman, *The Divorce Revolution* (New York: Free Press, 1985); and *Los Angeles Times,* 20 January 1995, 8.

24. Lenore Weitzman reports that about one third of divorced women reported that their husbands threatened to sue for custody as a ploy in negotiations. See Weitzman, *The Divorce Revolution,* 310–11; see also Doris Foster and Henry Freed, "Law and the Family: Politics of Divorce Process-Bargaining Leverage, Unfair Edge," *New York Law School Legal Review* 192 (1984): 6.

25. E. Mark Cummings and Patrick Davies, *Children and Marital Conflict: The Impact of Family Dispute and Resolution* (New York: Guilford Press, 1994).

26. AP, "Day Care," *New York Times,* 27 July 1994, A14.

27. John Bowlby, *Attachment and Loss,* vol. 1 of *Attachment* (New York: Basic Books, 1969).

28. Arlene Skolnick, "Solomon's Children: The New Biologism, Psychological Parenthood, Attachment Theory, and the Best Interests Standard," in Mary Ann Mason, Arlene Skolnick, and Steve Sugarman, eds., *All Our Families: New Policies for a New Century* (New York: Oxford University Press, 1998).

29. Sue Reid, "Children Taken from Mother Who Works Too Hard," *New York Times,* 25 September 1994, sec. 2, 12.

30. Ibid.

31. Brian E. Albrecht, "Debate Rages over Bias in Child Custody," *The Plain Dealer,* 1 November 1994.

32. Ibid.

33. Ireland v. Smith, 214 Mich. App. 235, 250, 542 N.W.2d 344, 351 (1995).

34. Ireland v. Smith, 214 Mich. App. 235, 245, 542 N.W.2d 344, 349 (1995).

35. Ireland v. Smith, 451 Mich. 457, 467, 547 N.W.2d 686, 691 (1996).

Chapter Two

1. As quoted in Taylor v. Taylor, 306 Md. 290, 508 A.2d 964, 975 (1986).

2. Quoting McCann v. McCann, 167 Md. 167, 172, 173, A. 7 (1934).

3. Doris J. Freed and Henry J. Walker, "Family Law in the Fifty States: An Overview," *Family Law Quarterly* 22, 4 (1990): 57, table 9. Statutory preference is given in Alabama, Connecticut, the District of Columbia, Louisiana, Minnesota, Nevada, New Hampshire, New Mexico, and New York.

4. Dodd v. Dodd, 403 N.Y.S.2d 401 (1978).

5. Lenore Weitzman, *The Divorce Revolution* (New York: Free Press, 1985), 231. Later, in 1989, California demoted joint custody from preferential treatment to equal standing with sole custody. Cal. Family Code § 3020.

6. Mary Ann Mason, *The Equality Trap* (New York: Simon and Schuster, 1988), 81; *From Fathers' Property to Children's Rights: A History of Child Custody in the United States* (New York: Columbia University Press, 1994), 121–60.

7. Eleanor Maccoby and Robert Mnookin, *Dividing the Child: Social and Legal Dilemmas of Custody* (Cambridge, MA: Harvard University Press, 1992).

8. Ibid., 113.

9. As the researchers explained it, "The fact that joint legal custody carries with it so little by way of actual consequences probably explains why it has become so popular. Lawyers for mothers no doubt tell their clients that they are giving up nothing of importance in agreeing to joint legal custody." Robert H. Mnookin, Eleanor E. Maccoby, Catherine R. Albiston, and Charlene E. Depner, "Private Ordering Re-Visited," in S. D. Sugarman and H. H. Kay, eds., *Divorce Reform at the Crossroads* (New Haven: Yale University Press, 1990), 73.

10. I have changed some of the identifying characteristics in this and other stories to protect the parties' identities, as noted earlier.

11. In re Marriage of Wood, 141 Cal.App. 3d 671 (1982).

12. In this instance also I have changed the name and some of the facts to protect the identity of the family.

13. Jean Piaget, considered the father of experimental developmental psychology, carefully detailed the development of the child's thought processes. He believed that children do not consistently differentiate between the subjective and objective until age seven or eight. The tender years doctrine for the most part encompassed this time frame as well. See, e.g., Jean Piaget and Bärbel Inhelder, *The Psychology of the Child* (New York: Basic Books 1969).

14. Patricia Shiono and Linda Sandham Quinn, "Epidemiology of Divorce," *Future of Children* 4 (Spring 1994): 18.

15. Arlene Skolnick, "Solomon's Children: The New Biologism, Psychological Parenthood, Attachment Theory, and the Best Interests Standard," in Mary Ann Mason, Arlene Skolnick, and Steve Sugarman, eds., *All Our Families: New Policies for a New Century* (New York: Oxford University Press, 1998).

16. Cal. Family Code § 3106.

17. Mnookin, Maccoby et al., "Private Ordering Re-Visited," in Sugarman and Kay, eds., *Divorce Reform at the Crossroads*, 73.

18. Stephen K. Erickson and Marilyn S. Mcknight Erickson, "Don and Linda: A Typical Divorce Case," *Mediation Quarterly* 21, 3 (1988): 10.

19. Ibid., 16.

20. David Chambers, *Making Fathers Pay: The Enforcement of Child Support* (Chicago: University of Chicago Press, 1979).

21. Maccoby and Mnookin, *Dividing the Child,* 197.

22. In the Westlaw Family Law state database, the work of Goldstein, Freud, and Solnit is mentioned 177 times.

23. Joseph Goldstein, Anna Freud, and Albert Solnit, *Beyond the Best Interests of the Child* (New York: Free Press, 1973), 38. See also Joseph Goldstein, Anna Freud, and Albert Solnit, *Before the Best Interests of the*

Child (New York: Free Press, 1979); Joseph Goldstein, Anna Freud, and Albert Solnit, *In the Best Interests of the Child* (New York: Free Press, 1986).

24. Quoted in Maxine Margolis, *Mothers and Such* (Gainsville: University of Florida Press, 1984), 90.

25. David L. Chambers, a leading proponent of a primary caretaker preference, contended following a review of the literature that there is no reason, based on gender alone, to prefer placing the child with the mother. David L. Chambers, "Rethinking the Substantive Rule for Custody Disputes in Divorce," *Michigan Law Review* 83 (1984): 477. On the other hand, the legal scholar Martha Fineman criticized Chambers's analysis of the father studies, claiming that the observations on which the researchers relied represented only minimal parenting skill: "skills that would be inadequate if we were talking about mothers rather than fathers." Moreover, she claimed that research findings were based on small, select, or unrepresentative samples. Martha L. Fineman and Anne Opie, "The Uses of Social Science Data in Legal Policymaking: Custody Determinations at Divorce," *Wisconsin Law Review* 32 (1987): 145.

26. Michael F. Lamb, "Father–Infant and Mother–Infant Interaction in the First Year of Life," *Child Development* 48 (1977): 167–81. See also Donald Berman, "Are Women More Responsive Than Men to the Young? A Review of Developmental and Situation Variables," *Psychological Bulletin* 88 (1980): 688. This article reviews almost sixty studies over twenty years. This research takes many forms, including measuring the pulse rates of mothers and fathers in response to pictures, and observations of real interactions between mothers, fathers, and children.

27. For a thorough discussion of father parenting studies see Ross A. Thompson, "Fathers and the Child's 'Best Interests': Judicial Decision Making in Custody Disputes," in Michael F. Lamb, *The Father's Role* (New York: J. Wiley, 1986), chap. 3.

28. Cal. Family Code § 3020.

29. J. Frank Furstenberg, Address to AAAS, May 1986, 18.

30. Quoting Zummo v. Zummo, 394 Pa. Super. 30, *44, 574 A.2d 1130, 1137, notes 8, 11, 12. Some of the studies cited are: Allison and Furstenberg, "How Marital Dissolution Affects Children," *Developmental Psychology* 25 (1989): 540–49; Harold Fishel, "Children's Adjustment in Divorced Families," *Youth & Society* 19 (1987): 173–96; McCant, "The Cultural Contradiction of Fathers as Nonparents," *Family Law Quarterly* 21 (1987): 127–43; Wooley, "Shared Parenting Arrangements," *Family Advocate* 1 (1978): 6; Grote and Weinstein, "Joint Custody," *Journal of Divorce* 1 (1977): 43–53; Coysh et al., "Parental Postdivorce Adjustment in Joint and Sole Physical Custody Families," *Journal of Family Issues* 10 (1989): 52–71; Tschann, Johnston, and Wallerstein, "Resources, Stressors, and Attachment as Predictors of Adult Adjustment After Divorce: A Longitudinal Study," *Journal of Marriage & Family* 51 (1989): 1033–46; Guttmann, "The Divorced Father," *Journal of Comparative Family Studies* 20 (1989): 247–61; Koch and Lowery, "Visitation and the Non-Custodial Father," *Journal of Divorce* 8 (1984): 47–65; Greif, "Fathers, Children, and Joint Custody," *American Journal of Orthopsychiatry* 49 (1979): 311–19; Seltzer, Schaeffer, and Channg, "Family Ties After Divorce: The Relationship Between Visiting and Paying Child Support," *Journal of Marriage and the Family* 51 (1989): 1013–32; Pearson and Thoennes, "Supporting Children After Divorce: The Influence of Custody on Child Support Levels," *Family Law Quarterly* 22 (1988): 319–39.

31. Zummo v. Zummo, 394 Pa. Super. 30, 44, 574 A.2d 1130, 1137.

32. Cal. Family Code § 3040. Joint custody was still retained as a presumption where the parents agreed. Cal. Family Code § 3080.

33. Judith S. Wallerstein and Tony J. Tanke, "To Move or Not to Move: Psychological and Legal Considerations in the Relocation of Children Following Divorce," *Family Law Quarterly* 30 (Summer 1996): 311–12.

34. In re Marriage of Burgess, 913 P.2d 473 (1996).

35. Maccoby and Mnookin, *Dividing the Child*, 151.

36. Janet Johnston, Marcia Kline, and J. Tschann, "Ongoing Post Divorce Conflicts: Effects on Children of Joint Custody and Sole Physical Custody Families," *American Journal of Orthopsychiatry* 59 (1991): 576–92; Carol S. Bruch and Janet M. Bowermaster, "The Relocation of Children and Custodial Parents: Public Policy, Past and Present," *Family Law Quarterly* 30 (Summer 1996): 245.

37. E. Mavis Heatherington and Janet Arasteh, eds., *The Impact of Divorce, Single Parenting, and Step Parenting on Children* (Hillsdale, NJ: Erlbaum, 1988).

Chapter Three

1. In re Marriage of Marshall & Nussbaum, 663 N.E.2d 1113, 278 Ill. App. 3d 1071 (1996).

2. Ibid., 1118.

3. Ibid.

4. Ibid.

5. Ibid., 1119–20.

6. Ibid., 1116.

7. Ibid.

8. Ibid.

9. Ibid., 1117.

10. Ibid.

11. Ibid., 1118

12. Tinker v. Des Moines, 393 U.S. 503 (1969).

13. Hazelwood v. Kuhlmeier, 484 U.S. 260 (1988).

14. New Jersey v. T.L.O., 469 U.S. 325 (1985).

15. In re Gault, 387 U.S. 1 (1967).

16. Thompson v. Oklahoma, 487 U.S. 815 (1988).

17. Planned Parenthood of Central Missouri v. Danforth, 428 U.S. 52 (1976).

18. Bellotti v. Baird II, 443 U.S. 622 (1979).

19. Walter J. Wadlington, "Consent to Medical Care for Minors," in Gary B. Melton, Gerald P. Koocher, and Michael J. Sak, eds., *Children's Competence to Consent* (New York: Plenum Press, 1983), 60–63.

20. Cal. Family Code § 3042.

21. See, e.g., Jean Piaget and Bärbel Inhelder, *The Psychology of the Child* (New York: Basic Books, 1969).

22. Judith S. Wallerstein, Presentation to the American Bar Association, 9 August 1992. For an analysis of the long-term effects of custody on children, see Judith S. Wallerstein and Sandra Blakeslee, *Second Chances* (New York: Houghton Mifflin, 1989).

23. Ibid.

24. Gary B. Melton, "Children's Competence to Consent: A Problem in Law and Social Science," in Melton, Koocher, and Sak, eds., *Children's Competence to Consent*, 15.

25. Lois A. Weithorn, "Involving Children in Decisions Affecting Their Own Welfare," in Melton, Koocher, and Sak, eds., *Children's Competence to Consent*, 245.

26. Ibid., 246.

27. For a critical interpretation of custody evaluations see John R. Levy, "Custody Investigations as Evidence in Divorce Cases," *Family Law Quarterly* 21 (1987): 149.

28. Mary Ann Mason, "Read My Lips: Are Mothers Losing Custody? Trends in Judicial Decision-making in Custody Disputes," *Family Law Quarterly* 31, 2 (Summer 1997): 215–37.

29. Private correspondence from the law offices of an Oakland family law attorney.

30. Ibid., 3.

31. Ibid., 4.

32. Ibid., 5.

33. Michael Wald, "Legal Policies Affecting Children: A Lawyer's Request for Aid," *Child Development* 47 (1976): 5.

34. James Garbarino, Frances M. Stot, and Faculty of the Erikson Institute, *What Children Can Tell Us* (San Francisco: Jossey-Bass, 1989), 223.

35. See, e.g., Piaget and Inhelder, *The Psychology of the Child*.

36. Ibid.

37. See Paul Roasin, *Erik Erickson* (New York: Free Press, 1986).

38. Ibid.

39. John Bowlby, *Attachment and Loss*, vol. 1 of *Attachment* (New York: Basic Books, 1969).

40. Paul Shiono and Linda Quinn, "Epidemiology of Divorce," *Future of Children* 4 (Spring 1994): 8.

41. Joseph Goldstein, Anna Freud, and Albert Solnit, *Beyond the Best Interests of the Child* (New York: Free Press, 1973).

42. Ibid., 112. See also Joseph Goldstein, Anna Freud, and Albert Solnit, *Before the Best Interests of the Child* (New York: Free Press, 1979); Joseph Goldstein, Anna Freud, and Albert Solnit, *In the Best Interests of the Child* (New York: Free Press, 1986).

43. Bowlby, *Attachment*.

44. Goldstein, Freud, and Solnit, *Beyond the Best Interests of the Child*, 38. See also Goldstein, Freud, and Solnit, *Before the Best Interests of the Child*; Goldstein, Freud, and Solnit, *In the Best Interests of the Child*.

45. Maxine Margolis, *Mothers and Such* (Gainsville: University of Florida Press, 1984).

46. Watts v. Watts, 350 N.Y.2d 285, 289 (N.Y. Fam. Ct. 1973).

47. Ibid.

48. Arlene Skolnick, "Solomon's Children: The New Biologism, Psychological Parenthood, Attachment Theory, and the Best Interests Standard," in Mary Ann Mason, Arlene Skolnick, and Steve Sugarman, eds., *All Our Families: New Policies for a New Century* (New York: Oxford University Press, 1998).

49. Ibid.

50. W. Va. Code Ann. § 48–2–15, Notes, References, & Annotations, Part III, *Custody and Maintenance of Children: Primary Caretaker Defined* (citing Garska v. McCoy, 167 W.Va. 59, 278 S.E.2d 357 (1981);

Lounsbury v. Lounsbury, 170 W.Va. 723, 296 S.E.2d 686 (1982); Graham v. Graham, 174 W.Va. 345, 326 S.E.2d 189 (1984); Cummings v. Cummings, 188 W.Va. 713, 426 S.E.2d 505 (1992)). See also Richard Neely, "The Primary Caretaker Parent Rule: Child Custody and the Dynamics of Greed," *Yale Law and Policy Review* 3 (1984): 168, 170.

51. In re Marriage of Marshall & Nussbaum, 663 N.E.2d 1113, 1122.

52. Ibid.

Chapter Four

1. Sara McLanahan and Gary Sandefur, *Growing Up with a Single Parent: What Hurts, What Helps* (Cambridge, MA: Harvard University Press, 1994), 2.

2. Jason DeParle, "Welfare Overhaul Initiatives Focus on Fathers," *New York Times*, 3 September 1998, A20.

3. Adoption of Michael H. v. Mark K., 10 Cal. 4th 1043, 43 Cal. Rptr. 2d 445 (1992).

4. Lehr v. Robertson, 463 U.S. 248, 261 (1983).

5. Caban v. Mohammed, 441 U.S. 380, 389 (1979) .

6. Adoption of Michael H. v. Mark K., 10 Cal. 4th 1043, 43 Cal. Rptr. 2d 445, 252 (1992).

7. Arlene Skolnick, "Solomon's Children: The New Biologism, Psychological Parenthood, Attachment Theory, and the Best Interests Standard," in Mary Ann Mason, Arlene Skolnick, and Steve Sugarman, eds., *All Our Families: New Policies for a New Century* (New York: Oxford University Press, 1998).

8. Ibid.

9. David Popenoe, "Evolution of Marriage and Stepfamily Problems," in Allan Booth and Judy Dunn, eds., *Stepfamilies: Who Benefits? Who Does Not?* (Hillsdale, NJ: Erlbaum, 1994), 19.

10. Martin Daly and Margo Wilson, *Homicide* (New York: A. de Guyter, 1988), 230.

11. Joseph H. Smith and Philip A. Crowl, eds., *Court Records of Prince George's County, Maryland, 1696–1699* (Washington, D.C.: American Historical Association, 1964), vi.

12. Ibid., 188.

13. Ibid., 434.

14. Michael Grossberg, *Governing the Hearth* (Chapel Hill: University of North Carolina Press, 1985), 219.

15. Mary Ann Mason, *From Father's Property to Children's Rights: A History of Child Custody in the United States* (New York: Columbia University Press, 1994), 68.

16. Hudson v. Hills, 8 N.H. 417, 418 (1836).

17. Olson v. Johnson, 23 Minn. 301, 303 (1877).

18. Stanley v. Illinois, 405 U.S. 645 (1971).

19. In Cabban v. Mohammed, 441 U.S. 380 (1979), where the father had lived with the mother and two children for five years the court allowed the father to block the adoption, while in Quilloin v. Walcott, 434 U.S. 246 (1978), the court denied an unmarried father a "veto power" over the adoption of his nonmarital child, when for eleven years he supported the child only irregularly and never lived with the child.

20. Lehr v. Robertson, 463 U.S. 248, 261–62 (1983).

21. Stanley v. Illinois, 405 U.S. 645 (1971).

22. Michael H. v. Gerald D. 49 U.S. 110 (1989).

23. E. Mavis Heatherington and Janet Arasteh, eds., *The Impact of Divorce, Single Parenting, and Step Parenting on Children* (Hillsdale, NJ: Erlbaum, 1988).

24. Andrew J. Cherlin, *Marriage, Divorce, Remarriage* (Cambridge, MA: Harvard University Press, 1992), 18.

25. DeParle, "Welfare Overhaul Initiatives Focus on Fathers," A20.

26. Robert I. Lerman, "A National Profile of Young Unwed Fathers," in Robert L. Lerman and Theodora J. Ooms, eds., *Young Unwed Fathers* (Philadelphia: Temple University Press, 1993), 35–39.

27. Cherlin, *Marriage, Divorce, Remarriage*, 18.

28. Lerman, "A National Profile of Young Unwed Fathers," 37.

29. Ibid., 48.

30. Uniform Parentage Act § 4(a).

31. DeParle, "Welfare Overhaul Initiatives Focus on Fathers," A20.

32. Karen M. Thomas, *The Buffalo News*, 31 August 1994, 7.

33. Ibid.

Chapter Five

1. Frank Furstenberg, "The New Extended Family: The Experience of Parents and Children After Remarriage," in K. Pasley and M. Ihinger-Tallman, eds., *Remarriage and Stepparenting: Current Research and Theory* (New York: Guilford Press, 1987), 185–96.

2. Margaret Mahoney, *Stepfamilies and the Law* (Ann Arbor: University of Michigan Press, 1994), 13–47.

3. Halpern v. Halpern, 184 Cal. Rptr., 740, 742 (Ct. App. 1982).

4. Carter v. Brodrick, 644 P.2d 850 n.5 (Alaska 1982).

5. Some states have looked to common law for guidance. Under common law there is some recognition for stepparents who in all meaningful ways served as parents under the doctrine of "in loco parentis." The term translates "is in the place of a parent." The person "in loco parentis" is one who has assumed the status and obligations of a parent without formal adoption. Whether or not one assumes this status depends on whether that person intends to assume that obligation. With this viewpoint, the act of becoming a residential stepparent is not enough; there must also be an intention to parent.

6. Howell v. Gossett, 214 S.E.2d 882 (Ga. 1975).

7. He had had no contact with them for at least a year.

8. Divorce is not always the background event. An increasing but still relatively small number of custodial mothers who marry stepfathers have not previously wed.

9. U.S. Bureau of Census, 1989.

10. Mary Ann Mason and Jane Mauldon, "The New Stepfamily Needs a New Public Policy," *Journal of Social Issues* 52, 3 (1996): 11–27.

11. Ibid., 6.

12. E. Mavis Heatherington and Kathleen M. Jodl, "Stepfamilies as Settings for Child Development," in Alan Booth and Judy Dunn, eds., *Stepfamilies: Who Benefits, Who Does Not?* (Hillsdale, N. J.: L. Erlbaum Associates, 1994) 55–81.

13. Ibid., 76.

14. E. Mavis Heatherington and William Clingempeel, "Coping with Marital Transitions: A Family Systems Perspective," *Monographs of the Society for Research in Child Development*, 57: 2–3, serial no. 227 (NY: The Society for Research in Child Development, 1992); and E. Thomson, Sara McLanahan, and R. B. Curtin, "Family Structure, Gender, and Parental Socialization," *Journal of Marriage and the Family* 54 (1992): 368–78.

15. Heatherington and Jodl, "Stepfamilies as Settings for Child Development," 69.

16. Ibid. This finding does not necessarily apply to stepdaughters.

17. Ibid., 64–65.

18. Thomson, McLanahan, and Curtin, "Family Structure, Gender, and Parental Socialization," 368–78.

19. Larry Bumpass and James Sweet, *American Families and Households* (New York: Russell Sage Foundation, 1987), 23.

20. Mason and Mauldon, "The New Stepfamily Needs a New Public Policy," 7.

21. Ibid.

22. Cal. Prob. Code § 6408.

23. Andrew J. Cherlin, "Remarriage as an Incomplete Institution," *American Journal of Sociology* 84 (1978): 634–49.

24. A complete exposition and discussion of this de facto parent model may be found in Mason and Mauldon, "The New Stepfamily Needs a New Public Policy"; and Mary Ann Mason, "The New Stepfamily: Problems and Possibilities," in Mary Ann Mason, Arlene Skol-

nick, and Steve Sugarman, eds., *All Our Families: New Policies for a New Century* (New York: Oxford University Press, 1998).

25. Cal. Family Code § c.

26. My own preliminary research results indicate that most stepfathers would like some continuing contact; stepmothers who have helped raise the children definitely want continuing close contact.

27. John Hollinger (ed. in chief) et al., *Adoption Law and Practice* (New York: Bancroft and Whitney, 1988).

28. Mason and Mauldon, "The New Stepfamily Needs a New Public Policy," 5.

29. Katherine Bartlett, "Re-thinking Parenthood as an Exclusive Status: The Need for Alternatives When the Premise of the Nuclear Family Has Failed," *Virginia Law Review* 70 (1984): 879–903.

30. Nancy S. v. Michele G., 228 Cal. App. 3d, 279 Cal. Rptr. 212, 218 (1991).

31. Ibid., 219.

32. Mary Ann Mason, "Legal Stranger or De Facto Parent?" (1997), *Law and Society*.

Chapter Six

1. In re James M., 65 Cal. App. 3d 254, 135 Cal. Rptr. 222 (1976).

2. Demie Kurz, "Physical Assaults by Husbands: A Major Social Problem," in Richard J. Gelles and Donileen R. Loseke, eds., *Current Controversies on Family Violence* (Newbury Park, CA: Sage, 1994), 88–100.

3. Murray A. Straus and Richard Gelles, eds., *Physical Violence in American Families: Risk Factors and Adaptations to Violence in 8,145 Families* (New Brunswick, NJ: Transaction, 1990).

4. Carey Goldberg, Simpson Wins Custody Fight for 2 Children by Slaying Wife, *New York Times*, 21 December 1996, A1.

5. Ibid.

6. Ibid.

7. In re James M., 258, 135 Cal. Rptr. at 224.

8. Ibid.

9. Ibid., 259, 135 Cal. Rptr. at 225.

10. Ibid.

11. Ibid.

12. Ibid., 258, 135 Cal. Rptr. at 224.

13. In the Matter of Mark G.V., 177 Cal. App. 3d 754, 225 Cal. Rptr. 460 (1986).

14. Ibid., 759–60, 225 Cal. Rptr. at 463–64.

15. This claim is made more frequently regarding allegations of fathers' sexual abuse of children, where evidence and eyewitness testimony are more difficult to establish. Mary Ann Mason, "A Judicial Dilemma: The Use of Expert Witness Testimony in Child Sex Abuse Cases," *Journal of Law and Psychiatry* 21 (1992): 35–65.

16. Collinsworth v. O'Connell, 508 So.2d 744, 746 (Fla. Dist. Ct. App. 1987).

17. Straus and Gelles, *Physical Violence in American Families*.

18. Kurz, "Physical Assaults by Husbands," 90.

19. Byron Egeland, "A History of Abuse Is a Major Risk Factor for Abusing the Next Generation," in Gelles and Loseke, eds., *Current Controversies on Family Violence*, 197–209.

20. La. Rev. Stat. Ann. § 9:361.

21. La. Rev. Stat. Ann. § 9:364.

22. Note, "Developments in the Law—Legal Responses to Domestic Violence, VI. Battered Women and Child Custody Decision-making," *Harvard Law Review* 106 (1993): 1597.

23. Cal. Family Code § 3000 et seq.

24. Blair v. Blair, 154 Vt. 201, 203–4, 575 A.2d 191, 192–93 (1990).

25. Lenore Walker, *The Battered Woman* (New York: Harper and Row, 1979).

26. Ibid.

27. Trina Grillo, "The Mediation Alternative: Process Dangers for Women," *Yale Law Journal* 100 (1991): 1545.

28. Pam Belluck, "Women's Killers Are Very Often Their Partners, A Study Finds," *New York Times*, 31 March 1997, B1.

29. Ibid.

30. Ibid.

31. Ibid.

32. Carole Ness, "Twice-Jailed Abusive Dad Wins Half-Time Custody," *San Francisco Examiner*, 9 February 1997, C1.

33. Ibid.

34. Marc J. Ackerman and Melissa C. Ackerman, "Child Custody Evaluation Practices: A 1996 Survey of Psychologists," *Family Law Quarterly* 30 (1997): 565.

35. Ness, "Twice-Jailed Abusive Dad Wins Half-Time Custody," 9.

36. Anna C. Salter, *Transforming Trauma: A Guide to Understanding and Treating Adult Survivors of Child Sexual Abuse* (Thousand Oaks, CA: Sage, 1995), citing D. E. H. Russel, *Sexual Exploitation: Rape Child Sexual Abuse and Workplace Harassment* (Beverly Hills, CA: Sage, 1984).

37. Newsom v. Newsom 557 So.2d 511 (Miss. 1990).

38. Ibid., 517.

39. Ibid.

40. Ibid., 513.

41. 28 U.S.C. § 1738A.

42. Cal. Penal Code § 207(e).

43. Mary S. Fahn, "Allegations of Child Abuse in Custody Disputes: Getting to the Truth of the Matter," *Family Law Quarterly* 25, 2 (1991): 193–216.

44. Martin J. Kaplan, "Children Don't Always Tell the Truth," *Journal of Forensic Sciences* 35, 3 (1990): 661–67.

45. Roland C. Summit, "The Child Sexual Abuse Accommodation Syndrome," *Child Abuse & Neglect* 7 (1983): 177. Summit did not intend his diagnostic categorization to be used in court as a "sex abuse test."

46. Mason, *A Judicial Dilemma*, 111–33.

47. Richard A. Gardner, *The Parental Alienation Syndrome: A Guide for Mental Health and Legal Professionals* (Cresskill, NJ: Creative Therapeutics, 1992), Addendum IIIa (April 1997).

48. Ibid.

Chapter Seven

1. Mireya Navarro, "Lesbian Loses Court Appeal for Custody of Daughter," *New York Times*, 31 August 1996, A7.

2. Ibid.

3. Ibid.

4. Ward v. Ward, 1996 Fla. App. LEXIS 9130, *12.

5. Smith v. Frates, 107 Wash. 13 (1919).

6. Lindsay v. Lindsay, 14 Ga., 660, (1854).

7. Ibid., 660.

8. Harmon v. Harmon, 208 P. 647, 111 Kan. 786 (1922).

9. Ibid.

10. Ibid.

11. The data from my own comparative study of 100 appellate court decisions from 1960 and 100 from 1990 indicate that while moral fitness was mentioned thirty-six times in 1960 as a factor in the court's decision, it was mentioned only six times in 1990. Mary Ann Mason, "Read My Lips: Are Mothers Losing Custody? Trends in Judicial Decision making in Custody Disputes," *Family Law Quarterly* 31, 2 (Summer 1997), 215–37.

12. See, e.g., Roe v. Roe, 324 S.E.2d 6691 (Va. Sup. Ct. 1985).

13. See, e.g., Doe v. Coe, 452 N.E.2d 293 (1983); S.N.E. v. R. L. B., 699 P.2d 875 (Alaska 1985). This position is also promoted by the influential Uniform Marriage and Divorce Act § 402, which states: "The court shall not consider conduct of a present or proposed custodian that does not affect his relationship to the child."

14. See Doe v. Doe, 222 Va. 736, 748, 284 S.E.2d 799, 806 (1981).

15. Va. Crim. Code § 18.2–361.

16. Bottoms v. Bottoms, 249 Va. 410 (1995).

17. Bottoms v. Bottoms, 18 Va. App. 481, 444 S.E.2d 276 (1994).

18. Ibid., 489, 444 S.E.2d at 281.

19. As quoted in Bottoms v. Bottoms, 18 Va. App. 481, 486–87, 444 S.E.2d 276, 279–80 (1994).

20. Bottoms v. Bottoms, 18 Va. App. 481, 484, 444 S.E.2d 276, 278 (1994).

21. Bottoms v. Bottoms 249 Va. 410, 457 S.E.2d 102 (1995).

22. Ibid., 418, 457 S.E.2d at 107.

23. D. H. v. J. H., 418 N.E.2d 286 (Ind. App. 1981).

24. Ibid., 289.

25. Ibid.

26. Ind. Code § 31–1–11.5–21(a), since repealed by P.L. 1–1997 § 157.

27. D. H. v. J. H., 418 N.E.2d 286, 293 (Ind. App. 1981).

28. Ibid., 296.

29. Charlotte Patterson, "Summary of Research Findings," paper presented at the Conference on Children and Divorce, in *Children, Divorce and Custody: Lawyers and Psychologists Working Together* (Los Angeles: American Bar Association, 1997), 1306; see also Patterson, "Children of Lesbian and Gay Parents," *Child Development* 63 (1993): 1025–42. The following is an example of a recent capsule statement summarizing research on lesbians as parents:

> Researchers who compared children raised in lesbian and heterosexual households found few or no differences in the development of gender identity, gender-role behavior, or sexual orientation. Studies have also found no deficits among children of lesbian mothers in other aspects of personal development, including separation-individuation, locus of control, self-concept, intelligence, or moral judgment. In addition, numerous studies have shown that children raised by lesbians have normal, healthy relationships with other children as well as with adults. According to Patterson's comprehensive literature review on lesbian and gay families, a child's adjustment is enhanced when the lesbian mother lives with her partner, when the lesbianism is acknowledged before the child reaches adolescence, and when the child has contact with peers from other lesbian families.

Nanette Gartrell et al., "The National Lesbian Family Study," *American Journal of Orthopsychiatry* 66 (1996): 272–73.

30. As quoted in Judy Stacey, "Gay and Lesbian Families: Queer Like Us," in Mary Ann Mason, Arlene Skolnick, and Steve Sugarman, eds., *All Our Families: New Policies for a New Century* (New York. Oxford University Press, 1998).

31. Thomas S. v. Robin Y., 599 N.Y.S.2d 377 (1993), overruled, 209 A.D.2d 298, 618 N.Y.S.2d 356 (1994).

32. Ibid., 378.

33. Ibid.

34. Jhordan C. v. Mary K., 179 Cal. App. 3d 386, 224 Cal. Rptr. 530 (Ct. App. 1986).

35. Ibid., 391.

36. Thomas S. v. Robin Y., 599 N.Y.S.2d 377, 380 (1993).

37. Ibid.

38. Thomas S. v. Robin Y., 209 A.D.2d 298, 618 N.Y.S.2d 356 (1994), quoting Matter of Nehra v. Uhlar, 43 N.Y.2d 242, 249, 401 N.Y.S.2d 168, 372 N.E.2d 4.

39. Thomas S. v. Robin Y., 209 A.D.2d 298, 618 N.Y.S.2d 356, 360 (1994).

40. Nancy S. v. Michele G., 228 Cal. App. 3d, 279 Cal. Rptr. 212 (1991).

41. Ibid.

42. Stacey, "Gay and Lesbian Families," in Mason, Skolnick, and Sugarman, eds., *All Our Families*, 125.

43. Julia J. Tate, "Taking up the Slack: Promoting the Welfare of Families Led by Gays and Lesbians," paper presented at the Conference on Children and Divorce, in *Children, Divorce and Custody*, 1318.

44. Johnson v. Calvert, 5 Cal. 4th 84, 19 Cal. Rptr. 2d 494 (1993).

45. Stephanie Salter, A Cruel Close to the Case of Mary Ward, *San Francisco Examiner*, 28 January 1997.

Chapter Eight

1. Maggie Fox, "British Scientists Clone First Adult Animal," Reuters World Service, 23 February 1997.

2. See, e.g., ibid.

3. Gursky v. Gursky, 39 Misc. 2d 1083, 242 N.Y.S.2d 406 (1963).

4. People v. Sorenson, 66 Cal. Rptr. 7 (1968).

5. Ibid., 10.

6. Unif. Parentage Act § 5, U.L.A. Parentage (1973).

7. Harry Krause, *Family Law*, 2d ed. (St. Paul, Minn.: West, 1986).

8. Jhordan C. v. Mary K., 179 Cal. App. 3d 386, *391, 224 Cal. Rptr. 530 (Ct. App. 1986).

9. Thomas S. v. Robin Y., 209 A.D.2d 298, 299, 618 N.Y.S.2d 356, 357 (1994).

10. Ibid.

11. Unif. Adoption Act, U.L.A. Adoption (1994).

12. Gen. 16:1–16.

13. Norma Katz, "Surrogate Motherhood and the Baby-Selling Law," *Columbia Journal of Law & Social Problems* 20 (1986): 1.

14. In the Matter of Baby M., 537 A.2d 1227 (1988).

15. Ibid., 1237.

16. Ibid., 1241.

17. Ibid., 1258, 1263.

18. Krause, *Family Law*, 287–88.

19. In the Matter of Baby M., 537 A.2d 1227, 1254 (1988).

20. Krause, *Family Law*, 337.

21. Johnson v. Calvert, 5 Cal.4th 84, 88, 851 P.2d 776, 778 (1993).

22. Ibid., 92, 851 P.2d at 781.

23. Ibid., 93, 851 P.2d at 782.

24. Ibid., 114, 851 P.2d at 796 (dissent by Kennard, J.).

25. For a full discussion of intent-based parenthood, see Marjorie Shultz, "Reproductive Technology and Intent-based Parenthood: An Opportunity for Gender Neutrality," *Wisconsin Law Review* 42 (1990): 297.

26. Unif. Adoption Act § 2–409, U.L.A. Adoption (1994).

27. In re Marriage of Moschetta, 25 Cal. App. 4th 1218, 30 Cal. Rptr. 893 (1994).

28. Ibid., 1223, 30 Cal. Rptr. at 895.

29. Ibid., 1231, 30 Cal. Rptr. at 901.

30. Ken Ellingwood, Surrogate Loses Joint Custody of O. C. Girl, 5, *Los Angeles Times*, 18 November 1995, A1.

31. R. Alta Charo, "Mommies Dearest," *Wisconsin Law Review* 32 (1992): 233.

32. Davis v. Davis, 842 S.W.2d 588 (1992).

33. Ibid., 603.

34. Ibid., 589.

35. Ibid., 589.

36. Ibid., 604.

37. 1986 L. Acts R. S. 9:121 et seq.

38. Davis v. Davis, 842 S.W.2d 588, 596–97 (1992), citing American Fertility Society, *Report on Ethical Considerations of the New Reproductive Technologies* (June 1990).

39. *International Herald Tribune*, 18 March 1997, 1.

40. Fred Barbash, British Frozen Embryos Face Disposal; Thousands of Fertilized Eggs Reach Deadline for Thawing, *Washington Post*, 1 August 1996, A1.

41. Hecht v. Sup. Ct. of Los Angeles, 50 Cal. App. 4th 1289, 1293, 59 Cal. Rptr. 2d 222, 224 (1996) rev. den. and ordered not to be officially published (15 January 1997).

42. Ibid., 1297, 59 Cal. Rptr. 2d at 227.

Chapter Nine

1. Child Abuse Prevention and Treatment Act, P.L. 93–415, U.S.C. § 5601(1974); Adoption Assistance and Child Welfare Act, P.L. 96–272, 442 U.S.C. § 670 (1980).

2. John Poertner and Allen Press, "Who Best Represents the Interest of the Child in Court?" *Child Welfare* 69, 6 (Nov.–Dec. 1990): 537–49.

3. Judith Wallerstein and Joan Berlin Kelly, *Surviving the Breakup* (New York: Basic Books, 1990), 39, 44.

4. H. Ted Rubin, "The Nature of the Court Today," *The Future of Children* 6, 3 (1996): 42, 43.

5. Ibid., 42.

6. Cal. Civil Code § 4607.

7. The five other states are Delaware, Florida, Maine, Washington, and Wisconsin.

8. A study of Connecticut, Los Angeles, and Minneapolis court-related custody mediations revealed that cases averaged 1.5 sessions and 2.3 hours in Connecticut, 1.7 sessions and 3 hours in Los Angeles, and 3.3 sessions and 4.3 hours in Minneapolis. In Maine mediations usually are held in a single session. Trina Grillo, "The Mediation Alternative: Process Dangers for Women," *Yale Law Journal* 100 (1991): 1583 n.180.

9. Hugh McIsaac, "Court-Connected Mediation," *Conciliation Courts Review* 21 (1983): 5.

10. Joan Kelly found that private sessions averaged 10 hours. Joan Kelly, "Mediated and Adversarial Divorce: Respondents' Perceptions of Their Processes and Outcomes," *Mediation Quarterly* 22 (Summer 1989): 74.

11. See, e.g., Martha Fineman, "Dominant Discourse, Professional Language, and Legal Change in Child Custody Decision-Making," *Harvard Law Review* 101, 4 (1988): 727; see also Grillo, "The Mediation Alternative," 1545.

12. Grillo, "The Mediation Alternative," 1563.

13. This concept of the battered woman is credited to Lenore Walker, *The Battered Woman* (New York: Harper and Row, 1979).

14. Grillo, "The Mediation Alternative," 1605–7.

15. Fineman, "Dominant Discourse," 769.

16. See, e.g., Randy Klaff, "The Tender Years Doctrine: A Defense," *California Law Review* 70 (1982): 335.

17. Minnesota and Oregon, for example, exclude cases of child and spousal abuse from court-ordered mediation: Minn. Stat. Ann. § 518–619, Or. Rev. Stat. Ann. § 107.755–95.

18. Wis. Stat. § 767.11(3) (West Supp. 1990).

19. Rubin, "The Nature of the Court Today," 43.

Afterword

1. Marc J. Ackerman and Melissa C. Ackerman, "Child Custody Evaluation Practices: A 1996 Survey of Psychologists," *Family Law Quarterly* 30 (1997): 565.

Index